SECONDING SINAI

Supplements to the
Journal for the Study
of Judaism

Editor
JOHN J. COLLINS
The Divinity School, Yale University

Associate Editor
FLORENTINO GARCÍA MARTÍNEZ
Qumran Institute, University of Groningen

Advisory Board
J. Duhaime
A. Hilhorst
P. W. van der Horst
A. Klostergaard Petersen
M. A. Knibb
J. T. A. G. M. van Ruiten
J. Sievers
G. Stemberger
E. J. C. Tigchelaar
J. Tromp

Volume 77

SECONDING SINAI

SECONDING SINAI

The Development of Mosaic Discourse in Second Temple Judaism

Hindy Najman

SBL

Society of Biblical Literature
Atlanta

Library of Congress Cataloging-in-Publication Data

Najman, Hindy.
    Seconding Sinai : the development of Mosaic discourse in Second Temple
Judaism / by Hindy Najman.
        p. cm. — (Supplements to the Journal for the study of Judaism ; v.
77)
        Originally published : Leiden ; Boston : Brill, 2003.
        Includes bibliographical references and index.
        ISBN 978-1-58983-424-8 (paper binding : alk. paper)
    1. Moses (Biblical leader) 2. Direct discourse in the Bible. 3. Bible. O.T.
Pentateuch—Criticism, interpretation, etc., Jewish. 4. Jewish law—
Interpretation and construction—History—To 1500. 5. Judaism—History—
Post-exilic period, 586 B.C.–210 A.D. I. Title.
    BS580.M6N35 2009
    296.09'014—dc22   2009011560

Printed in the United States of America
on acid-free paper

CONTENTS

GENERAL ABBREVIATIONS

AB	Anchor Bible
ABD	*Anchor Bible Dictionary.* Edited by D. N. Freedman. 6 vols. New York, 1992
Abr.N	*Abr-Nahrain*
ABRL	Anchor Bible Reference Library
AJSR	*Association for Jewish Studies Review*
ANRW	*Aufstieg und Niedergang der römischen Welt: Geschichte und Kultur Roms im Spiegel der neueren Forschung.* Edited by H. Temporini and W. Haase. Berlin, 1972–
BAR	*Biblical Archaeology Review*
BASOR	*Bulletin of the American Schools of Oriental Research*
BBR	*Bulletin for Biblical Research*
BEATAJ	Beiträge zur Erforschung des Alten Testaments und des antiken Judentum
BETL	Bibliotheca ephemeridum theologicarum lovaniensium
BFCT	Beiträge zur Förderung christlicher Theologie
BHS	*Biblica Hebraica Stuttgartensia.* Edited by K. Elliger and W. Rudolph. Stuttgart, 1983
BIS	Biblical Interpretation Series
BJS	Brown Judaica Series
BZAW	Beihefte zur Zeitschrift für die alttestamentliche Wissenschaft
CBQ	*Catholic Biblical Quarterly*
CBQMS	Catholic Biblical Quarterly Monograph Series
CJAS	Christianity and Judaism in Antiquity Series
CRINT	Compendia rerum iudaicarum ad Novum Testamentum
CSCO	Corpus scriptorum christianorum orientalium. Edited by I. B. Chabot et al. Paris, 1903
CTHPT	Cambridge Texts in the History of Political Thought
DJD	Discoveries in the Judaean Desert
DSD	*Dead Sea Discoveries*
ErIsr	*Eretz-Israel*
EstBib	*Estudios bíblicos*
FRLANT	Forschungen zur Religion und Literatur des Alten und Neuen Testaments
HAR	*Hebrew Annual Review*
HSM	Harvard Semitic Monographs
HTR	*Harvard Theological Review*
HUCA	*Hebrew Union College Annual*
IBHS	*An Introduction to Biblical Hebrew Syntax.* B. K. Waltke and M. O'Connor. Winona Lake, Indiana, 1990
IEJ	*Israel Exploration Journal*
IES	Israel Exploration Society
Int	*Interpretation*
JANES	*Journal of the Ancient Near Eastern Society*
JANESCU	*Journal of the Ancient Near Eastern Society of Columbia University*
JBL	*Journal of Biblical Literature*
JCS	*Journal of Cuneiform Studies*
JECS	*Journal of Early Christian Studies*

JJS	*Journal of Jewish Studies*
JNES	*Journal of Near Eastern Studies*
JQR	*Jewish Quarterly Review*
JSJ	*Journal for the Study of Judaism in the Persian, Hellenistic, and Roman Periods*
JSJSup	Journal for the Study of Judaism in the Persian, Hellenistic, and Roman Periods Supplement Series
JSOT	*Journal for the Study of the Old Testament*
JSOT/ASOR	Journal for the Study of the Old Testament/American Schools of Oriental Research
JSOTSup	Journal for the Study of the Old Testament Supplement Series
JSPSup	Journal for the Study of the Pseudepigrapha Supplement Series
JSQ	*Jewish Studies Quarterly*
JSS	*Journal of Semitic Studies*
JTS	*Journal of Theological Studies*
LCL	Loeb Classical Library
LD	Lectio divina
LEC	Library of Early Christianity
Leš	*Lešonénu*
LXX	Septuagint
MT	Masoretic Text
NJPS	*Tanakh: The Holy Scriptures: The New JPS Translation according to the Traditional Hebrew text*
NovT	*Novum Testamentum*
NovTSup	Novum Testamentum Supplements
OBO	Orbis biblicus et orientalis
OBT	Overtures to Biblical Theology
OTL	Old Testament Library
OtSt	*Oudtestamentische Studiën*
PACS	Philo of Alexandria Commentary Series
PEGLMBS	*Proceedings, Eastern Great Lakes and Midwest Biblical Societies*
RevQ	*Revue de Qumran*
RHPR	*Revue d'histoire et de philosophie religieuses*
RivB	*Rivista biblica italiana*
RP	Religious Perspectives
RT	Religious Traditions
RTR	*Reformed Theological Review*
SAe	Scriptores Aethiopici
SAOC	Studies in Ancient Oriental Civilizations
SBL	Society of Biblical Literature
SBLDS	Society of Biblical Literature Dissertation Series
SBLEJL	Society of Biblical Literature Early Judaism and Its Literature
SBLPS	Society of Biblical Literature Pseudepigrapha Series
SBLSCS	Society of Biblical Literature Septuagint and Cognate Studies
SBLSP	Society of Biblical Literature Seminar Papers
SBLSymS	Society of Biblical Literature Symposium Series
SBLTT	Society of Biblical Literature Texts and Translations
SBS	*Stuttgarter Bibelstudien*
SBTS	Sources for Biblical and Theological Study
SC	Sources chrétiennes. Paris: Cerf, 1943–
ScEs	*Science et esprit*
SCL	Sather Classical Lectures
SDSSRL	Studies in the Dead Sea Scrolls and Related Literature
SHR	Studies in the History of Religions (supplement to *Numen*)

SJLA	Studies in Judaism in Late Antiquity
SJOT	*Scandinavian Journal of the Old Testament*
SPM	Studia Philonica Monographs
SR	*Studies in Religion*
SSEJC	Studies in Scripture in Early Judaism and Christianity
STDJ	Studies on the Texts of the Desert of Judah
StPatr	Studia patristica
StPB	Studia post-biblica
StPh	*Studia Philonica*
StPhA	*Studia Philonica Annual*
Text	*Textus*
TSAJ	Texte und Studien zum antiken Judentum
USFSHJ	University of South Florida Studies in the History of Judaism
VT	*Vetus Testamentum*
VTSup	Vetus Testamentum Supplements
WMANT	Wissenschaftliche Monographien zum Alten und Neuen Testament
WUNT	Wissenschaftliche Untersuchungen zum Neuen Testament
ZABR	*Zeitschrift für altorientalische und biblische Rechtgeschichte*
ZAW	*Zeitschrift für die alttestamentliche Wissenschaft*
ZDMG	*Zeitschrift der deutschen morgenländischen Gesellschaft*
ZTK	*Zeitschrift für Theologie und Kirche*

PREFACE

This project began as a dissertation on the various ways in which interpretive authority was claimed in Second Temple Judaism. While revising my dissertation for publication, however, I came to conceptualize the project in a new way, so that the result is a different book. In particular, the concept of a biblical-interpretive discourse tied to a founder, which organizes this book, is not to be found in the dissertation.

Here I focus on Mosaic Discourse alone. Even in the study of Mosaic Discourse, I make no claim to exhaustiveness. My goal is, rather, to provide an initial example of the methodological use of a concept that will, I hope, prove itself fruitful elsewhere, in the scriptural traditions of Second Temple and early Rabbinic Judaisms. In this book I focus on Second Temple texts because it is the Second Temple period that serves as the pivot between the literature and history of ancient Israel, and the post-destruction developments of rabbinic Judaism and Christianity.

ACKNOWLEDGMENTS

Grateful acknowledgment is due to my teachers, my colleagues and my friends. James Kugel's work on motific continuities in biblical interpretation provided the initial impetus and inspiration for this project. Professor Kugel supervised my dissertation and continues to give of his mind and creative spirit with great energy and modesty. He is an exemplary teacher and scholar. I also thank the other members of my committee, Jon Levenson and Jay Harris, as well as two teachers with whom I worked closely, Peter Machinist and John Strugnell.

The editors of the series in which this book appears, John Collins and Florentino García Martínez, raised questions and made suggestions that forced me to reconsider the entire project. They helped me to broaden and refocus this project in significant ways.

Recently, Michael Fishbane suggested that I thematize the problem of Mosaic authority. The conceptualization of Mosaic discourse in this book expresses my attempt to respond to his very helpful suggestion.

I am profoundly grateful to my colleagues in the Department of Theology at the University of Notre Dame, in particular, to my colleagues in the area of Christianity and Judaism in Antiquity. Since I joined the Department of Theology in 1998, my colleagues have been a great source of inspiration, generously offering careful comments and suggestions. James C. VanderKam has carefully read all of the work I gave him and has consistently been a source of great knowledge and extraordinary breadth in the field of Second Temple history, interpretation and, in particular, the book of *Jubilees*. I continue to learn from my wonderful colleague, Gregory E. Sterling, about the subtle balance of Hellenism and Judaism in the late Second Temple Period and about that brilliant interpreter and philosopher of the ancient world, Philo of Alexandria. His comments and suggestions have been very helpful. Michael Signer is a constant source of valuable support and wisdom. I cannot imagine a more enabling chair and colleague than John Cavadini.

I am grateful to colleagues who have read specific chapters or discussed concepts related to the book: Moshe Bernstein, Joseph Blenkinsopp, Marc Brettler, George Brooke, Mary Rose D'Angelo,

Graham Hammill, Gary Knoppers, Bernard Levinson, Blake Leyerle, John Meier, Margaret Mitchell, Judith Newman, David O'Connor, Hugh Page, Jean Porter, Michael Satlow, and Eugene Ulrich.

I must also express my deep appreciation for leave and research support from the Department of Theology, the Institute of Scholarship in the Liberal Arts at the University of Notre Dame, and the Jordan Kapson Chair of Jewish Studies. In the earlier stages of this project I received support from the Memorial Foundation for Jewish Culture, the Harvard Center for Jewish Studies, the Department of Near Eastern Languages and Civilizations at Harvard University, and the Harry Austryn Wolfson Fellowship.

I have incorporated sections from my dissertation, "Authoritative Writing and Interpretation: A Study in the History of Scripture" (Ph.D. diss., Harvard University, 1998) and the following previously published essays: "Interpretation as Primordial Writing: Jubilees and its Authority Conferring Strategies," *JSJ* 30 (1999): 379–410; "Philo of Alexandria on the Law of Nature and the Law of Moses," *StPhA* 11 (1999): 55–73; "Legal Innovation in Ezra-Nehemiah," in *The Interpretation of Scripture in Early Judaism and Christianity* (ed. C. A. Evans; JSPSup 33; SSEJC 7; Sheffield: Sheffield Academic, 2000), 202–16. I thank the editors for permission to reproduce parts of these essays.

In the Fall of 2000, I taught a seminar at the University of Notre Dame entitled "Torah of Moses." I thank my students for their insights and excellent conversation throughout the semester.

Over the past few years I have been very fortunate to have doctoral students from the Department of Theology at the University of Notre Dame assist me in the preparation of my manuscript. My students gave generously of their time as they assisted me in the proofreading of the manuscript and the preparation of the indices and bibliography. John Bergsma, Brad Milunski, OFM Conv., Samuel Thomas, and Robert Groegle gave much appreciated assistance. Steven Schweitzer provided invaluable assistance at the early and final stages of the book production.

My parents, Cantor Chaim and Dr. Sherrell Najman, my in-laws, Dr. David and Elizabeth Franks, and my siblings, along with their families, were a source of constant support and encouragement. My sister, Dina Najman-Licht, gave much appreciated assistance.

While writing this book my husband, Paul Franks, and I were blessed with two children, Marianna Bluma and Ezra Yehuda. Our lives and work have been enriched in ways I never imagined possible.

Nothing looks quite the same anymore, except for the one source of constant support and inspiration. Paul has seen this project through its numerous re-conceptions and re-writings. His philosophical insight and invaluable suggestions have contributed in countless ways to this new book. His friendship and generosity know no bounds. I dedicate this book to him.

Hindy Najman
August 16, 2002
8 Elul 5762

CHAPTER ONE

MOSAIC DISCOURSE

> How many authors are there among the writers?
> Author means originator.
>
> Friedrich Schlegel[1]

The History of Texts and the History of Textuality

Biblical studies has developed a sophisticated sensitivity to the history of texts. But it has not yet developed a similar sophistication with respect to the history of *concepts* of textuality. Most importantly for this study, discussions of the *authorship* of biblical texts, and of the *authority* they claim for themselves, are often riddled with anachronism.

For the last few centuries, the question of authorship has been central to the study of ancient texts. If we only knew who wrote, say, the *Odyssey*, or the Book of Deuteronomy, and under what conditions, then, it has seemed, it would be possible to understand these works rigorously, historically. As Jon Levenson wrote: "Indeed, nothing has been more characteristic of the modern study of the Bible than a passion for questions of authorship and dating."[2] To answer

---

[1] Friedrich Schlegel, "On Philosophy. To Dorothea," in *Theory as Practice: A Critical Anthology of Early German Romantic Writings* (ed. and trans. J. Schulte-Sasse et al.; Minneapolis: University of Minnesota Press, 1997), 316, fragment 68.

[2] Jon D. Levenson, "Theological Consensus or Historicist Evasion? Jews and Christians in Biblical Studies," in *The Hebrew Bible, The Old Testament, and Historical Criticism: Jews and Christians in Biblical Studies* (Louisville: Westminster/John Knox, 1993), 89. For recent discussion of authorship and authority see Timothy H. Lim, Hector L. MacQueen, and Calum M. Carmichael, eds., *On Scrolls, Artefacts and Intellectual Property* (JSPSup 38; Sheffield: Sheffield Academic, 2001); Martha Woodmansee and Peter Jaszi, eds., *The Construction of Authorship: Textual Appropriation in Law and Literature* (Durham, N.C.: Duke University Press, 1994).

For an excellent discussion of the innovative interest in the identification of the author and attribution see Burton L. Mack, "Under the Shadow of Moses: Authorship and Authority in Hellenistic Judaism," *SBL Seminar Papers, 1982* (SBLSP 21; Chico, Calif.: Scholars Press, 1982), 299–318. See also David G. Meade, *Pseudonymity and Canon: An Investigation into the Relationship of Authorship and Authority in Jewish and Earliest Christian Tradition* (Tübingen: J. C. B. Mohr, 1986; repr., Grand Rapids: Eerdmans, 1987).

these questions, long-established textual unities have been decom-
posed into chronologically distinct strata, and long-lost sources have
been posited. Old authorial ascriptions, sometimes recorded within
the texts themselves—such as the ascription of the *Odyssey* to Homer,
or of parts of Deuteronomy to Moses—have been rejected.[3] These
individuals, whose names are among the most famous in human history, have been replaced as authors by otherwise unknown schools,[4]
which persisted over centuries and consisted of anonymous bards or
scribes.[5] Not only did ancient authors attribute their writings to older
figures, but they also reworked earlier authoritative writings in ways
that leave contemporary scholars unsure about the status of their
writings and their relation to older traditions. Are these texts forg-

---

[3] For a helpful overview of developments in biblical criticism in the nineteenth
century, see John W. Rogerson, *Old Testament Criticism in the Nineteenth Century: England
and Germany* (Philadelphia: Fortress, 1985).

[4] In "Pseudepigraphy in the Israelite Tradition," in *Pseudepigrapha I* (ed. K. von
Fritz; Vandoeuvres-Geneve: Fondation Hardt, 1972), Morton Smith argues that
Israelite literature was ". . . originally and customarily anonymous. When interest in
history became acute in the 7th century and later centuries B.C. a considerable
number of anonymous works were falsely attributed to famous historical figures . . . The
first great representative of this genre is probably, but not certainly, the Deuteronomic
Code (*Dt.* 12–26 and 28), written shortly before 621 B.C." (214–15).

For recent scholarship on the "Deuteronomic School," see Moshe Weinfeld,
Deuteronomy and the Deuteronomic School (Oxford: Clarendon, 1972); Norbert F. Lohfink,
"Was There a Deuteronomistic Movement?" in *Those Elusive Deuteronomists: The
Phenomenon of Pan-Deuteronomism* (ed. L. S. Schearing and S. L. McKenzie; JSOTSup
268; Sheffield: Sheffield Academic, 1999), 36–66; Raymond F. Person, *Second Zechariah
and the Deuteronomic School* (JSOTSup 167; Sheffield: JSOT Press, 1993); Rolf Rendtorff,
The Problem of the Process of Transmission in the Pentateuch (JSOTSup 89; Sheffield:
JSOT Press, 1990); Erhard Blum, *Studien zur Komposition des Pentateuch* (BZAW 189;
Berlin: de Gruyter, 1990); Suzanne Boorer, *The Promise of the Land as Oath: A Key to
the Formation of the Pentateuch* (BZAW 205; Berlin: de Gruyter, 1992); Robert R. Wilson,
"Who Was the Deuteronomist? (Who Was Not the Deuteronomist?): Reflections on
Pan-Deuteronomism," in *Those Elusive Deuteronomists: The Phenomenon of Pan-Deuteronomism*
(ed. L. S. Schearing and S. L. McKenzie; JSOTSup 268; Sheffield: Sheffield
Academic, 1999), 67–82, esp. 78. For further readings regarding the "Priestly" or
"Holiness School," see David Frankel, *The Murmuring Stories of the Priestly School: A
Retrieval of Ancient Sacerdotal Lore* (VTSup 89; Leiden: Brill, 2002); Israel Knohl, *The
Sanctuary of Silence: The Priestly Torah and the Holiness School* (Minneapolis: Fortress, 1995).

[5] See the important work of Albert B. Lord, *The Singer of Tales* (Cambridge, Mass.:
Harvard University Press, 1960), Jack Goody, *Literacy, Family, Culture and the State:
The Interface Between the Written and the Oral* (Cambridge: Cambridge University Press,
1987), and Walter J. Ong, *Orality and Literacy: The Technologizing of the Word* (London:
Methuen, 1982). There is a fascinating and intimate relationship between Homeric
and biblical studies. See the discussion of the relationship between Friedrich August
Wolf and Johann Gottfried Eichhorn in Anthony Grafton, introduction to *Prolegomena
to Homer (1795)* (translated with introduction and notes by A. Grafton, G. W. Most
and J. E. G. Zetzel; Princeton: Princeton University Press, 1985), 3–35.

eries?[6] Do they reflect a deliberate attempt to obscure the later origins of a book for the purpose of authorization and reception of the new text as revealed Scripture?

To be sure, it is a crucial insight that texts received as unities can have histories of production. And of course the methods developed to reconstruct text production are immensely valuable. But it is also

---

[6] The term "forgery" has traditionally been considered problematic in theological circles. Morton Smith recounts an exchange between Franz Delitzsch and his professor: "'Pseudepigraphy' is, in theological circles, a discreditable term, and 'forgery' is little short of unmentionable. The younger Delitzsch reported an amusing example of this attitude. He learned from his professor's lecture that *Deuteronomy* was not written by Moses, but was a work of the 7th century, composed for a specific purpose and for that purpose attributed to Moses. Deeply shocked, he went to call on the professor and asked, 'Is *Deuteronomy*, then, a forgery?' 'For God's sake, no!' said the professor, 'That may very well be so, but you mustn't say so'" ("Pseudepigraphy in the Israelite Tradition," 193). For a distinction between forgery and "genuine religious pseudepigraphy," see Wolfgang Speyer's classic study, *Die Literarische Fälschung im Heidnischen und Christlichen Altertum: Ein Versuch Ihrer Deutung* (Munich: C. H. Beck'sche Verlagsbuchhandlung, 1971), 37, 150–52.

See also Bruce Metzger's discussion of the reason why scholars have shied away from the term forgery and instead used the term "pseudepigrapha," in his essay, "Literary Forgeries and Canonical Pseudepigrapha," *JBL* 91 (1972): 3–24. He states: "A literary forgery is essentially a piece of work created or modified with the intention to deceive. Accordingly, not all pseudepigrapha (that is, works wrongly attributed to authors) are to be regarded as forgeries. In the case of genuine forgery (if this oxymoron may be permitted) the attribution must be made with the calculated attempt to deceive. This consideration excludes from the category of literary forgeries both the copy made in good faith for purposes of study and the large class of writings that, in the course of their descent from antiquity, have become associated with the name of some great classical author or Father of the Church . . . These commentaries are certainly pseudepigraphic, but just as certainly they are not forgeries" (4). M. Smith writes: "Accordingly it is from false attribution, not form [*sic*] forgery, that we must begin our study of the pseudepigrapha in the Israelite-Jewish tradition" ("Pseudepigraphy in the Israelite Tradition," 195). See also D. G. Meade, *Pseudonymity and Canon*.

In addition, see the recent discussions of this issue by John Van Seters, "Creative Imitation in the Hebrew Bible," *SR* 29 (2000): 395–409, and by Anthony Grafton, *Forgers and Critics: Creativity and Duplicity in Western Scholarship* (Princeton: Princeton University Press, 1990). According to Grafton: "Forgery does not include all works wrongly attributed to authors . . . It does not even include all works that authors have deliberately ascribed to persons other than themselves. In some periods and traditions writers have ascribed religious texts to divine or semidivine figures not because they were preoccupied with matters of authorship but because they wished to stress the continuity of their writings with an original tradition or an orthodox doctrine. A number of Jewish writers did this in the last centuries B.C. when they wrote apocalyptic and other works under the names of the biblical patriarchs, perhaps to fill the gap left by the cessation of prophecy. Such practices need not imply an intention to deceive, though they sometimes do; their products should be called pseudepigrapha rather than forgeries until the *mens rea* of the author is established" (5–6).

true that the authority of ancient texts has sometimes been bound
up with authorial ascription. And we are in danger of missing a
great deal about these texts if we do not seek to understand *why* so
many people, over so many centuries, worked so hard to erase the
signs of their own labor, to conceal the history of textual production.[7]

Of course, scholars do have *something* to say about why these unknown redactors hid the history of their texts and ascribed them to
privileged individuals. The redactors, we are told, engaged in pseudonymous attribution of texts—a device intended to secure for new myths
or laws an authority that they would not otherwise possess.[8] The

---

[7] The Book of Isaiah is a case in point. See Joseph Blenkinsopp: "It is not always,
indeed not generally, possible to determine the historical setting and time of these
exegetical expansions. Since the entire process is attributed to Isaiah, it is understandable that, in marked contrast to Second Isaiah, the scholiasts and learned seers
and scribes of a later day would find ways to efface themselves and give their say-
ings the semblance of antiquity or anonymity" (*Isaiah 1–39: A New Translation with
Introduction and Commentary* [AB 19; New York: Doubleday, 2000], 90). For a helpful discussion of the process by which reworked traditions were authorized in first
millennium B.C.E. Mesopotamian writings, see Francesca Rochberg-Halton, "Canonicity
in Cuneiform Texts," *JCS* 36 (1984): 127–44. On page 134, Rochberg-Halton writes:
"Mesopotamia is distinguished by its extensive written tradition whose primary validity was precisely that it recorded traditions originating in the distant past and preserved for present and future generations of scribes the language and culture of
their forebears." On page 136, she continues: "But divine authorship, placed as it
is in the literary catalog in the context of legendary authors, human authors of
great antiquity, and descendants of ancestral scribes, fits into a broader pattern of
antiquity of authorship. The antiquity rather than the divinity of authorship clearly
emerges as the important criterion for a text's authoritative status." On page 144,
regarding the concept of canon, she states: "The aspect of 'canonicity' of cuneiform
texts that concerns antiquity of authorship simply points to the high regard for traditions of scholarship which the scholars themselves traced back to the sages of the
time before the legendary Flood. This absolutely contrasts with the particular doc-
trinal aspect of canonicity in the Old and New Testaments which concerns theological claims about the origin, sacredness, authority and inspirational nature of that
canonized literature." See also the important essay of Wilfred G. Lambert, "Ancestors,
Authors, and Canonicity," *JCS* 11 (1957): 1–14, and Jeffrey H. Tigay, *The Evolution
of the Gilgamesh Epic* (Philadelphia: University of Pennsylvania Press, 1982).

[8] See James A. Sanders, "Introduction: Why the Pseudepigrapha?" in *The
Pseudepigrapha and Early Biblical Interpretation* (ed. J. H. Charlesworth and C. A. Evans;
JSPSup 14; SSEJC 2; Sheffield: JSOT Press, 1993), 13–19. Concerning the term
"pseudepigrapha" Sanders writes: "It is an inept term that has come since the early
eighteenth century to mean roughly the following: the Early Jewish literature (largely
in the 200 B.C.E. to 200 C.E. period) that resembles the Apocrypha or Deuterocanonical
literature but is not included in the Jewish or Western Christian canons, or in
Rabbinic literature. But even that is not a definition . . . No one in the field has
found another term that has gained acceptance to designate this important body
of literature . . ." (13–14). On the use and understanding of the term "pseudepigrapha" see the following: Michael E. Stone, "The Dead Sea Scrolls and the

suggestion—sometimes made explicit but often lurking just below the surface—is that the "real authors" committed what we would call *forgery*, an activity that is not only unhistorical, but also morally tainted. The ancient texts are *frauds*—perhaps pious ones[9]—but nonetheless frauds. Consider, for example, this passage from Bernard Levinson:

> Deuteronomy's use of precedent subverts it. The old saw of Deuteronomy as a pious fraud may thus profitably be inverted. Is there not something of an impious fraud—of *pecca fortiter!*—in the literary accomplishment of the text's authors? . . . The authors of Deuteronomy retroject into the past their modernist transformation of the tradition . . . The function of the pseudepigraph is that it displaces not only the previous tradition (the authoritative text) but also that tradition's just claim to priority.[10]

Here Levinson assumes a contemporary conception of fraudulence, and a contemporary conception of piety towards tradition. He assumes, first, that it is fraudulent to tamper with the actual words of an existing text and then to present the rewritten version as if it were the original. To be sure, this would be fraudulent today. But we cannot simply assume that it would be fraudulent in every culture and at all times.

It is worth noting that on a view such as Levinson's cited above, historical criticism is not offering an objective or neutral study of ancient texts. Rather it is debunking the authority of Scripture as

---

Pseudepigrapha," *DSD* 3 (1996): 270–95; Devorah Dimant, "Apocrypha and Pseudepigrapha at Qumran," *DSD* 1 (1994): 151–59; Kyle Keefer, "A Postscript to the Book: Authenticating the Pseudepigrapha," in *Reading Bibles, Writing Bodies: Identity and The Book* (ed. T. K. Beal and D. M. Gunn; London: Routledge, 1997), 232–41; James H. Charlesworth, "The Significance of the New Edition of the Old Testament Pseudepigrapha," in *La Littérature Intertestamentaire: Colloque de Strasbourg (17–19 Octobre 1983)* (Paris: Presses Universitaires de France, 1985), 11–28; John Strugnell, "Moses-Pseudepigrapha at Qumran: 4Q375, 4Q376, and Similar Works," in *Archaeology and History in the Dead Sea Scrolls: The New York University Conference in Memory of Yigael Yadin* (ed. L. H. Schiffman; JSPSup 8; JSOT/ASOR Monographs 2; Sheffield: JSOT Press, 1990), 221–56; Edward M. Forster, *Anonymity: An Enquiry* (London: Hogarth, 1925).

[9] Anthony Grafton, in his essay, "Jacob Bernays, Joseph Scaliger, and Others," in *Bring Out Your Dead: The Past as Revelation* (Cambridge, Mass.: Harvard University Press, 2001), 279–98, n. 295, notes that August Böckh contrasts the work of the Hebrews, which he characterizes as "impious deceit," with the work of Christians, which he characterizes as "pious fraud" (quoted in J. Freudenthal, *Alexander Polyhistor und die von ihm erhaltenen Reste jüdischer und samaritanischer Geschichtswerke* [Breslau, 1875], 194).

[10] Bernard M. Levinson, *Deuteronomy and the Hermeneutics of Legal Innovation* (New York: Oxford University Press, 1997), 150.

fraudulent. Thus the fact that Moses was not the author of the speeches attributed to him in Deuteronomy renders the book itself a fraudulent piece of propaganda associated with the Deuteronomistic historians. Similarly, rewriting earlier traditions is conceived as a combination of practices that we might call *plagiarizing* and *tampering* with existing texts. Again, the implication is that the resulting texts are unhistorical, morally tainted, and undeserving of the authority they have enjoyed.[11]

This picture of the practices and intentions of the producers and redactors of biblical texts fits very well with the hostile attitude towards religious authorities characteristic of many key figures of the Enlightenment, the period in which modern biblical criticism was crystallized.[12] Indeed, it fits *so* perfectly that we have good reason to worry that biblical studies remain captive to an Enlightenment prejudice that should not be accepted without critical examination. Has it been shown that, considered in their historical contexts, practices

---

[11] Debunking pseudepigrapha was one of the activities in which philological methods were first honed; see, e.g., Isaac Casaubon's famous exposure of the *Corpus Hermeticum* as having been pseudonymously attributed to Hermes. On this event see Anthony Grafton, "Protestant Versus Prophet: Isaac Casaubon on Hermes Trismegistus," *Journal of the Warburg and Courauld Institutes* 46 (1983): 78–93.

[12] The biblical criticism of the Enlightenment has a long pre-history. See, e.g., James L. Kugel, "The Bible in the University," in *The Hebrew Bible and Its Interpreters* (ed. W. H. Propp, B. Halpern, and D. N. Freedman; Winona Lake, Ind.: Eisenbrauns, 1990), 143–65. Kugel writes: "... *all* of the major trends of modern biblical scholarship, and many of its conclusions, existed in latency as soon as the rules of acceptable assumptions and procedures began to change in the fifteenth and sixteenth centuries: all that remained was to ask, one by one, the questions permitted by the new outlook and by the increasing freedom from established tradition and Church dogma" (150). See also the two seminal essays on historical criticism by Jon D. Levenson, "Theological Consensus or Historicist Evasion?," 82–105 and "Historical Criticism and the Fate of the Enlightenment Project," in *The Hebrew Bible, The Old Testament, and Historical Criticism*, 106–26. Levenson discusses the origin of the historical-critical method and states the following: "The method derives from the Renaissance sense of the past as this is transformed through Enlightenment rationalism and then Romantic hermeneutics, with its emphasis on self-expression and authorial intention" (96). On the transition from the eighteenth to nineteenth centuries and the accompanying appearance of such individuals as de Wette, J. W. Rogerson writes: "... by the close of the eighteenth century, critical German scholarship had already achieved much. It had gained the freedom to investigate questions of authorship of books, unity of books, and sources underlying books, without the restraints imposed by traditional opinions on these matters deriving from narrow views of the nature of inspiration.... Yet, arguably, it had not achieved the breakthrough that was to constitute the fundamental difference between critical scholarship in the nineteenth as opposed to the eighteenth century. That breakthrough was, however, only a few years away as the eighteenth century came to an end" (*Old Testament Criticism in the Nineteenth Century*, 27).

of pseudonymous attribution constituted forgery? Or is the application of such a concept to antiquity an instance of anachronism, one of the cardinal sins of historiography?

Like the classification of texts as pseudepigraphic, the characterization of Second Temple texts as "Rewritten Bible" is problematic.[13] Use of the term can suggest an *anachronistic conception of a text*—as a fixed set of claims embodied in specific language, such that tampering with that language is tantamount to interfering with an author's property. When scholars who employ such a concept encounter biblical and extra-biblical texts that recount biblical narratives with variations and insertions, they may be tempted to infer that these texts aspire to replace an older, authentic biblical tradition with a new version.[14] Instead, we should ask whether these biblical and extra-biblical writers shared our contemporary conception of a text. Although

---

[13] The term "Rewritten Bible" was coined by Geza Vermes, *Scripture and Tradition in Judaism: Haggadic Studies* (2d. rev. ed.; StPB 4; Leiden: Brill, 1973; 1st ed. 1961). He states that one of his aims in this volume is to address "the structure and purpose of the re-writing of the Bible" (10). The French notion of "texte continué" originates with Charles Perrot, *Pseudo-Philon: Les antiquités bibliques. Tome II: Introduction littéraire, commentaire et index* (SC 230; Paris: Cerf, 1976), 22–28, 24. For a comprehensive definition of the genre of Rewritten Bible see Philip S. Alexander, "Retelling the Old Testament," in *It is Written: Scripture Citing Scripture. Essays in Honour of Barnabas Lindars, SSF* (ed. D. A. Carson and H. G. M. Williamson; Cambridge: Cambridge University Press, 1988), 99–121.

In addition, a helpful characterization of this process as "creative imitation" has been suggested in the excellent essay by John Van Seters, "Creative Imitation in the Hebrew Bible," 395–409. Although I do not agree with Van Seters' assessment of the dating of J, his characterization of rewriting as creative imitation is extremely helpful as a way of remarking on the methodological and narrative repetitions in the Hebrew Bible.

[14] I do not mean to suggest that everyone who refers to "Rewritten Bible" thinks in terms of the replacement of an authentic text. See Moshe J. Bernstein, "4Q252: From Re-Written Bible to Biblical Commentary," *JJS* 45 (1994): 2–27; James C. VanderKam, "Questions of Canon Viewed through the Dead Sea Scrolls," *BBR* 11 (2001): 269–92; Florentino García Martínez, "Temple Scroll," *Encyclopedia of the Dead Sea Scrolls* 2:927–33; George J. Brooke, "Rewritten Bible," *Encyclopedia of the Dead Sea Scrolls* 2:777–81; idem, "Between Authority and Canon: The Significance of Reworking the Bible for Understanding the Canonical Process," (paper presented at the Seventh Orion International Symposium: Reworking the Bible at Qumran in the Context of Second Temple Judaism, Hebrew University of Jerusalem, 17 January 2002, n.p.; forthcoming in Orion Conference Proceedings. Online: http://orion.mscc.huji.ac.il/orion/symposiums/7th/). On the contrary, in recent scholarship there is a general consensus among scholars who work on Second Temple literature that the essential function of Rewritten Bible is interpretive. Yet, despite this agreement, the term itself tends to be misleading. For a helpful discussion see James H. Charlesworth, "In the Crucible: The Pseudepigrapha as Biblical Interpretation," in *The Pseudepigrapha and Early Biblical Interpretation* (ed. J. H. Charlesworth

biblicists assume the existence of a somewhat fixed biblical text as early as the Persian period,[15] they acknowledge the fluidity of biblical traditions.[16] Even if it is still possible to speak of rewriting, the distinction between the *transmission* and the *interpretation* of biblical traditions was not as sharp as the term Rewritten Bible implies.[17]

---

and C. A. Evans; JSPSup 14; SSEJC 2; Sheffield: JSOT Press, 1993), 120–43. Charlesworth does not *explicitly* claim that the terminology has been instrumental in misleading readers of Second Temple literature. I maintain, however, that it has contributed significantly to much of the confusion found in the scholarship.

[15] See the following: Joseph Blenkinsopp, "The Mission of Udjahorresnet and Those of Ezra and Nehemiah," *JBL* 106 (1987): 409–21; idem, *The Pentateuch: An Introduction to the First Five Books of the Bible* (ABRL; New York: Doubleday, 1992), 239–42; idem, "Was the Pentateuch the Civic and Religious Constitution of the Jewish Ethnos in the Persian Period?" in *Persia and Torah: The Theory of Imperial Authorization of the Pentateuch* (SBLSymS 17; Atlanta: Society of Biblical Literature, 2001), 41–62; Peter Frei, "Zentralgewalt und Lokalautonomie im Achämenidenreich," in P. Frei and K. Koch, *Reichsidee und Reichsorganisation im Perserreich* (2d enl. ed.; OBO 55; Freiburg: Universitätsverlag and Göttingen: Vandenhoeck & Ruprecht, 1996; 1st ed. 1984), 5–132; idem, "Die persische Reichsautorisation: Ein Überblick," *ZABR* 1 (1995): 1–35 [translated as: "Persian Imperial Authorization: A Summary," in *Persia and Torah: The Theory of Imperial Authorization of the Pentateuch* (trans. J. W. Watts; SBLSymS 17; Atlanta: Society of Biblical Literature, 2001), 5–40]. For a more cautious view see Gary N. Knoppers, "An Achaemenid Imperial Authorization of Torah in Yehud?" in *Persia and Torah: The Theory of Imperial Authorization of the Pentateuch* (SBLSymS 17; Atlanta: Society of Biblical Literature, 2001), 115–34.

[16] See Eugene Ulrich, "The Bible in the Making: The Scriptures at Qumran," in *The Community of the Renewed Covenant* (ed. E. Ulrich and J. C. VanderKam; CJAS 10; Notre Dame: University of Notre Dame Press, 1994), 77–94. Ulrich writes: "The first statement to make about the Bible at Qumran is that we should probably not think of a 'Bible' in the first century B.C.E. or the first century C.E., at Qumran or elsewhere. There were collections of Sacred Scripture, of course, but not Bible in our developed sense of the term" (77). See also Julio Trebolle Barrera, "The Authoritative Functions of Scriptural Works at Qumran," in *The Community of the Renewed Covenant* (ed. E. Ulrich and J. C. VanderKam; CJAS 10; Notre Dame: University of Notre Dame Press, 1994), 95–110; J. A. Sanders, "Introduction: Why the Pseudepigrapha?" 13–19; Frank Moore Cross, "The Old Testament at Qumrân," in *The Ancient Library of Qumran* (3d rev. ed.; Sheffield: Sheffield Academic and Minneapolis: Fortress, 1995; 1st ed. 1958), 121–42; Frank Moore Cross and Shemaryahu Talmon, eds., *Qumran and the History of the Biblical Text* (Cambridge, Mass.: Harvard University Press, 1975); James C. VanderKam, "Authoritative Literature in the Dead Sea Scrolls," *DSD* 5 (1998): 382–402; Julio Trebolle Barrera, "A 'Canon Within a Canon': Two Series of Old Testament Books Differently Transmitted, Interpreted and Authorized," *RevQ* 19 (2000): 383–99; Stephen B. Chapman, "'The Law and the Words' as a Canonical Formula within the Old Testament," in *The Interpretation of Scripture in Early Judaism and Christianity: Studies in Language and Tradition* (ed. C. A. Evans; JSPSup 33; SSEJC 7; Sheffield: Sheffield Academic, 2000), 26–74; Eugene Ulrich, *The Dead Sea Scrolls and the Origins of the Bible* (SDSSRL; Grand Rapids: Eerdmans and Leiden: Brill, 1999).

[17] On the application and understanding of the term "Rewritten Bible," see M. J. Bernstein, "4Q252," 2–27; George W. E. Nickelsburg, "Chapter Three: The Bible

At this point, it is helpful to recall an insight of Michel Foucault, who points out the danger of anachronism when reading texts with contemporary assumptions about authorship and text production, assumptions that seem to us so obvious that they have no alternatives and need no justification.

> We now ask of each poetic or fictional text: From where does it come, who wrote it, when, under what circumstances, or beginning with what design? The meaning ascribed to it and the status or value accorded it depends on the manner in which we answer these questions. And if a text should be discovered in a state of anonymity—whether as a consequence of an accident or the author's explicit wish—the game becomes one of rediscovering the author. Since literary anonymity is not tolerable, we can accept it only in the guise of an enigma. As a result, the author function today plays an important role in our view of literary works.[18]

Foucault remarks that there are alternatives to the current role and significance of what he calls the author function. Indeed, there have been alternative dispensations, even within the relatively recent past:

> The author function does not affect all discourses in a universal and constant way, however. In our civilization, it has not always been the same types of texts that have required attribution to an author. There was a time when the texts we today call 'literary' (narratives, stories, epics, tragedies, comedies) were accepted, put into circulation, and valorized without any question about the identity of their author; their anonymity caused no difficulties since their ancientness, whether real or imagined, was regarded as a sufficient guarantee of their status.[19]

As Foucault reminds us, it is not only *texts* that develop over time. The connected *concepts* of the authority and authorship of texts *also* have long and complex histories. Both models of anonymity and of pseudonymity can be found in the texts of the Hebrew Bible and in the extra-biblical texts of the Second Temple period. But even

---

Rewritten and Expanded," in *Jewish Writings of the Second Temple Period: Apocrypha, Pseudepigrapha, Qumran Sectarian Writings, Philo, Josephus* (ed. M. E. Stone; CRINT 2.2; Assen: Van Gorcum and Philadelphia: Fortress, 1984), 89–156; P. S. Alexander, "Retelling the Old Testament," 99–121.

[18] Michel Foucault, "What is an Author?" in *Michel Foucault: Aesthetics, Method, and Epistemology. Vol. 2* (ed. J. D. Faubion; trans. J. V. Harari, modified by R. Hurley; 2 vols.; New York: The New Press, 1998), 213.

[19] Ibid., 212. For a critical evaluation of Foucault's essay on authorship see Mark Vessey, "The Forging of Orthodoxy in Latin Christian Literature: A Case Study," *JECS* 4 (1996): 495–513.

when an author is identified in a biblical text, it is unclear if that identification is to be considered *the same* as what moderns would characterize as *the author function*.

To be sure, it might be objected, it would indeed be anachronistic to apply a contemporary concept of authorship to an ancient text, but only if it could be shown that a different concept of authorship was operative at the time of the text's production and/or reception. Perhaps it can be shown that currently employed notions of pseudonymous attribution and rewriting presuppose contemporary concepts of authorship. But this is not sufficient to justify a charge of anachronism. What is required in addition is a reconstruction of the concepts operative at the time of the text's production and/or reception. But how can this requirement be met?

Here I will attempt an example of just such a reconstruction. In particular I will focus on the role of Moses in concepts of authorship and authority that develop in the exilic and post-exilic periods. In particular I will study later Second Temple participants in Mosaic Discourse, a discourse that, I will argue, originates with the gradual production of the collection now referred to as Deuteronomy.

It has been noted that, in Deuteronomy, compared to earlier traditions, Moses plays a strikingly expanded role. Also noteworthy, however, is the continued expansion of Moses' role in Second Temple texts, both biblical and para-biblical. The development has at least two dimensions. On the one hand, authoritative law comes to be called the Torah of Moses, and the list of laws under that heading is subject to expansion and augmentation.[20] On the other hand, the figure of Moses becomes increasingly central and Moses himself is

[20] On the Torah of Moses see: Michael Fishbane, *Biblical Interpretation in Ancient Israel* (Oxford: Clarendon, 1985; repr., Clarendon Paperbacks, 1988), esp. 256–65; S. B. Chapman, "The Law and the Words," 26–74; James L. Kugel, "Early Interpretation: The Common Background of Late Forms of Biblical Exegesis," in James L. Kugel and Rowan A. Greer, *Early Biblical Interpretation* (LEC 3; Philadelphia: Westminster, 1986), 11–106; Jon D. Levenson, "The Sources of Torah: Psalm 119 and the Modes of Revelation in Second Temple Judaism," in *Ancient Israelite Religion: Essays in Honor of Frank Moore Cross* (ed. P. D. Miller Jr., P. D. Hanson, and S. D. McBride; Philadelphia: Fortress, 1987), 559–74; Eugene Ulrich, "From Literature to Scripture: Reflections on the Growth of a Text's Authoritativeness," *DSD* 10 (2003): forthcoming. See also my essay on the relationship between the Torah of Moses and Ezra, "Torah of Moses: Pseudonymous Attribution in Second Temple Writings," in *The Interpretation of Scripture in Early Judaism and Christianity: Studies in Language and Tradition* (ed. C. A. Evans; JSPSup 33; SSEJC 7; Sheffield: Sheffield Academic, 2000), 202–16.

idealized in various ways linked to various notions of authority: for example, as prophet, as lawgiver, as divine amanuensis, as king and as divine man.[21] I want to draw particular attention to a connection that has not been noted before: the connection between the Deuteronomic elaboration of the Torah and the figure of Moses, and the

---

[21] For one of the most illuminating discussions of Mosaic authority, see Sara Japhet's article, "Law and 'The Law' in Ezra-Nehemiah," in *The Proceedings of the Ninth World Congress of Jewish Studies* (Jerusalem: Magnes, 1985), 99–115. See also the discussion of pseudonymous attribution to Moses in M. Smith, "Pseudepigraphy in the Israelite Tradition," 200–10.

In addition, there is some literature that discusses traditions that invoked Mosaic authority. See, e.g., Gary A. Anderson, "The Status of the Torah Before Sinai," *DSD* 1 (1994): 1–29; Joseph Blenkinsopp, *Ezra-Nehemiah: A Commentary* (OTL; Philadelphia: Westminster, 1988); Samuel S. Cohon, "Authority in Judaism," *HUCA* 11 (1936): 593–646; Mary Rose D'Angelo, *Moses in the Letter to the Hebrews* (SBLDS 42; Missoula, Mont.: Scholars Press, 1979); Burton Mack, "Moses on the Mountaintop," in *The School of Moses: Studies in Philo and Hellenistic Religion* (ed. J. P. Kenney; BJS 304; SPM 1; Atlanta: Scholars Press, 1995), 16–28; J. L. Kugel, "Early Interpretation," 11–106; Robert C. Marshall, "Moses, Oedipus, Structuralism and History," *RT* 5 (1983): 245–66; Moshe Bernstein, "4Q159 Fragment 5 and the 'Desert Theology' of the Qumran Sect," *DSD* 9 (2002): 75–103; Crispin Fletcher-Louis, "4Q374: A Discourse on the Sinai Tradition: The Deification of Moses and Early Christology," *DSD* 3 (1996): 236–52; idem, *All the Glory of Adam: Liturgical Anthropology in the Dead Sea Scrolls* (STDJ 42; Leiden: Brill, 2002), esp. 6–9, 31–32, 135–49; Naphtali Wieder, "The 'Law-Interpreter' of the Sect of the Dead Sea Scrolls: The Second Moses," *JJS* 3 (1952): 158–75; Rolf Rendtorff, "Esra und das 'Gesetz'," *ZAW* 96 (1984): 165–84; Dale C. Allison Jr., *The New Moses: A Matthean Typology* (Minneapolis: Fortress, 1993); David L. Tiede, "The Figure of Moses in *The Testament of Moses*," in *Studies on the Testament of Moses* (ed. G. W. E. Nickelsburg; SBLSCS 4; Cambridge, Mass.: Society of Biblical Literature, 1973), 86–92; Jan Assmann, *Moses the Egyptian: The Memory of Egypt in Western Monotheism* (Cambridge, Mass.: Harvard University Press, 1997); James W. Watts, "The Legal Characterization of Moses in the Rhetoric of the Pentateuch," *JBL* 117 (1998): 415–26; Wayne A. Meeks, *The Prophet-King: Moses Traditions and the Johannine Christology* (NovTSup 14; Leiden: Brill, 1967); Harry Austryn Wolfson, *Philo. Vol. 2* (2 vols.; Cambridge, Mass.: Harvard University Press, 1947), 2:322–37; M. Fishbane, *Biblical Interpretation*, 256–65, 525–43; idem, *The Garments of Torah: Essays in Biblical Hermeneutics* (Bloomington, Ind.: Indiana University Press, 1989; repr., 1992), 1–18, 70–75; B. Mack, "Under the Shadow of Moses," 310–18; and my article, "The Law of Nature and the Authority of Mosaic Law," *StPhA* 11 (1999): 55–73.

M. Fishbane comments on the process of appropriating the Mosaic tradition: "This revision of the Mosaic recitation of an earlier divine command [in Deut. 5:12] is thus an exemplary case of the exegetical extension some legal teachings underwent in biblical literature. They preserve the hierarchical preeminence of the divine voice at all costs. But by the very activation of the earlier source via its citation, the hermeneutical imagination at work in Jer. 17:21–22 betrays itself: its desire to prolong the divine voice into a present which presupposes the entire Sinaitic revelation, and its willingness to subordinate the human exegetical voice, whose undisguised presence would then underscore a gap in the authority of the revealed law" (*Garments of Torah*, 110).

further elaboration of those dimensions of Mosaic authority in late
Second Temple literature. In some crucial respects, I will argue, it
is helpful to think of the Book of Deuteronomy, in the hands of late
Second Temple tradents, as providing models for the practices of
pseudonymous attribution and rewriting developed by later Second
Temple authors and redactors—although it is also essential to attend
to differences between the Deuteronomists and their successors, as
well as to differences between those successors.

The expansion of the Law and the idealization of the figure of
Moses together constitute a development of the utmost importance,
extending far beyond the period studied in this book. We might
think of this development as culminating, say, in the position of
Maimonides, who entitles his authority-claiming codification of Jewish
law, *Mishneh Torah*—a title traditionally used for the Deuteronomic
discourse of Moses—and who characterizes Moses, not only as the
ultimate prophet and lawgiver, but also as the exemplary human
being.[22]

What is the alternative to seeing this long-term expansion of Moses'
role—this long history of pseudonymous attribution and rewriting—
as a history of fraud and tampering? Although Foucault is not primarily concerned, in his discussion of the author function, with
ancient texts, and although he does not directly address the Hebrew
Bible, one of his examples provides a useful contemporary analogue
to the cases I am considering. It is the example of *discourses that are
inextricably linked to their founders*, such as Marxism or Freudianism.
When someone proclaims "Back to Marx!" or "Back to Freud!" she
claims to represent the *authentic* doctrine of Marx or Freud, although
she may express it in different words. Of course, today such people
make known their own names, under which they author books.[23]
But, in some ancient cultures, the way to continue or return to the
founder's discourse was precisely to ascribe what one said or wrote,
not to oneself, but rather to the founder.[24] Thus, for example, Iambli-

---

[22] See, e.g., Kalman P. Bland, "Moses and the Law According to Maimonides,"
in *Mystics, Philosophers, and Politicans: Essays in Jewish Intellectual History in Honor of
Alexander Altmann* (ed. J. Reinharz and D. Swetschinski, with collaboration of K. P.
Bland; Durham, N.C.: Duke University Press, 1982), 49–66.
[23] A fascinating exception is the mathematical work ascribed to Nicolas Bourbaki,
who is of course the collective pseudonym for a group of French mathematicians
who do not wish to publish that work under their own names.
[24] See, for example David K. O'Connor's discussion of Socrates as a founder in

chus the Pythagorean said that it was more honorable and praise-
worthy to publish one's philosophical treatises in the name of
Pythagoras than to publish them in one's own name.[25] And Tertullian
wrote that Luke's gospel ought to be ascribed to Paul and Mark's
to Peter, because: "that which disciples publish should be regarded
as their masters' work."[26] It was in this spirit that Plato wrote, not
in his own name, but in the name of his master, Socrates, while
members of the Academy later wrote in Plato's name, and members of the Lyceum in Aristotle's.[27]

The idea of a discourse tied to a founder provides, I want to suggest, a helpful way to think about the developing conceptions of the
Mosaic Law and figure of Moses. On this understanding of a discourse tied to a founder, to rework an earlier text is to update, inter-
pret and develop the content of that text in a way that one claims
to be an authentic expression of the law already accepted as author-
itatively Mosaic. Thus, when what *we* might call a "new" law—
perhaps even what we might regard as a significant "amendment"
of older law—is characterized as the Law of Moses, this is not to
imply that it is to be found within the actual words of an historical
individual called Moses. It is rather to say that the implementation
of the law in question would enable Israel to return to the authentic teaching associated with the prophetic status of Moses.[28]

"The Seductions of Socrates," *First Things* 114 (2001): 29–33. O'Connor writes:
"Most of the major philosophical schools during the first six centuries after his death
traced their origins to Socrates, and vigorously disputed other claimants to the
Socratic legacy. Stoics, Skeptics, and Cynics all proudly claimed him as their founder
and looked to him as their exemplary sage" (29).

[25] Iamblicus, *De Vita Pythagorica*, paragraph 98. The Pythagorean practice was
cited by commentators on Aristotle as a precedent for Peripatetic pseudepigraphy.
See W. Speyer's classic study, *Die Literarische Fälschung im Heidnischen und Christlichen
Altertum*, 34, n. 6, n. 7.

[26] Tertullian, *Marc.* 6.5. See the discussion of this passage in John J. Collins,
"The Impact of Dogmatism on Rational Discourse: Comments on the Paper of
Michael Dummett," in *Hermes and Athena: Biblical Exegesis and Philosophical Theology*
(ed. E. Stump and T. P. Flint; Notre Dame: University of Notre Dame Press, 1993),
23–30. See also W. Speyer, *Die Literarische Fälschung im Heidnischen und Christlichen
Altertum*, 34.

[27] In the Second Letter, Plato writes that there is not and will not be any written work of his own, and that the works called Plato's are works of a modernized
and embellished Socrates. (*Ep.* II 314 b–c). If, as some think, the letter is pseudepigraphic, then it is a pseudepigraphic justification for pseudepigraphy!

[28] E.g., see my discussion of Ezra's prohibition of foreign marriage in "Torah of
Moses," 202–16. Also see the following for a detailed discussion of this issue and
its subsequent development in later traditions: Gedaliah Alon, "The Levitical

To take personal responsibility for a new interpretation would have been contrary to the Second Temple conception of authority, which always demanded roots in the pre-exilic past.[29] This appeal to antiq-

---

Uncleanness of Gentiles," in *Jews, Judaism and the Classical World* (trans. I. Abrahams; Jerusalem: Magnes, 1977), 146–89; Adolph Büchler, "The Levitical Impurity of the Gentile in Palestine Before the Year 70," *JQR* 17 (1926): 1–81; idem, "Family Purity and Family Impurity in Jerusalem Before the Year 70 c.e.," in *Studies in Jewish History: the Adolph Büchler Memorial Volume* (ed. I. Brodie and J. Rabbinowitz; London: Oxford University Press, 1956), 64–98; Shaye J. D. Cohen, "The Origins of the Matrilineal Principle in Rabbinic Law," *AJSR* 10 (1985): 19–53; idem, "From the Bible to the Talmud: The Prohibition of Intermarriage," *HAR* 7 (1983): 23–39; idem, "Conversion to Judaism in Historical Perspective: From Biblical Israel to Postbiblical Judaism," *Conservative Judaism* 36.4 (1983): 31–45; idem, "Crossing the Boundary and Becoming a Jew," *HTR* 82 (1989): 13–33; Louis Epstein, "Intermarriage," in *Marriage Laws in the Bible and Talmud* (Cambridge, Mass.: Harvard University Press, 1942), 145–219; Tamara C. Eskenazi and Eleanore P. Judd, "Marriage to a Stranger in Ezra 9–10," in *Second Temple Studies: 2. Temple Community in the Persian Period* (ed. T. C. Eskenazi and K. H. Richards; JSOTSup 175; Sheffield: JSOT Press, 1994), 266–85; Christine E. Hayes, *Gentile Impurities and Jewish Identities: Intermarriage and Conversion from the Bible to the Talmud* (New York: Oxford University Press, forthcoming); idem, "Intermarriage and Impurity in Ancient Jewish Sources," *HTR* 92 (1999): 3–36; Martha Himmelfarb, "Levi, Phineas, and the Problem of Intermarriage at the Time of the Maccabean Revolt," *JSQ* 6 (1999): 1–24; idem, "Sexual Relations and Purity in the Temple Scroll and the Book of Jubilees," *DSD* 6 (1999): 11–36; Jonathan Klawans, *Impurity and Sin in Ancient Judaism* (New York: Oxford University Press, 2000); idem, "Notions of Gentile Impurity in Ancient Judaism,' *AJSR* 20 (1995): 285–312; Gary N. Knoppers, "Intermarriage, Social Complexity, and Ethnic Diversity in the Genealogy of Judah," *JBL* 120 (2001): 15–30; James L. Kugel, "The Holiness of Israel and the Land in Second Temple Times," in *Texts, Temples, and Traditions: A Tribute to Menahem Haran* (ed. M. V. Fox et al.; Winona Lake, Ind.: Eisenbrauns, 1996), 21–32; idem, "The Story of Dinah in the Testament of Levi," *HTR* 85 (1992): 1–34; Jacob Milgrom, "Religious Conversion and the Revolt for the Formation of Israel," *JBL* 101 (1982): 169–76; idem, "The Concept of Impurity in *Jubilees* and the *Temple Scroll*," *RevQ* 16 (1993): 277–84; idem, "Scriptural Foundation and Deviation in the Laws of Purity of the Temple Scroll," in *Archaeology and History in the Dead Sea Scrolls* (ed. L. H. Schiffman; Sheffield: JSOT Press, 1990), 83–99; Duane L. Smith-Christopher, "The Mixed Marriage Crisis in Ezra 9–10 and Nehemiah 13: A Study of the Sociology of Post-Exilic Judaean Community," in *Second Temple Studies: 2. Temple Community in the Persian Period* (ed. T. C. Eskenazi and K. H. Richards; JSOTSup 175; Sheffield: JSOT Press, 1994), 243–65; idem, "Between Ezra and Isaiah: Exclusion, Transformation, and Inclusion of the 'Foreigner' in Post-Exilic Biblical Theology," in *Ethnicity and the Bible* (ed. M. G. Brett; BIS 19; Leiden: Brill, 1996), 117–42; Cana Werman, "*Jubilees* 30: Building a Paradigm for the Ban on Intermarriage," *HTR* 90 (1997): 1–22; J. Blenkinsopp, *Ezra-Nehemiah*, 184–85; James L. Kugel, "Foreigners Are Different," and "Intermarriage is Forbidden," in *The Bible As It Was* (Cambridge, Mass.: Harvard University Press, 1997), 236–38; Jon D. Levenson, "The Last Four Verses in Kings," *JBL* 103 (1984): 353–61, esp. 358 n. 19; Sheldon H. Blank, "The Dissident Laity in Early Judaism," *HUCA* 19 (1945–46): 1–42.

[29] An interesting exception can be found in Ben Sira, where the author of the text is named as Yeshua [Jesus] son of Eleazar, son of Sira (Prologue, 50:27). See

uity was inextricably linked to an ongoing attempt to recover the loss of the First Temple period. As we will also see in some of the later Second Temple interpretive traditions, the independence and empowerment experienced in the Maccabean period gave rise to courageous exegesis and extraordinary creativity.[30] But even the most innovative material could not present itself as innovative. Indeed, innovators found models in the Deuteronomic literature associated with the Josianic reforms, an earlier period of rare independence and empowerment. For the Deuteronomic texts had developed ways to recast tradition, while simultaneously honoring tradition and claiming continuity with it. The only passable roads to textual authority led through the past. Mosaic Discourse was one such route.

At this point, two further clarifications are necessary. First, to say that a number of texts, written over a long period of time, are members of a single *Mosaic* Discourse, is not merely to say that these texts exhibit what has been called intertextuality.[31] It is also to say

---

discussion of the name of the author in Patrick W. Skehan and Alexander A. Di Lella, *The Wisdom of Ben Sira: A New Translation with Notes* (AB 39; New York: Doubleday, 1987), 3–30; see also Martin Hengel, "Anonymität, Pseudepigraphie und 'Literarische Fälschung' in der jüdisch-hellenistischen Literatur," in *Pseudepigrapha I* (ed. K. von Fritz; Vandoeuvres-Geneve: Fondation Hardt, 1972), 231–308, esp. 234; Norbert Brox, "Falsche Verfasserangaben: zur Erklärung der frühchristlichen Pseudepigraphie," *SBS* 79 (1975): 11–67, esp. 62–67.

[30] See James C. VanderKam, *An Introduction to Early Judaism* (Grand Rapids: Eerdmans, 2001), especially 216–17. I am also indebted to Gary N. Knoppers for his instructive insights on this matter in a private conversation, April 2002.

[31] Jan Assmann has also employed the notion of discourse in his study of representations of Moses the Egyptian in biblical and post-biblical traditions. See his *Moses the Egyptian*: "Discourse is more than intertextuality. Besides the textual dimension there is always the material or thematic dimension (*Sachdimension*). A discourse is defined by the double relationship of a text to the chain of its predecessors (textual dimension) and to the common theme (material dimension). Normally discourse creates a stronger affinity between texts than does authorship . . . The similarity among texts participating in a discourse (as opposed to those forming the oeuvre of a specific writer) is reminiscent of Claude Lévi-Strauss' concept of myth as the totality of its versions. This raises the question as to whether the notion of 'myth' would not be equally adequate with regard to the Moses-Egypt tradition. It is a story that unfolds in innumerable versions much in the same way as the stories of Hercules or Prometheus. The only difference is that the Moses-Egypt story is told not by poets but by scholars. Nevertheless, the dynamics that are operative in the unfolding of the story seem much the same as those operating in what Hans Blumenberg has called *Arbeit am Mythos* ('work on myth') . . . Metaphorically speaking, a discourse has a life of its own which reproduces itself in those who are joining in it. It is this 'life of its own' that might be related to the mythical aspect of discourse in Lévi-Strauss' sense. Behind, beside, and beneath the discourse that takes place in the realm of the written word, there is the myth of Egypt, which transcends

that these texts employ the features listed below. Second, to say that these strategies are features that constitute a single discourse is not to say that that these strategies are invariant and timeless. Rather, the strategies vary considerably and develop over time, in a way that leaves open the possibility of significant innovation.[32] Thus, to count as a participant in Mosaic Discourse, a text must *either* incorporate all of the four features below, *or* it must compensate appropriately for any missing feature.

Four Features of Mosaic Discourse

I. By reworking and expanding older traditions through interpretation, a new text claims for itself the authority that already attaches to those traditions.[33]

---

this realm and which works its 'mythomotoric' spell from behind the stage. In the eighteenth century one would have personified this mythomotoric fascination as the 'genius of the discourse.' For us, this kind of helpful mystification is, of course, illicit and so is the use of unanalyzed concepts like 'discourse' and 'cultural memory.' I can only hope that the foregoing remarks have sufficiently clarified my use of the terms" (16–17). See also his discussion of discourse, which is much less distancing from Foucault, in *The Search for God in Ancient Egypt* (trans. D. Lorton; Ithaca: Cornell University Press, 2001), 163–64.

[32] Here I am indebted to Stanley Cavell's conception of genre: "The idea is that the members of a genre share the inheritance of certain conditions, procedures and subjects and goals of composition, and that in primary art each member of such a genre represents a study of these conditions, something I think of as bearing the responsibility of the inheritance. There is, on this picture, nothing one is tempted to call *the* features of a genre which all its members have in common. First, nothing would count as a feature until an act of criticism defines it as such. (Otherwise it would always have been obvious that, for instance, the subject of remarriage was a feature, indeed a leading feature, of a genre.) Second, if a member of a genre were just an object with features then if it shared *all* its features with its companion members they would presumably be indistinguishable from one another. Third, a genre must be left open to new members, a new bearing of responsibility for its inheritance; hence, in the light of the preceding point, it follows that the new member must bring with it some new feature or features. Fourth, membership in the genre requires that if an instance (apparently) lack a given feature, it must compensate for it, for example, by showing a further feature 'instead of' the one it lacks. Fifth, the test of this compensation is that the new feature introduced by the new member will, in turn, contribute to a description of the genre as a whole" (*Pursuits of Happiness: The Hollywood Comedy of Remarriage* [Cambridge, Mass.: Harvard University Press, 1981], 28–29). Also, see Stanley Cavell, "The Fact of Television," in *Themes Out of School: Effects and Causes* (San Francisco: North Point Press, 1984; repr., Chicago: University of Chicago Press, 1988), 235–68, esp. 242–44.

[33] On the concept of a "reworked" text, with 4QReworked Pentateuch as a primary example, see the following: Emanuel Tov and Sidnie White Crawford,

II. The new text ascribes to itself the status of Torah. It may portray itself as having either a heavenly or an earthly origin, but in any event as an authentic expression of the Torah of Moses.

III. The new text is said to be a re-presentation of the revelation at Sinai. There is repeated emphasis on gaining access to revelation through a re-creation of the Sinai experience. This strategy emphasizes the presentness of the Sinai event, even in the face of destruction and exile.

IV. The new text is said to be associated with, or produced by, the founding figure, Moses. This claim serves to authorize the new interpretations as divine revelation or dictation and as prophecy or inspired interpretation. The new text can then be seen as an extension of earlier ancestral discourse.

Mosaic Discourse, thus characterized, comes to play an increasingly important role in the development of Second Temple Judaism and, indeed, in the nascent periods of rabbinic Judaism and early Christianity. I do not claim that the discourse of Moses is the only discourse operative in ancient Judaism, or even that it is the most important one.[34] Rather I hope to offer a new way of characterizing

---

"Reworked Pentateuch," in *Qumran Cave 4, VIII: Parabiblical Texts, Part 1* (ed. H. Attridge et al.; DJD 13; Oxford: Clarendon, 1994), 187–351; J. C. VanderKam, "Questions of Canon," 276–81; Eugene Ulrich, "The Dead Sea Scrolls and the Biblical Text," in *The Dead Sea Scrolls after Fifty Years: A Comprehensive Assessment* (ed. P. W. Flint and J. C. VanderKam; 2 vols.; Leiden: Brill, 1998–99), 1:79–100; Emanuel Tov, "The Textual Status of 4Q364–367 (4QPP)," in *The Madrid Qumran Congress: Proceedings of the International Congress on the Dead Sea Scrolls Madrid 18–21 March, 1991* (ed. J. Trebolle Barrera and L. Vegas Montaner; 2 vols.; STDJ 11.1; Leiden: Brill, 1992), 1:43–82; idem, "Rewritten Bible Compositions and Biblical Manuscripts, with Special Attention to the Samaritan Pentateuch," *DSD* 5 (1998): 334–54; idem, "Biblical Texts as Reworked in Some Qumran Manuscripts with Special Attention to 4QRP and 4QparaGen-Exod," in *The Community of the Renewed Covenant* (ed. E. Ulrich and J. C. VanderKam; CJAS 10; Notre Dame: University of Notre Dame Press, 1994), 111–34; Sidnie White Crawford, "Reworked Pentateuch," *Encyclopedia of the Dead Sea Scrolls* 2:775–77; idem, "The 'Rewritten Bible' at Qumran: A Look at Three Texts," *ErIsr* 26 (1999): 1–8; Michael Segal, "4QReworked Pentateuch or 4QPentateuch?" in *The Dead Sea Scrolls Fifty Years after Their Discovery: Proceedings of the Jerusalem Congress, July 20–25, 1997* (ed. L. H. Schiffman, E. Tov, and J. C. VanderKam; Jerusalem: IES and the Shrine of the Book, 2000), 391–99; idem, "Biblical Exegesis in 4Q158: Techniques and Genre," *Text* 19 (1998): 45–62; Moshe Bernstein, "Pentateuchal Interpretation at Qumran," in *The Dead Sea Scrolls after Fifty Years: A Comprehensive Assessment* (ed. P. W. Flint and J. C. VanderKam; 2 vols.; Leiden: Brill, 1998–99), 1:128–59.

[34] One such example is what I might characterize as a Davidic discourse that combines messianism and kingship into texts and subsequent interpretive traditions;

ancient biblical relationships to the esteemed past, and to lay the
groundwork both for studies of other developments of Mosaic Discourse,
and for studies of other discourses, tied to other founders.

In what follows I will offer a schematic discussion of the origination of Mosaic Discourse in the book of Deuteronomy. I will then
turn to later extra-biblical traditions that I identify as participants in
the discourse of Moses. In particular, I will examine *Jubilees* and
11QTemple, typically classified as pseudepigrapha that "rewrite the
bible." In particular both *Jubilees* and 11QTemple rework pentateuchal narratives in ways that are analogous to reworkings of earlier traditions now preserved in Deuteronomy. Reading these Second
Temple texts as participants in Mosaic Discourse will make available new perspectives on their attempts to authorize themselves
through accounts of their own origination and through the incorporation of hallowed language. Finally, I will consider the writings
of Philo of Alexandria. Jewish writers of the later Second Temple
period, who were influenced by the Greco-Roman tradition, conceived the independence of the author (the historiographer, the poet,
the playwright) in a way that was new to Judaism.[35] For, in that tradition, the production of texts, and even the interpretations of ancient
traditions, came to be attributed not only to the heavenly muse but
also to individuals.[36] Thus Philo, while recounting inherited traditions of the fathers, does not shy away from telling his audience that
some of his interpretations came from his own exegetical insight—

---

another would be characterized as a Solomonic discourse that combines the ever-
growing wisdom traditions with a notion of divine revelation and selection. Consider
also the substantial texts associated with Enoch. On Isaiah traditions see Joseph
Blenkinsopp, "The Prophetic Biography of Isaiah," in *Mincha: Festgabe für Rolf Rendtorff
zum 75. Geburtstag* (ed. E. Blum; Neukirchen Vluyn: Neukirchener Verlag, 2000),
13–26. On Enochic traditions see James C. VanderKam, "Chapter 2: 1 Enoch,
Enochic Motifs, and Enoch in Early Christian Literature," in *The Jewish Apocalyptic
Heritage in Early Christianity* (ed. J. C. VanderKam and W. Adler; CRINT 3.4; Assen:
Van Gorcum and Minneapolis: Fortress, 1996), 33–101.

[35] Arnaldo Momigliano, "Chapter 2: The Herodotean and the Thucydidean
Tradition," in *The Classical Foundations of Modern Historiography* (SCL 54; Berkeley and
Los Angeles: University of California Press, 1990), 29–53. On the concept of intel-
lectual property in ancient Judaism, Hellenism and Early Christianity, see W. Speyer,
Die Literarische Fälschung im Heidnischen und Christlichen Altertum, 150; N. Brox, "Falsche
Verfasserangaben," 69; M. Hengel, "Anonymität, Pseudepigraphie," 234–35.

[36] One aspect of this development is the proliferation of Roman political histories
and biographies, in which both authors and subjects are identified as individuals.
See Arnaldo Momigliano, *The Development of Greek Biography: Four Lectures* (Cambridge,
Mass.: Harvard University Press, 1971).

perhaps inspired[37]—or from his own application of the allegorical
method to the ancient, biblical traditions. In such a context, so
different from that of the Deuteronomists, is it still possible to produce texts that participate in Mosaic Discourse? By raising this question, I hope to shed light, not only on Philo's fascinating synthesis
of Second Temple Judaism with Hellenism, but also to explore the
limits—and thus the conditions of the possibility—of Mosaic Discourse.
Although I argue that Philo links his interpretations to the founder,
i.e., Moses, and to his exemplary Law, there are two important ways
in which Philo's participation in the Discourse of Moses is different
from the first three examples I consider in the first two chapters. In
the first case, Philo subordinates the Law of Moses to the figure of
Moses, in contrast to the other Palestinian examples (e.g., *Jubilees*
and 11QTemple) where the figure of Moses is subordinated to the
Law of Moses. In the second case, Philo distinguishes between his
own interpretations and the Law of Moses. Thus, Philo's interpretations do not straightforwardly have Sinaitic status. In both cases
Philo's use of the logic of copy and original enables him to participate in Mosaic Discourse, notwithstanding the differences between
Palestinian and Hellenistic Judaisms.

Deuteronomy and the Origin of Mosaic Discourse

In order to prepare the way for the study of post-exilic works, I will
now consider Deuteronomy, a work that may be seen as the origin
of Mosaic Discourse and as a model for later instances of that Discourse. My goal here is not to present a comprehensive study of the
various redactional layers of Deuteronomy or of the narrative that
is said to describe the origin of Deuteronomy, namely 2 Kings
22–23.[38] Instead, I want to illustrate how the four features mentioned

---

[37] David M. Hay, "Philo's View of Himself as an Exegete: Inspired, But Not
Authoritative," *StPhA* 3 (1991): 40–52; John R. Levison, "Inspiration and the Divine
Spirit in the Writings of Philo Judaeus," *JSJ* 26 (1995): 271–323, Markus Bockmuehl,
Revelation and Mystery in Ancient Judaism and Pauline Christianity (Grand Rapids: Eerdmans,
1997), 71–78. See the further discussion of this point in Chapter 3.
[38] The development of the Deuteronomistic History (DtrH) and its relationship
to the Book of Deuteronomy is a highly complex issue. The view of Martin Noth
that a single author composed the entire corpus of DtrH (*Überlieferungsgeschichtliche
Studien: Die sammelnden und bearbeitenden Geschichtswerke im Alten Testament* [3d ed.;
Darmstadt: Wissenschaftliche Buchgesellschaft, 1967; 1st ed. 1943]; Eng. trans. *The
Deuteronomistic History* [JSOTSup 15; Sheffield: Sheffield Academic, 1991]) has been

above are invoked in Deuteronomy, over the course of an editing process that lasted more than a century, and how these strategies may be understood, not as pulling the wool over the eyes of gullible readers, but rather as establishing membership in a *discourse tied to a founder*, i.e., Moses.

Reworking as Expansion and Omission

Reworkings of earlier traditions are everywhere in the book of Deuteronomy.[39] I want briefly to consider a much-discussed example: the

---

replaced by two main schools of thought. The first, building on the analysis of Rudolf Smend ("Das Gesetz und die Völker: Ein Beitrag zur deuteronomistischen Redaktionsgeschichte," in *Probleme biblischer Theologie: Festschrift Gerhard von Rad* [ed. H. W. Wolff; Munich: Kaiser, 1971], 494–509) and revised by Walter Dietrich (*Prophetie und Geschichte* [FRLANT 108; Göttingen: Vandenhoeck & Ruprecht, 1972]), recognize three redactions, termed DtrG/H, DtrP, and DtrN. The second, following Frank Moore Cross ("The Themes of the Book of Kings and the Structure of the Deuteronomistic History," in *Canaanite Myth and Hebrew Epic: Essays in the History of the Religion of Israel* [Cambridge, Mass.: Harvard University Press, 1973], 274–89), advocates a "double redaction" which occurred at the time of Josiah and during the exile close to the time of the final events narrated in 2 Kings 25:27–30. See these two volumes on the history of such debates: Richard D. Nelson, *The Double Redaction of the Deuteronomistic History* (JSOTSup 18; Sheffield: JSOT Press, 1981) and Mark A. O'Brien, *The Deuteronomistic History Hypothesis: A Reassessment* (OBO 92; Göttingen: Vandenhoeck & Ruprecht, 1989). See also the detailed discussion of the importance that the reforms of Josiah (2 Kings 22–23) have played in these analyses by Erik Eynikel, *The Reform of King Josiah and the Composition of the Deuteronomistic History* (OtSt 33; Leiden: Brill, 1996). However, it must be noted that in addressing the production of DtrH, the production and redaction of the Book of Deuteronomy must not be neglected by scholars; the Book of Deuteronomy is intimately connected to DtrH, appearing to serve as an introduction. The process of textual growth appears to begin with the Deuteronomic Code, which has been supplemented by (several) subsequent Deuteronomic redactions, which in turn was edited by the final redactor of the Deuteronomistic History to serve as a preface. This function is particularly evident at the close of the narrative in Deuteronomy 34. See the influential comments of Gerhard von Rad, *Deuteronomy: A Commentary* (OTL; Philadelphia: Westminster, 1966), 12. See also the excellent article by Thomas Römer and Marc Z. Brettler which argues for a "Priestly-Deuteronomistic" redaction in the Pentateuch and in Joshua which accounts for both the P passage of Joshua 24 and the function of Deut 34:7–9 in its current location as the hinge text for a Hexateuch which originated during the Persian Period ("Deuteronomy 34 and the Case for a Persian Hexateuch," *JBL* 119 [2000]: 401–19). I accept the characterization of distinct redactional layers stemming from different time periods and social locations in both Deuteronomy and DtrH as argued by Gary N. Knoppers, "Rethinking the Relationship between Deuteronomy and the Deuteronomistic History: The Case of Kings," *CBQ* 63 (2001): 393–415.

[39] See also discussions of the relationship between the authority of Moses and the Book of Deuteronomy in the following: M. Fishbane, *Biblical Interpretation*, 213–16,

Deuteronomic law collection (Deuteronomy 12–26), which reworks the collection of laws in Exodus in the Book of the Covenant (Exod 20:22–23:33). Scholars have long recognized significant parallels between the Deuteronomic Code and the religious and political reforms associated with Josiah in 2 Kings.[40] Indeed, since the seminal work of Wilhelm Martin Leberecht de Wette,[41] most scholars, with some exceptions,[42] have accepted the dating of the Deuteronomic law collection to the seventh century, during the reign of Josiah.[43] What

---

224, 256–61; Marc Z. Brettler, *The Creation of History in Ancient Israel* (London: Routledge, 1995), especially chapter 4, "Deuteronomy as Interpretation," 62–78; J. Van Seters, "Creative Imitation," 400–02; M. Smith, "Pseudepigraphy in the Israelite Literary Tradition," 200–09.

[40] See the review of scholarship by Gary N. Knoppers, *Two Nations Under God: The Deuteronomistic History of Solomon and the Dual Monarchies. Volume 2: The Reign of Jeroboam, the Fall of Israel, and the Reign of Josiah* (HSM 53; Atlanta: Scholars Press, 1994), 125–33. See also Mordechai Cogan and Hayim Tadmor, *II Kings: A New Translation* (AB 11; New York: Doubleday, 1988), 293–94; Frank Moore Cross, "The Themes of the Book of Kings," 274–89; Sid Z. Leiman, *The Canonization of Hebrew Scripture: The Talmudic and Midrashic Evidence* (Hamden, Conn.: Archon, 1976), 143 n. 73; J. Blenkinsopp, *The Pentateuch*, 214–17; Moshe Weinfeld, "The Scribes and 'The Book of the Torah,'" in *Deuteronomy and the Deuteronomic School* (Oxford; Clarendon, 1972; repr., Winona Lake, Ind.: Eisenbrauns, 1992), 158–71; Norbert Lohfink, "The Cult Reform of Josiah of Judah: 2 Kings 22–23 as a Source for the History of Israelite Religion," in *Ancient Israelite Religion: Essays in Honor of Frank Moore Cross* (ed. P. D. Miller Jr., P. D. Hanson, and S. D. McBride; Philadelphia: Fortress, 1987), 459–75.

[41] Wilhelm Martin Leberecht de Wette, *Dissertatio critico-exegetica, qua Deuteronomium a prioribus Pentateuchi libris diversum, alius cuiusdam recentioris auctoris opus esse monstratur* (Ienae: Literis Etzdorfii, 1805).

[42] For a few examples of scholars who believe that the discovery narrative is an exilic or postexilic creation with little or no connection to the historical events of Josiah's reign, see the following: Robert H. Kennett, *Deuteronomy and the Decalogue* (Cambridge: Cambridge University Press, 1920), 2–3; Gustav Hölscher, "Komposition und Ursprung des Deuteronomiums," *ZAW* 40 (1922): 161–255, 231; idem, "Das Buch der Könige, seine Quellen und seine Redaktion," in ΕΥΧΑΡΙΣΤΗΡΙΟΝ: *Studien zur Religion und Literatur des Alten und Neuen Testaments* (FRLANT 36/1; ed. H. Schmidt; Göttingen: Vandenhoeck & Ruprecht, 1923), 158–213; Friedrich Horst, "Die Kultsreform des Königs Josia (II Rg. 22–23)," *ZDMG* 77 (1923): 220–35, 226; Ernst Würthwein, "Die josianische Reform und das Deuteronomium," *ZTK* 73 (1976): 395–423, 421; Martin Rose, "Bermerkungen zum historischen Fundament des Josia-Bildes in II Reg. 22 f.," *ZAW* 89 (1977): 55–62; Christoph Levin, "Joschija im deuteronomistischen Geschichtswerk," *ZAW* 96 (1984): 351–71, 354–56; Philip R. Davies, *In Search of 'Ancient Israel'* (JSOTSup 148; Sheffield: JSOT Press, 1992), 94–112.

[43] G. N. Knoppers states: "Given the tremendous upheaval Josiah creates with his cultic revolution, the Deuteronomist downplays, even obfuscates, his differences with Deuteronomy. The spotlight on Deuteronomy enables the Deuteronomist to portray Josiah's innovations as renovations, his revolution in religion as a restoration to an ancient ideal" (*Two Nations*, 2:124).

remains controversial, however, is the significance of the connection between the Deuteronomic Code and what have come to be called the Josianic reforms.[44]

Arguably the most radical and significant Josianic reform is the centralization of the cult, expressed by the Deuteronomic Code's careful reworking of earlier traditions from the Covenant Code that explicitly allowed for sacrificing outside the temple and outside Jerusalem.[45] In a recent study, Bernard Levinson examines these reworkings with much care and in great detail.[46] He concludes that the Deuteronomic Code is a deliberately subversive and transformative text that is intended to *replace* the Covenant Code.[47]

However, this thesis encounters a difficulty. If one intends to *replace* an earlier code, why should one exert so much effort to incorporate and preserve its wording? Why should one constantly remind the

---

[44] See the extensive discussion of Josiah's reforms in G. N. Knoppers, *Two Nations*, 2:171–228. Also relevant are the following: N. Lohfink, "The Cult Reform of Josiah," 459–75; idem, "Recent Discussions on 2 Kings 22–23: The State of the Question," in *A Song of Power and the Power of Song: Essays on the Book of Deuteronomy* ("Zur neuern Diskussion über 2 Kön 22–23," in *Das Deuteronomium: Entstehung, Gestalt und Bostschaft* [ed. N. Lohfink; BETL 68; Louvain: Louvain University Press, 1985], 24–48; repr., trans. L. M. Maloney; ed. D. L. Christensen; SBTS 3; Winona Lake, Ind.: Eisenbrauns, 1993), 36–61; Frank Moore Cross and David Noel Freedman, "Josiah's Revolt against Assyria," *JNES* 13 (1954): 56–58; W. Eugene Claburn, "The Fiscal Basis of Josiah's Reforms," *JBL* 92 (1973): 11–22; Jon D. Levenson, "Who Inserted the Book of the Torah?," *HTR* 68 (1975): 203–33; Hermann Spieckermann, *Juda unter Assur in der Sargonidenzeit* (FRLANT 129; Göttingen: Vandenhoeck & Ruprecht, 1982), 30–160; Lyle Eslinger, "Josiah and the Torah Book: Comparison of 2 Kgs 22:1–23:28 and 2 Chr 34:1–35:19," *HAR* 10 (1986): 37–62. For a recent attempt to place the final form of the Book of the Covenant during the Persian Period in connection with Ezra's reforms see Joy Joseph, *'Re-Lecturing' of Deuteronomy (Chapter [sic] 12–26) in the Post-Exilic Period* (Berlin: Logos Verlag, 1997).

One cannot assume that Deuteronomy and the Deuteronomistic History originate from the same community or that those responsible for the production of these works had a shared agenda. See G. N. Knoppers: "If much of Deuteronomy's political, social and cultic legislation seems to reflect the concerns and priorities of scribes, officials, and priests at the temple court in Jerusalem, the Deuteronomistic historiography of the monarchy reflects the concerns and priorities of scribes and governmental officials at Jerusalem's court" ("Rethinking the Relationship," 408).

[45] On the centralization of the cult as part of the southern and northern reforms during Josiah's reign, see G. N. Knoppers, *Two Nations*, 2:191–228.

[46] B. M. Levinson, *Deuteronomy and the Hermeneutics of Legal Innovation*.

[47] See a similar position advocated by Otto Eissfeldt that the purpose of the inclusion of earlier material in Deuteronomy is to make those texts which are "embedded superfluous, or at any rate to correct it and to lead to its being understood in a particular sense" (*The Old Testament: An Introduction* [trans. P. Ackroyd; New York: Harper & Row, 1966], 221).

reader of the earlier text, already accepted as authoritative, which one wishes to supplant? Would these constant reminders not be self-defeating? Levinson addresses this difficulty when he writes:

> Through their exegetical reworking, the authors of Deuteronomy transform the Exodus altar law. They rework its key terms in such a way as finally to make it prohibit what it originally sanctioned (multiple altar sites as legitimate) and command the two innovations it could never have contemplated: cultic centralization and local, secular slaughter. Both the technique and the boldness of this hermeneutical transformation are remarkable. The lemma is viewed atomistically: legal or textual authority operates at the level of individual words that, even when recontextualized, retain their operative force. Such studied concern with textual authority, not to mention the immense meditation upon the laws that it presupposes, is astonishing in seventh-century Israel. In its reuse, the Exodus lemma is so fundamentally transformed that it commands both cultic sacrifice (at the central sanctuary) and local slaughter (voided of ritual meaning). The antithetical reworking of the original text suggests an extraordinary ambivalence on the part of the authors of Deuteronomy, who retain the old altar law only to transform it and who thereby subvert the very textual authority that they invoke.[48]

Here Levinson recognizes a tension between the goal he ascribes to the Deuteronomists and the rewriting strategy they employ. He conceptualizes this tension as "an extraordinary ambivalence" within the minds of the Deuteronomists themselves. It seems to me, however, that the tension is purely internal to Levinson's account. It is a tension between the details of his analyses and the terms of his conclusion. If the intention to *replace* the Covenant Code were not ascribed to the Deuteronomists, then the tension would disappear. Perhaps what underlies Levinson's interpretation of the Deuteronomist's intention is a contemporary conception of textual authority, according to which the actual words and "plain meaning" of a text have a certain integrity. On this conception, a text may be faithfully reproduced, in whole or in part, or it may be repudiated and replaced. To produce an edited version of the text, however, in a way that alters the wording and even counters the "plain meaning" of the text, is simply unacceptable. Since the Deuteronomists choose precisely the latter, unacceptable option, they must be viewed as ambivalent between the first two options, between reproduction and replacement. But

---

[48] B. M. Levinson, *Deuteronomy and the Hermeneutics of Legal Innovation*, 46.

this conclusion seems compulsory only if the contemporary conception of textual authority is assumed to be operative for the Deuteronomist. In fact, there is no explicit evidence whatsoever that replacement is the Deuteronomist's goal. Indeed, the only evidence supporting the replacement thesis is, at the same time, evidence that counts against it. For the only evidence is the transformative character of some Deuteronomic reworkings. But, as we have seen, the very fact that these are *reworkings* and not independent texts also creates a difficulty for the replacement thesis.[49]

In addition, Levinson's argument for the replacement thesis turns on the subtlety with which the Deuteronomists appropriated and amended the precise language of the Covenant Code to fit their own purposes. This presupposes that the text of the Covenant Code was already fixed in the seventh century B.C.E., and indeed that we can now reconstruct that text accurately. But there is simply no evidence to support these presuppositions.[50]

Finally, as Joseph Blenkinsopp has pointed out, approximately two-thirds of the laws in the Covenant Code are not repeated in the Deuteronomic Code.[51] But there is no reason to think that Deuteronomists intended these laws to be forgotten. Instead, there is good reason to think that they intended the Covenant Code to be preserved alongside the Deuteronomic Code, with the latter serving as the authentic exposition of certain laws in the former.[52] One might also argue that the exilic frame of Deuteronomy alludes to narratives

---

[49] Here it may be objected that, paradoxical though it may sound, would-be replacements characteristically rework the very texts they seek to displace, thus usurping their authority. See A. Grafton: "Almost every other major forger known to us, from Ctesias in antiquity to such crude and incompetent modern epigones as Kujau, has inserted as much attested fact as possible into his creations to give the pure fantasies ballast and structure. The most ambitious forger imaginable, then, the one who seeks to reorient his contemporaries' mental maps of a whole sector of the past, must apparently depict many familiar landmarks even when he insists that he is not doing so" (*Forgers and Critics*, 61–62). I accept the point, but do not consider it an objection to my argument. For my thesis is not that there is no possibility whatsoever that Deuteronomy is intended as a replacement. My thesis is rather that it has not been proven that Deuteronomy is intended as a replacement if the reworking of older traditions serves as the *only* evidence.

[50] See E. Ulrich, *Dead Sea Scrolls and the Origins of the Bible*.

[51] J. Blenkinsopp, *The Pentateuch*, 210.

[52] See also Patrick D. Miller Jr., "'Moses My Servant': The Deuteronomic Portrait of Moses," *Int* 41 (1987): 245–55; repr. in *A Song of Power and the Power of Song: Essays on the Book of Deuteronomy* (ed. D. L. Christensen; SBTS 3; Winona Lake, Ind.: Eisenbrauns, 1993), 301–12, esp. 306–07.

that are only elaborated in earlier traditions, which were presumably intended to survive, not to be replaced.[53] Indeed, this is exactly what we know to have happened: Deuteronomy came to be accepted as Scripture alongside earlier traditions, including the Covenant Code. Perhaps the co-existence of these two collections served as a license to continue the creative hermeneutical endeavor in the future.[54]

Still, if one remains committed to the replacement thesis, one will find ways of acknowledging—if not of alleviating—these difficulties. One may take the fact that the Deuteronomists presuppose, in various ways, the continued existence of the traditions they intend to replace, as an expression of their ambivalence. And one may view the reception of the Deuteronomic Code alongside the code it was intended to replace as a delicious irony: the subversion of the Deuteronomist's subversive intent.[55] Why, in the face of these difficulties, might one

---

[53] According to Thomas Römer, allusions to patriarchal narratives are characteristic of a post-exilic redaction: "This is the context in which the separation of Deuteronomy from the Deuteronomistic History and its attachment to the Pentateuch is probably situated, perhaps initially with the intention of reinforcing the deuteronomistic position somewhat. But how could the integration of Deuteronomy into this new Torah corpus be further emphasized? This is what might be called the 'final redaction,' concerned for the harmony of the whole, which took on the task by inserting into Deuteronomy (and elsewhere) the names of the patriarchs, in apposition to the deuteronomistic father. The theory that this identification is the work of a redaction of the Pentateuch is confirmed by the fact that neither in Joshua through 2 Kings nor in Jeremiah are the fathers assimilated in this way to the patriarchs. As we have already seen, the insertion of the names of Abraham, Isaac, and Jacob into Deuteronomy was carried out in a very considered way; it happened at strategic locations, such as the very beginning (Deut 1:8) and the end (34:4) of the book . . . By mentioning Abraham, Isaac, and Jacob seven times and thenceforth imposing the identification 'fathers = patriarchs,' the final redaction is manifestly striving to separate Deuteronomy from the Deuteronomistic History and reinforce the cohesiveness of the Pentateuch. In fact, the promises made to the patriarchs now function as a leitmotif covering the entirety of 'Genesis to Deuteronomy' (see especially Gen 50:24; Exod 32:13, 33:1; Lev 26:42; Num 32:11; Deut 32:4)" ("Deuteronomy in Search of Origins," in *Reconsidering Israel and Judah: Recent Studies on the Deuteronomistic History* ["Le Deutéronome à la quête des origins," in *Le Pentateuque: Débats et recherches* (ed. P. Haudebert; LD 151; Paris: Cerf, 1992), 65–98; repr., trans. P. T. Daniels; ed. G. N. Knoppers and J. G. McConville; SBTS 8; Winona Lake, Ind.: Eisenbrauns, 2000], 112–38, n. 156–57). For Dtr2 as responding to exile, see also J. D. Levenson, "Who Inserted," 232 n. 31. In addition, see the insights of Hans W. Wolff, "Das kerygma des deuteronomistichen Geschichteswerkes," *ZAW* 73 (1961): 171–86. Finally, see the critique of Wolff by F. M. Cross, "The Themes of the Book of Kings," 277–78.

[54] This suggestion was made by Hugh R. Page, Jr., in private communication, May 2002.

[55] Again, see B. M. Levinson's various comments in his *Deuteronomy and the Hermeneutics of Legal Innovation*: "The authors of Deuteronomy sought to locate their

remain committed to the replacement thesis? Ultimately, I suggest, what underlies the debate between those who regard the law code as intending to replace earlier traditions, and those who regard it as intending to expound and expand those traditions, are the questions: Should a contemporary conception of textual authority be attributed to the Deuteronomists? What alternative could there be?

Alas, there are no short or decisive answers to these questions. There are, for example, no biblical parallels to the explicit statements of Iamblichus and Tertullian quoted above. Consequently, the proposal that there are alternatives and that the replacement thesis is anachronistic could be demonstrated by nothing short of a thoroughgoing reconstruction of conceptions of textual authority and authorship operative in the various strata of Deuteronomy. If such a reconstruction is plausible, and if the resulting conceptions of textual authority and authorship are compatible with an interpretation of the Deuteronomic project as exposition and expansion, then the replacement thesis should lose its attraction. For the reworking of the language of earlier traditions in the Deuteronomic Code, a failure to mention specific laws, and the presence of allusions to narratives that are not retold, are only difficulties on the assumption that the replacement thesis is true.

This is not the place for a thoroughgoing reconstruction, since my focus in this book is on Second Temple texts. However, consideration of 2 Kings 22–23—the crucial text concerning the origin of the Deuteronomic Code—seems to me illuminating, if not decisive. Here is narrated the event that is said to have initiated the Josianic reforms: the discovery of the scroll whose content is identified by scholars with the Deuteronomic Code.[56]

---

innovative vision in prior textual authority by tendentiously appropriating texts like the Covenant Code . . ." (16); ". . . the authors of Deuteronomy used the Covenant Code as a textual resource in order to pursue their own very different religious and legal agenda. The authors of Deuteronomy employed the garb of dependence to purchase profound hermeneutical independence" (149); "Imitation becomes the sincerest form of encroachment" (150); "It therefore represents a major irony of literary history that Second Temple editors incorporated both the Covenant Code and the legal corpus of Deuteronomy into the Pentateuch. In doing so, they preserved Deuteronomy alongside the very text that it sought to replace and subvert" (153).

[56] As Sara Japhet notes: "Since de Wette's epoch making *Dissertatio Critica* (1805), it has been generally accepted by biblical scholarship that the book which prompted Josiah's reform was Deuteronomy, either in its canonical form or some variation of it . . ." (*I & II Chronicles: A Commentary* [OTL; Louisville: Westminster/John Knox, 1993], 1030).

2 Kgs 22:8–10[57]

(8) ויאמר חלקיהו הכהן הגדול על שפן הספר ספר התורה מצאתי בבית יהוה
ויתן חלקיה את הספר אל שפן ויקראהו (9) ויבא שפן הספר אל המלך וישב
את המלך דבר ויאמר התיכו עבדיך את הכסף הנמצא בבית ויתנהו על יד עשי
המלאכה המפקדים בית יהוה (10) וינד שפן הספר למלך לאמר ספר נתן לי
חלקיה הכהן ויקראהו שפן לפני המלך

(8) Then the high priest Hilkiah said to the scribe Shaphan, "I have
found a scroll of the Teaching in the House of the LORD." And Hilkiah
gave the scroll to Shaphan, who read it. (9) The scribe Shaphan then
went to the king and reported to the king: "Your servants have melted
down the silver that was deposited in the House, and they have deliv-
ered it to the overseers of the work who are in charge at the House
of the LORD." (10) The scribe Shaphan also told the king, "The high
priest Hilkiah has given me a scroll"; and Shaphan read it to the king.

What, according to this text, is the basis of the scroll's authority? It
is the connection of the scroll to three authoritative institutions: the
temple, the monarchy, and the prophet. First, the scroll is discovered in the House of the LORD, where it had presumably been
deposited for priestly safekeeping, for it is discovered in the "House
of the LORD."

Second, the king is deeply affected when the scroll is read to him.
Indeed, he is moved to begin the process of reform.[58]

2 Kgs 22:11

ויהי כשמע המלך את דברי ספר התורה ויקרע את בגדיו

When the king heard the words of the scroll of the Teaching, he rent
his clothes.

---

[57] All of the subsequent citations follow the *BHS* with translations from NJPS.

[58] This is the perspective of the Deuteronomistic History, but it is not shared by
the Chronicler who has a different order of events: the cultic reforms occur first
with the "discovery" of the "scroll of the Torah" as its by-product rather than its
cause (2 Chr 34:1–21). On this issue, DtrH's view has typically been favored over
that of Chr, but there are some exceptions. See, e.g., L. Eslinger, "Josiah and the
Torah Book," 59–60 and Theodor Oestreicher, *Das deuteronomistische Grundgesetz*
(BFCT 27/4; Gütersloh: Bertelsmann, 1923), 60–65. It is noteworthy that the
reforms associated with Josiah (e.g., covenant renewal, northern campaigns, appeals
to the remnant of Israel, cultic and administrative reforms) are unprecedented in
DtrH, but they appear as major themes in Chr (G. N. Knoppers, *Two Nations*,
2:191, n. 42). See the discussion of these themes in the following: Klaus Baltzer,
The Covenant Formulary in Old Testament, Jewish, and Early Christian Writings (trans. D. E.
Green; Philadelphia: Fortress, 1971), 51–52, 72–78; Sara Japhet, *The Ideology of the
Book of Chronicles and its Place in Biblical Thought* (trans. A. Barber; BEATAJ 9; Frankfort:

Third, the scroll's message is interpreted by the prophetess Huldah.[59]
What is remarkable here is what is *not* said. Nothing explicit is
said about the author or origin of the scroll, rather only about the
location of its discovery, i.e., in the temple. Questions that seem to
us to be pressing—even unavoidable—are apparently of no interest
to Josiah and his cohorts. They do not ask of the scroll the questions that, as Foucault says, we ask of a text today: "From where
does it come, who wrote it, when, under what circumstances, or
beginning with what design?" By the seventh century B.C.E., it became

---

Lang, 1989), 105–16; Gary N. Knoppers, "A Reunited Kingdom in Chronicles?"
PEGLMBS 9 (1989): 74–88; H. G. M. Williamson, *Israel in the Book of Chronicles*
(Cambridge: Cambridge University Press, 1977), 97–131.

The importance of the Torah in Chr has been noted by several scholars; see
especially: Gerhard von Rad, *Das Geschichtsbild des chronistischen Werkes* (Stuttgart:
Kohlhammer, 1930), 41–63; Thomas Willi, *Die Chronik als Auslegung* (FRLANT 106;
Göttingen: Vandenhoeck & Ruprecht, 1972), 48–52; S. Japhet, *Ideology*, 234–47;
Isac L. Seeligman, "ניצני מדרש בספר דברי הימים," *Tarbiz* 49 (1979–80): 14–32; Judson
R. Shaver, *Torah and the Chronicler's History Work: An Inquiry into the Chronicler's References
to Laws, Festivals, and Cultic Institutions in Relationship to Pentateuchal Legislation* (BJS 196;
Atlanta: Scholars Press, 1989), 73–86. See also the discussion of written documents
in the Chronicler by Steven J. Schweitzer, "Reading Chronicles as Utopian
Historiography: Continuity and Innovation in Service of the Cult," (paper presented
at the National annual meeting of the SBL, Denver, Colo., 18 November, 2001),
1–12.

On the relationship between writing and prophetic interpretation in Chronicles
see William M. Schniedewind, *The Word of God in Transition: From Prophet to Exegete
in the Second Temple Period* (JSOTSup 197; Sheffield: Sheffield Academic, 1995); idem,
"Prophets and Prophecy in the Books of Chronicles," in *The Chronicler as Historian*
(ed. M. P. Graham, K. G. Hoglund, and S. L. McKenzie; JSOTSup 238; Sheffield:
Sheffield Academic, 1997), 204–24; idem, "The Chronicler as an Interpreter of
Scripture," in *The Chronicler as Author: Studies in Text and Texture* (ed. M. P. Graham
and S. L. McKenzie; JSOTSup 263; Sheffield: Sheffield Academic, 1999), 158–80.
For the efficacy of writing in prophetic texts, see, e.g., Isaiah 8, Exodus 19 and 32,
Haggai 2, Zechariah 5, Ezekiel 2–3 and 37. In this context, it is common to speak
of a "textualization of Judaism" during the Persian and Hellenistic periods. See
J. L. Kugel, "Early Interpretation," 13–72; and my survey of the issue in "Torah
of Moses," 202–16; idem, "Authoritative Writing and Interpretation: A Study in
the History of Scripture" (Ph.D. diss., Harvard University, 1998), especially 15–118.

[59] Huldah's oracle was edited at least twice by exilic editors. On this point see
G. N. Knoppers, *Two Nations*, 2:140–56. On page 145, he provides a summary of
the different ways of understanding the nature of Huldah's oracle (which he cor-
rectly notes is actually two separate oracles which are related in a complex manner). His own view of this textual development argues for one exilic redaction which
attempts to "rehabilitate the reputation of Josiah" by recasting the second oracle
and creating the first (2 Kgs 22:18–20 and 22:16a–17b) followed by a second exilic
redaction which focused on Josiah's contrition as a model of repentance and shaped
the passage apologetically to explain his death at the hands of Pharaoh Neco
(152–56).

essential to insist on certain answers to at least some of these questions—for example, that Moses wrote the authoritative text at Sinai,
on God's instruction, or at some divinely appointed angel's dictation. But in 2 Kings 22–23, these answers are not even suggested.
The questions to which they respond are not even raised. Instead
those who discover and read the text presuppose that the discovered
text is part of the original Mosaic revelation at Sinai.[60] The priest,
scribe and king are ultimately sufficient to authorize a text, be it
new or old, and later exilic hands attribute the reinterpretation(s) of
that discovered scroll to the prophetess Huldah.

To be sure, this is an argument from silence. But it strongly suggests that the scribes behind the production of Dtr1 operated with
a conception of textual authority strikingly different from our own
and, indeed, from conceptions operative in later Deuteronomic strata.
If so, then we should be sensitive to the historical development of
conceptions of authority and authorship, and we should avoid the
anachronistic imposition of conceptions from one period upon texts
from another. Once alternatives to our contemporary conceptions
are considered, the replacement thesis seems obligatory no longer.

Self-Ascribed Status of Torah

In other pentateuchal traditions, what is characterized as Torah is
typically a law or body of laws concerned with a specific content.[61]
A Torah is thus a *conceptual unity* that is constituted by the common

---

[60] See G. N. Knoppers on this point in his chapter five, "Innovation as Renovation:
Josiah and 'The Scroll of the Torah,'" in *Two Nations*, 2:121–169. Knoppers suggests that 2 Kings 22–23 connects the discovery of the scroll in 2 Kings to the
Sinai event by using the phrase 'the scroll of the covenant' to refer to the temple
document (2:131; 131, n. 20). Furthermore, Knoppers states the following: "In any
event, Josiah's profound respect for 'the scroll of the torah' is evident in his ratio-
nale for consulting Huldah [citing 2 Kgs 22:13]" (2:135).

[61] According to Jacob Milgrom and Israel Knohl, the Priestly Torah referred to
traditions (perhaps separate scrolls of law) as *Torah*. Traditions of Torah are part
of the Priestly Torah, which was subsequently edited by the Holiness School and,
at a later stage, incorporated into the Pentateuch. For some discussion of these collection of "laws" see Israel Knohl, *The Sanctuary of Silence*, 6 and 89 n. 91; Jacob
Milgrom, *Leviticus 1–16: A New Translation with Introduction and Commentary* (AB 3; New
York: Doubleday, 1991), 2 and 688 on Lev 11:46. For a discussion of the characteristics of ancient Torah Scrolls see Étan Levine, "The Transcription of the Torah
Scroll," *ZAW* 94 (1982): 99–105; Menahem Haran, "Book-Scrolls in Israel in Pre-
Exilic Times," *JJS* 33 (1982): 161–73.

features or shared subject matter of its members.[62] It is not a collection of *toroth*, but is linked to a single founder and referred to as a single unit of law and history. What is new in Deuteronomic traditions is that the status of Torah is sometimes ascribed to a unit of instruction that lacks this specificity of content or conceptual unity. "Deuteronomy is in fact the only book of the Pentateuch that refers to itself as *torah*."[63] Instead of being characterized conceptually, this unit is designated by means of a *demonstrative*—the linguistic device typically used when conceptual designation is not available. Thus, for example, at the beginning of Deuteronomy, Moses undertakes to expound "this Torah" (1:5):

בעבר הירדן בארץ מואב הואיל משה באר את התורה הזאת לאמר

On the other side of the Jordan, in the land of Moab, Moses undertook to expound this Teaching. He said . . .

It is "this Torah" which he places before the children of Israel (4:44):[64]

וזאת התורה אשר שם משה לפני בני ישראל

This is the Teaching that Moses set before the Israelites:

Here the status of Torah is ascribed, not to specific laws or bodies of law, but to authoritative tradition as a whole, including laws of

---

[62] For a discussion of how the term "Torah" is used as a strategic means of textual production and collection, see Jean-Pierre Sonnet, *The Book Within the Book: Writing in Deuteronomy* (BIS 14; Leiden: Brill, 1997), esp. 12–26 and 235–36.

See also on the nature of deixis, *IBHS* 54–55, 235–52, 306–14. The deictic sign refers "to the situation of communication, pointing outside the discourse" (*IBHS*, 55) and makes it "possible for speaker and hearer to situate an utterance without explicitly mentioning all characterizing features" (*IBHS*, 235). The deictic particle thus produces a separation and specifies one thing from another; i.e., "this is not that." Through the use of the deictic particle, a collection is organized; an entity emerges that is coherent and complete, without need to refer again to that which is outside its assigned delimiter.

[63] Dennis T. Olson, *Deuteronomy and the Death of Moses: A Theological Reading* (OBT; Minneapolis: Fortress, 1994), 8.

[64] S. B. Chapman, "The Law and the Words," states: "Within Deuteronomy all the references to תורה—with three exceptions—appear in the literary frame to the book now found in chs. 1–11 and 27–34. All three exceptions are located in ch. 17, long suspected of exhibiting later redaction. The references to תורה in the framing material are interesting not only because they appear to have selected this word from among other legal terms to refer to the Mosaic covenant, but also because they use תורה to refer to the book of Deuteronomy itself as the embodiment of that covenant. Within the literary frame, a deictic pronoun is often used together with תורה to refer to the book of Deuteronomy as such" (30–31).

many kinds, as well as narratives—thus to a whole whose members share no common features or content, a whole whose unity can only be indicated as that which is present to the reader.[65] Such ascriptions of the status of Torah to authoritative tradition as a whole are characteristic, not only of Deuteronomic texts, but of all texts participating in what I am calling Mosaic Discourse.

Such a conception of Torah may easily be extended to the exposition and expansion characteristic of Deuteronomic reworkings of earlier traditions. Not only is a specific law Torah, but so too is its reworking, understood as its authentic expression.[66]

It is noteworthy that the discovered scroll in 2 Kgs 23:3 is said to be a *sefer Torah*:

ויעמד המלך על העמוד ויכרת את הברית לפני יהוה ללכת אחר יהוה ולשמר
מצותיו ואת עדותיו ואת חקתיו בכל לב ובכל נפש להקים את דברי הברית הזאת
הכתבים על הספר הזה ויעמד כל העם בברית

> The king stood by the pillar and solemnized the covenant before the LORD: that they would follow the LORD and observe His commandments, His injunctions, and His laws with all their heart and soul; that they would fulfill all the terms of this covenant as inscribed upon the scroll. And all the people entered into the covenant.

Here the deictic—הכתבים על הספר הזה—is also used. Thus the text of 2 Kings 22–23 invokes the very same authority that Deuteronomy accords to itself, the authority of "this Torah," of the whole tradition placed by Moses before the children of Israel.

Re-Presentation of Sinaitic Revelation

The use of a demonstrative or deictic term is informative only when it is clear from which point of view the term is being used. In general,[67] Deuteronomic texts do not use such terms from the point of

---

[65] For additional uses of the deictic, see Deut 4:8; 17:18–19; 27:3, 8, 26; 28:58, 61; 29:28; 31:9, 26.

[66] S. B. Chapman, "The Law and the Words," concludes: "It appears likely that תורה sometimes refers to a re-interpretation or an extension of the biblical traditions as a whole" (51).

[67] There are of course exceptions: 1:1–5; 2:10–12, 20–23; 4:44–49; 5:1a; 10:6–9; 27:1a, 9a, 11; 28:69; 29:1a; 31:1, 7a, 9, 10, 14–21, 22, 23a, 24–25, 30; 32:44–46a, 48–52; 33:1–2a, 7a, 8a, 12a, 13a, 18a, 20a, 22a, 23a, 24a; 34:1–9. For further discussion of attribution to Moses see note 76 below.

view of a specified speaker—say, of Moses. Rather, they use such terms within anonymous third person descriptions of the speech and actions of Moses. That is to say, they use such terms *from the point of the view of the text's reader or listener.*[68]

This is of great importance, for it follows that the unity of Torah, in the special sense of the Deuteronomist, is secured through *the presence of tradition to those who read or hear the words of Torah.* This presence is itself authority-conferring insofar as it is a re-presentation of the event of revelation. Thus, Deuteronomy claims, through Moses' discourse in Moab, to re-present Sinai (Deut 5:3).[69]

לֹא אֶת אֲבֹתֵינוּ כָּרַת יְהוָה אֶת הַבְּרִית הַזֹּאת כִּי אִתָּנוּ אֲנַחְנוּ אֵלֶּה פֹה הַיּוֹם כֻּלָּנוּ חַיִּים

It was not with our fathers that the LORD made this covenant, but with us, the living, every one of us who is here today.

Later in Deuteronomy, we see another explicit reenactment of the Sinai event (Deut 31:12–13):

---

[68] Scholars have long pointed out that Torah was not originally connected to Sinai. Jon D. Levenson notes: "The mention of Sinai (vv 9, 18 [in Psalm 68]) clearly implies a connection between YHWH and that mountain much closer than what we would expect from the Pentateuchal narratives in which Mount Sinai seems to be no more than the place in which the revelation of law took place . . . The 'One of Sinai' is the numen, the deity, of that mountain, the God of whom Sinai is characteristic. The same expression occurs in an identical context in the famous Song of Deborah (Judg 5:4–5). It is possible that 'Sinai' in Ps 68:9, 18 and Judg 5:5 is a gentilic adjective related to the 'Wilderness of Sin,' a desert probably in the Sinai peninsula (e.g., Exod 16:1). If so, the expression refers to a broader area than the mountain itself in its designation of the divine abode" (*Sinai and Zion: An Entry into the Jewish Bible* [San Francisco: Harper & Row, 1985], 19–20). On the origins of Psalm 68 see William F. Albright, "A Catalogue of Early Hebrew Lyric Poems (Psalm LXVIII)," *HUCA* 23 (1950): 1–39, and the discussion by Sigmund Mowinckel, *The Psalms in Israel's Worship* (trans. D. R. Ap-Thomas; rev. Eng. ed. in 2 vols.; Oxford: Basil Blackwell, 1962; repr., 1 vol. 1982; 1st ed. 1951), 1:5, 125, 152, 170–74, and 2:152–54.

[69] F. M. Cross affirms the position that the use of the phrase "to this day" is indicative of both the sources and the portions created by the Deuteronomistic author since at least two of its occurences presume "the existence of the Judacan state, notably 2 Kings 8:22 and 16:6" ("The Themes of the Book of Kings," 275). Thus, the phrase does not provide evidence of diverse material having been grouped together into only one redactional layer. Rather, the phrase may indicate material that has an ancient origin and has now gone under at least two subsequent redactions, both in the Deuteronomic tradition. Such a phrase allows for a certain degree of temporal flexibility and provides a means of participation by the readership of that particular text.

(12) הקהל את העם האנשים והנשים והטף וגרך אשר בשעריך למען ישמעו ולמען
ילמדו ויראו את יהוה אלהיכם ושמרו לעשות את כל דברי התורה הזאת (13)
ובניהם אשר לא ידעו ישמעו ולמדו ליראה את יהוה אלהיכם כל הימים אשר
אתם חיים על האדמה אשר אתם עברים את הירדן שמה לרשתה

(12) Gather the people—men, women, children, and the strangers in
your communities—that they may hear and so learn to revere the
LORD your God and to observe faithfully every word of this Teaching.
(13) Their children, too, who have not had the experience, shall hear
and learn to revere the LORD your God as long as they live in the
land that you are about to cross the Jordan to possess.

And Deut 31:28–30:[70]

(28) הקהילו אלי את כל זקני שבטיכם ושטריכם ואדברה באזניהם את הדברים
האלה ואעידה בם את השמים ואת הארץ (29) כי ידעתי אחרי מותי כי השחת
תשחתון וסרתם מן הדרך אשר צויתי אתכם וקראת אתכם הרעה באחרית הימים
כי תעשו את הרע בעיני יהוה להכעיסו במעשה ידיכם (30) וידבר משה באזני
כל קהל ישראל את דברי השירה הזאת עד תמם

(28) Gather to me all the elders of your tribes and your officials, that
I may speak all these words to them and that I may call heaven and
earth to witness against them. (29) For I know that, when I am dead,
you will act wickedly and turn away from the path that I enjoined
upon you, and that in time to come misfortune will befall you for having done evil in the sight of the LORD and vexed Him by your deeds.
(30) Then Moses recited the words of this poem to the very end, in
the hearing of the whole congregation of Israel.

In Nehemiah 8, set in a time of restoration and reform, we can
once again observe the repetition of this feature of Mosaic Discourse.
This text is a remarkable scene in which, at least from the perspective of Ezra-Nehemiah, the Torah was textualized and invested
in the Torah of Moses. According to Ezra-Nehemiah, the central
unifying event for the returning exiles was neither revelation mediated by a prophet, nor the coronation of a Davidic king—both of
which did not seem possible, or, perhaps even desirable from the
standpoint of fifth century B.C.E. Judahite leadership. Instead, the
central event was a public reading of the Mosaic Torah by Ezra

---

[70] G. N. Knoppers argues that the discovery of the scroll in 2 Kings 22–23 may
also be viewed as a re-presentation of Sinai; see *Two Nations Under God*, 2:168–69.

who was said to be both priest and scribe and who had interpreters at hand to supply explanations.[71] Neh 8:1–8:

(1) ויאספו כל העם כאיש אחד אל הרחוב אשר לפני שער המים ויאמרו
לעזרא הספר להביא את ספר תורת משה אשר צוה יהוה את ישראל
(2) ויביא עזרא הכהן את התורה לפני הקהל מאיש ועד אשה וכל מבין
לשמע ביום אחד לחדש השביעי (3) ויקרא בו לפני הרחוב אשר לפני
שער המים מן האור עד מחצית היום נגד האנשים והנשים והמבינים
ואזני כל העם אל ספר התורה (4) ויעמד עזרא הספר על מגדל עץ אשר
עשו לדבר ויעמד אצלו מתתיה ושמע ועניה ואוריה וחלקיה ומעשיה
על ימינו ומשמאלו פדיה ומישאל ומלכיה וחשם חשבדנה זכריה משלם
(5) ויפתח עזרא הספר לעיני כל העם כי מעל כל העם היה וכפתחו עמדו
כל העם (6) ויברך עזרא את יהוה האלהים הגדול ויענו כל־העם אמן אמן
במעל ידיהם ויקדו וישתחו ליהוה אפים ארצה (7) וישוע ובני ושרביה ימין
עקוב שבתי הודיה מעשיה קליטא עזריה יוזבד חנן פלאיה והלוים
מבינים את העם לתורה והעם על עמדם (8) ויקראו בספר בתורת האלהים
מפרש ושום שכל ויבינו במקרא:

All the people gathered together in the broad open space in front of the Water Gate. They asked Ezra the scribe to bring the book of the Torah of Moses that the LORD had commanded Israel. Ezra the priest brought the Torah before the assembly, men, women, and all who could hear with understanding, on the first day of the seventh month. He read aloud from it before the broad open space in front of the Water Gate from dawn until midday facing the men, women, and the interpreters, and the ears of all the people were attentive to the book of the Torah. Ezra the scribe stood upon a wooden tower which they

---

[71] The introduction to Ezra's mission in the Masoretic text of 7:1–10 provides information about Ezra's lineage and indicates what was involved in authorizing a leader for the returning exiles in the early post-exilic period. We are told that Ezra possessed the required authority and sufficient preparation for the job. First, Ezra is included in the Aaronide line of priests and is therefore a priest with the highest pedigree, who is therefore authorized to conduct temple sacrifice and ritual. However, Ezra is never included in any of the high priestly lineages. It is notable that in later Jewish interpretive traditions, the Rabbis write that if Aaron had been living during the time of Ezra, he would have been considered inferior to Ezra (*Qoh. Rab.* 1.4). Second, Ezra is a scribe who is an "expert in the Teaching of Moses" (Ezra 7:6). He therefore provides an authoritative link to the pre-exilic past of the returnees. Third, Ezra is said to have "dedicated himself to study the Teaching of the LORD" (7:6). Thus, Ezra is prepared for the task of interpreting, explaining, and applying the ancient law to a new context in which Israel is ruled, not by a Davidic monarch, but by a Persian king. Finally, Ezra is said to be "in the benevolence of the LORD" (7:6) and of God (7:9). Ezra continues to be celebrated in later Jewish traditions. Perhaps most remarkable are the repeated comparisons between Ezra and Moses. See, for example, *t. Sanh.* 4.4, which states: "Ezra was sufficiently worthy that the Torah could have been given through him if Moses had not preceded him."

had crafted for this thing. Next to him, on his right stood Mattithiah, Shema, Anaiah, Uriah, Hilkiah, and Maaseiah and on his left Pedaiah, Mishael, Malkijah, Hashum, Hashbaddanah, Zechariah, and Meshullam. Ezra the scribe opened the scroll before the eyes of the entire people, for he was above all of the people. When he opened it all of the people stood. Ezra blessed the LORD, the great God, and the entire people answered: "Amen, Amen" while raising their hands, bowing down, and prostrating themselves before the Lord with their faces upon the ground. Jeshua, Bani, Sherebiah, Jamin, Akkub, Shabbethai, Hodiah, Maaseiah, Kelita, Azariah, Jozabad, Hanan, Pelaiah, and the Levites, the ones interpreting the Torah for the people while the people stood. They read aloud from the book of the Torah of God, explaining, applying insight, and making the lection comprehensible.

Here the scroll of Torah is read, not to a king, but rather to all of the members of the assembly.[72] The people publicly hear and then publicly accept the Torah. It is as if they reenact the covenant on Sinai, except that this time their mediator is not the prophetic scribe and divine amanuensis,[73] but rather a scribe who is able to read what Moses had written.

However, merely seeing and hearing Ezra's reading did not guarantee that the people would understand what was read. They required the intervention of the interpreters who stood on the side. These interpreters must have translated Mosaic Torah into a language the people could understand. Perhaps, like later Targumim, their translations also resolved difficulties of comprehension and interpretation, and perhaps they resolved these difficulties in ways that had already become traditional.

We cannot say much that is definite about the contribution of these interpreters, but we can say that it was fateful for the development

---

[72] J. L. Kugel notes: "The incident does provide a useful index for the growing role of Scripture in this community. For it is noteworthy that this Torah is not a text for rulers or community leaders alone; its statutes are not meant even to provide only the operative legal framework for community life, as for example our legal systems do. . . . The Torah, if it is to function as the central text for the community, must truly be their common property, and be properly understood by everyone" ("Early Interpretation," 22).

[73] E.g., Exodus 32–34 where Moses is depicted as rewriting what God had inscribed. See also Brevard S. Childs, *The Book of Exodus: A Critical, Theological Commentary* (OTL; Louisville: Westminster, 1976), 557–62, 604–10; R. Edelman, "To 'annot Exodus xxxii 18," *VT* 16 (1966): 355; Roger N. Whybray, "annôt in Exodus xxxii 18," *VT* 17 (1967): 122; Sigo Lehming, "Versuch zu Ex. xxxii," *VT* 10 (1960): 16–50; Lothar Perlitt, *Bundestheologie im Alten Testament* (WMANT 36; Neukirchen Vluyn: Neukirchener Verlag, 1969), 203 ff.

of Second Temple Judaism. Mosaic Torah could not function as the
authoritative center of religious life unless apparent anachronisms
and legal or narrative inconsistencies could be regarded as manifes-
tations of the text's cryptic nature. In Neh 8:1–8, the interpreter
supplanted the prophet as mediator of God's word. But the authority of the interpreter, unlike that of the prophet, depended upon the
authenticity of the text as Mosaic. The Torah of ancient Judaism
was authorized, at least in part, insofar as it claimed to be the faithfully transmitted text of Sinai and insofar as it was linked, explicitly, to the revelation of Moses at Sinai.

These re-presentations of Sinai serve to authorize the re-intro-
duction of Torah into the Jewish community at times of legal reform
and of covenant renewal. The revelation at Sinai is not a one-time
event, but rather an event that can be re-presented, even in exile.[74]
In fact, that repetition became central to Jewish self-understanding
in the exile and in the post-exilic period as well. Jon Levenson writes:

> Sinai was a kind of archetype, a mold into which new experiences
> could be fit, hundreds of years after the original event, if such there
> was. That mold served as a source of continuity which enabled new
> norms to be promulgated with the authority of the old and enabled
> social change to take place without rupturing the sense of tradition
> and the continuity of historic identity . . . The experience of Sinai, what-
> ever its historical basis, was perceived as so overwhelming, so charged
> with meaning, that Israel could not imagine that any truth or com-
> mandment from God could have been absent from Sinai.[75]

Pseudonymous Attribution to Moses

It has long been recognized in biblical scholarship that the attribution to Moses in the book of Deuteronomy is pseudonymous.[76] But

---

[74] D. T. Olson states: "Thus, the writing of the Mosaic *torah* did not freeze the
tradition into a dead letter. Instead, the writing of the text freed it to become a
dynamic witness by which God's word could tangibly transcend boundaries of time,
generations, and space. Moreover, the provisions for its continued reading, studying and interpreting by human priests, elders, and all people ensured that its words
would be constantly reinterpreted and reapplied to new situations and times" (*Death
of Moses*, 136).

[75] J. D. Levenson, *Sinai and Zion*, 18–19.

[76] See, e.g., the discussion of pseudonymous attribution to Moses in M. Smith,
"Pseudepigraphy in the Israelite Tradition," 199–205. There are, of course, a number of direct addresses where God speaks to the people. However, if one argues

it remains to be resolved how to characterize what seems to a contemporary eye to be a forgery. Patrick Miller writes:

> It is, of course, highly unlikely that we have here an accurate historical report of words and actions by Moses on the plains of Moab before the settlement. The creation of the Book of Deuteronomy appears to have been a complex, prolonged process, most of which probably took place at a much later time. What was in the minds of the now unknown persons who over a period of time composed Deuteronomy can only be a matter of speculation. However, it is likely that the ascription and reception of this book as Mosaic was done in a most serious fashion and that the portrait of Moses as the teacher-prophet who alone received the divine word from the Lord and expounded it to the people served to enhance the seriousness with which the book would be received by the community.[77]

So, Moses is celebrated as a unique lawgiver, prophet, and faithful amanuensis, and this celebration serves to authorize Deuteronomic reworkings and interpretations.

Indeed, Moses is not only unique. He is, according to Deut 34:10–12, the ultimate prophet.[78]

(10) ולא קם נביא עוד בישראל כמשה אשר ידעו יהוה פנים אל פנים (11) לכל
האתות והמופתים אשר שלחו יהוה לעשות בארץ מצרים לפרעה ולכל עבדיו
ולכל ארצו (12) ולכל היד החזקה ולכל המורא הגדול אשר עשה משה לעיני
כל ישראל

(10) Never again did there arise in Israel a prophet like Moses—whom the LORD singled out, face to face, (11) for the various sign and portents that the LORD sent him to display in the land of Egypt, against Pharaoh and all his courtiers and his whole country, (12) and for all the great might and awesome power that Moses displayed before all Israel.

---

that these speeches are also part of Moses' relevation then this does not compromise the collection in Deuteronomy as being Mosaic. See Robert Polzin, *Moses and the Deuteronomist: A Literary Study of the Deuteronomic History* (New York: Seabury, 1980), 63–65; M. Fishbane, *Biblical Interpretation*, 436; J. W. Watts, "Legal Characterization," 415–26.

[77] P. D. Miller Jr., "Moses My Servant," 306.

[78] So J. D. Levenson: "The Mosaic era was different from anything that followed: Never again has there arisen a prophet in Israel like Moses, whom YHWH knew face to face (Deut 34:10). In fact, so unavailable is that Mosaic mode of revelation that even the site of the grave of the great prophet is unknown (v 6). It is surely no coincidence that the site of Mount Sinai is similarly unknown. The legacy of Mount Sinai, what Jewish tradition calls Torah in the broadest sense, endured" (*Sinai and Zion*, 90).

Thus the authority of Deuteronomy is also ultimate. Miller notes that Deuteronomy is authoritative insofar as "the community needs no further instruction than Moses' teaching and its authority rests in part upon its completion and its ascription to Moses."[79]

Although explicit characterization of Moses' status as ultimate prophet appears to be novel, it is rooted in earlier traditions concerning Moses' role in the revelation at Sinai.[80] Here too, Deuteronomic reworking is both subtle and of profound significance. In earlier traditions, Sinai is portrayed as an event in which the people as a whole have direct access to the divine presence, although Moses

---

[79] Patrick D. Miller Jr., "Deuteronomy and Psalms," *JBL* 118 (1999): 3–18; repr. in *Israelite Religion and Biblical Theology: Collected Essays* (JSOTSup 267; Sheffield: Sheffield Academic, 2000), 318–36, citation 319 n. 1; see also the articles by David P. Moessner on the tradition associated with Moses' death: "Jesus and the 'Wilderness Generation': The Death of the Prophet like Moses according to Luke," *SBL Seminar Papers, 1982* (SBLSP 21; Chico, Calif.: Scholars Press, 1982): 319–40; idem, "Paul and the Pattern of the Prophet like Moses in Acts," *SBL Seminar Papers, 1983* (SBLSP 22; Chico, Calif.: Scholars Press), 203–12; idem, "Luke 9:1–50: Luke's Preview of the Journey of the Prophet like Moses of Deuteronomy," *JBL* 102 (1983): 575–605.

[80] There is a great deal of scholarship on Moses and his various depictions. In the primary sources we find the following differences in the pentateuchal sources: In the JE traditions we see the earliest traditions of Moses. He experiences divine revelation, appeals to Pharaoh on behalf of the Lord, and assumes authority as the paradigmatic prophet. The Deuteronomic tradition appropriates the JE traditions and recasts them with a focus on Moses as the lawgiver and judge of Israel. In this editing of earlier traditions and in the formation of the Pentateuch, Moses emerges as a prophet who interprets the law and is known for his role in the reception of the testimonial tablets. Hence, the Law comes to be seen as the Law of Moses. The Priestly stratum is concerned to provide the details of Moses' involvement in the tabernacle, the chronology of desert travels, and Mosaic genealogy. On this see, e.g., George W. Coats, *Moses: Heroic Man, Man of God* (JSOTSup 57; Sheffield: Almond, 1988); Dewey M. Beegle, "Moses," *ABD* 4:909–18. In addition, there is a very helpful discussion in John Van Seters, *In Search of History: Historiography in the Ancient World and the Origins of Biblical History* (New Haven, Conn.: Yale University Press, 1983; repr., Winona Lake, Ind.: Eisenbrauns, 1997), especially the discussion of the pentateuchal narratives and their historical development in "Chapter 7: Israelite Historiography," 209–48 and "Chapter 10: The Deuteronomist From Joshua to Samuel," 322–53. See also David M. Hay, "Moses Through New Testament Spectacles," *Int* 44 (1990): 240–52 on the portrayal of Moses in the NT. He rejects D. P. Moessner's views cited in the previous note, arguing that Jesus is compared to a prophet rather than specifically to "the prophet like Moses" (242). Hay notes: "Thus we find many claims that Moses bears witness to Jesus' glory but very few that Jesus is like Moses" (245). It is in this context that the Torah of Moses can be addressed. He continues: "Almost every New Testament writer refers to the Pentateuch, and none calls into question its general status as divine revelation. Yet there is a pronounced tendency to represent the Sinai revelation as *comparatively inferior* to the revelation given in Jesus" (245). He claims: "Nonetheless, New Testament writers, including Paul, never appear to polemicize directly against Moses" (248).

plays an essential role. But, in Deuteronomy, Moses becomes the mediator, who is alone granted access to the divine presence, and who conveys the word of God to Israel. Moshe Weinfeld argues that this transformation is connected to the Josianic abolition of the high places and the provincial sanctuaries, as reflected in 2 Kings 22–23.[81] Thus the centrality of Moses underwrites the centralization of the cult. So, the fact that the traditions of Deuteronomy come to be associated with the figure and founder, Moses, bolsters the reforms of the law collection in Deuteronomy.

Thus, when Deuteronomy portrays Moses' discourse on the plains of Moab, prior to Moses' death and Israel's entry into the promised land, it is in effect portraying a re-presentation of the revelation at Sinai. Now, however, by means of the demonstrative, it is not the Decalogue alone, but a larger body of law and instruction, that is authorized through the mediation of Moses and, ultimately, through the event at Sinai.[82] This larger body is the Torah of Moses, because it carries the singular authority connected to Moses' unique and ultimate prophetic status. It is with good reason, then, that Deuteronomy itself came to be known as משנה תורה.[83] For Deuteronomy portrays the re-presentation of Torah, not only to the children of Israel on the plains of Moab, but also to readers and listeners of the text at any time.

Conclusion

Although Deuteronomy claims a certain ultimacy for itself, rooted in the ultimacy of Moses' status as prophet, this does not mean that Deuteronomy marks an end. On the contrary, it marks the beginning of what I am calling Mosaic Discourse. Once there is a unitary status of Torah to which all law and instruction can be said to belong, once rewriting—expository, expansive and even revisionary—may be

---

[81] M. Weinfeld, *Deuteronomy and the Deuteronomic School*, 44, 190.

[82] On the twofold interpretation of the Decalogue in Deuteronomy (chs. 6–11 and again in chs. 12–26) see the following: M. Fishbane, *Garments of Torah*, 9–11; idem, *Biblical Interpretation*, 343–50, 531; Bernard M. Levinson, "The Case for Revision and Interpolation within the Biblical Legal Corpora," in *Theory and Method in Biblical and Cuneiform Law* (ed. B. M. Levinson; JSOTSup 181; Sheffield: Sheffield Academic, 1994), 37–59; D. T. Olson, *Death of Moses*, 40–61 and 62–125.

[83] Throughout rabbinic literature Deuteronomy is simply referred to as *Mishneh Torah*. See, e.g., *Sifre Deb.* 160; *b. ʿAbod. Zar.* 25a; *b. Ḥul.* 63b.

authorized through the ever-present possibility of the re-presentation
of Sinai, once all that is sacred is linked to the incomparable Moses,
once all that is authoritative must be linked to Moses as to a founding figure, then the operations performed by Deuteronomists upon
earlier traditions may—indeed, must—be repeated by others upon
those earlier traditions and upon Deuteronomic traditions themselves.
For the Deuteronomists have established a model for the authoritative interpretation of tradition and for its authoritative application
to new circumstances. As we shall see, this model plays an important role in the later development of Second Temple Judaism—
whose claims to authority must take the form of claims to repetition,
even in the face of radically changed circumstances, hence of claims
to re-presentation after the death of the founder. So, when Deuteronomy 34 insists on the impossibility of another prophet like Moses,
this means in effect that one crucial way of claiming authority within
Second Temple Judaism will be to write in the name—indeed, in
the voice—of Moses himself.

CHAPTER TWO

REWRITING REWRITTEN: *JUBILEES* AND 11QTEMPLE AS PARTICIPANTS IN MOSAIC DISCOURSE

> The angel handed me a book, saying, "It contains everything that you could possibly wish to know." And he disappeared. So I opened the book, which was not particularly fat. It was written in an unknown character. Scholars translated it, but they produced altogether different versions. They differed even about the very senses of their own readings, agreeing upon neither the tops nor the bottoms of them, nor upon the beginnings of them nor the ends. Toward the close of this vision it seemed to me that the book melted, until it could no longer be distinguished from this world that is about us.
>
> Paul Valéry[1]

The Proliferation of Second Temple Interpretation

Throughout the post-exilic period, interpretations of authoritative writings proliferated. The extant literature suggests that, while various Jewish groups acknowledged a corpus of revealed literature as authoritative and as the theological basis for their community and practice, they disagreed sharply about who had the correct interpretation of an already ancient tradition whose meaning was sometimes elusive.[2] Interpreters had to show why their interpretations of revealed literature were authoritative and should be preferred to the available alternatives. Accordingly, they developed a panoply of both interpretive methods and authority-conferring strategies.[3]

---

[1] Translated by Carolyn Forché in her collection of poetry and translations, *The Angel of History* (New York: HarperCollins, 1994), 78.

[2] See J. L. Kugel, "Chapter 1: The World of Ancient Biblical Interpreters," in *The Bible As It Was* (Cambridge, Mass.: Harvard University Press, 1997), 1–51. See also my discussion in "Angels at Sinai: Exegesis, Theology and Interpretative Authority," *DSD* 7 (2000): 313–33, esp. 313–15.

[3] On the concept and implementation of such strategies see my article, "Interpretation as Primordial Writing: Jubilees and Its Authority Conferring Strategies," *JSJ* 30 (1999): 379–410.

It is in the context of this proliferation and competition of interpretations that we first find new, post-Deuteronomic participants in
Mosaic Discourse. But this is not to say that there had been no relevant developments in the meantime. Numerous exilic and early
post-exilic texts exhibit one or more of the features constitutive of
Mosaic Discourse. Only from the Maccabean period, however, are
texts extant that exhibit all four features. Perhaps a full-scale repetition of the Deuteronomic project—a bold and independent enterprise—could be undertaken only at a time of political independence.
Such independence and strength had not been part of the Israelite
self-understanding since the time of Josiah.

The two participants in Mosaic Discourse I will consider in this
section both originated in the second century B.C.E.: *Jubilees* and the
Temple Scroll (11QT).[4] Scholars have long noted their methodological and theological similarities.[5] Some have even argued that

---

[4] Most scholars date both of these works to the Second Temple period during
the second century B.C.E. There has been some debate about whether the Temple
Scroll or *Jubilees* is earlier. On the issue of their relative chronology and criteria for
establishing such dates, see the following: James C. VanderKam, "The Origins and
Purposes of the *Book of Jubilees*," in *Studies in the Book of Jubilees* (ed. M. Albani,
J. Frey, and A. Lange; Tübingen: Mohr Siebeck, 1997), 3–24; idem, "The Temple
Scroll and the Book of Jubilees," in *Temple Scroll Studies: Papers presented at the International
Symposium on the Temple Scroll. Manchester, December 1987* (ed. G. J. Brooke; JSPSup
7; Sheffield: Sheffield Academic, 1989), 211–36; Gershon Brin, "Regarding the
Connection between the *Temple Scroll* and the Book of *Jubilees*," *JBL* 112 (1993):
108–09; Robert Doran, "The Non-Dating of Jubilees: Jub. 34–38; 23:14–32 in
Narrative Context," *JSJ* 20 (1989): 1–11; James H. Charlesworth, "The Date of
Jubilees and the Temple Scroll," *SBL Seminar Papers, 1985* (SBLSP 24; Chico, Calif.:
Scholars Press, 1985), 193–204; Yigael Yadin, *The Temple Scroll* (3 vols.; Jerusalem:
IES and The Shrine of the Book, 1983), 1:386–402; idem, "Is the Temple Scroll
a Sectarian Document?," in *Humanizing America's Iconic Book* (ed. G. M. Tucker and
D. A. Knight; trans. V. Hurowitz; Chico, Calif.: Scholars Press, 1982), 153–69;
Lawrence H. Schiffman, "The Sacrificial System of the *Temple Scroll* and the Book
of Jubilees," *SBL Seminar Papers, 1985* (SBLSP 24; Chico, Calif.: Scholars Press,
1985), 217–33; idem, "The King, his Guard, and the Royal Council in the *Temple
Scroll*," *American Academy for Jewish Research* 54 (1987): 237–59; Johann Maier, *The
Temple Scroll: An Introduction, Translation and Commentary* (trans. R. T. White; JSOTSup
34; Sheffield: JSOT Press, 1985), 1–7; trans. of *Die Tempelrolle vom Toten Meer* (Munich:
Ernst Reinhart Verlag, 1978); Annette Steudel, "There are No Further Columns
in the *Temple Scroll*," *RevQ* 19 (1999): 131–36. On the view that 11QT is an extant
Sadducean Torah see Hans Burgmann, "11QT: The Sadducean *Torah*," in *Temple
Scroll Studies: Papers presented at the International Symposium on the Temple Scroll. Manchester,
December 1987* (ed. G. J. Brooke; JSPSup 7; Sheffield: Sheffield Academic, 1989),
257–63.

[5] On shared exegetical and cultic tradition, see J. C. VanderKam, "The Temple
Scroll and the Book of Jubilees," esp. 232; see also the recent discussion by Sidnie

Jubilees and the Temple Scroll were originally a single work.[6] Ultimately, however, as I will argue, the two texts are far too different in their style, method of interpretation, and overall theological agenda to be parts of the same work. The right way to express their deep affinity, I believe, is to say, not that they are parts of a single work, but rather that they both participate in Mosaic Discourse and exhibit all four of that Discourse's constitutive features, albeit in significantly different ways.

Reworking Authoritative Literature in Jubilees *and* 11QTemple

Both *Jubilees* and the Temple Scroll have been recognized as examples of Rewritten Bible,[7] a genre of Second Temple texts that recounts biblical narratives with variations and insertions. In some sense, this characterization is clearly correct. *Jubilees* retells the narratives from the beginning of Genesis through the middle of Exodus, while the Temple Scroll reworks the sections of the Pentateuch drawing from the second half of the book of Exodus and the books of Leviticus, Numbers, and Deuteronomy. However, it is both crucial and difficult to avoid anachronistic assumptions about the significance of rewriting authoritative texts.[8]

White Crawford, *The Temple Scroll and Related Texts* (Companion to the Qumran Scrolls 2; Sheffield: Sheffield Academic, 2000), 77–78.

[6] Ben Zion Wacholder, "The Relationship between 11QTorah (The Temple Scroll) and the Book of Jubilees: One Single or Two Independent Compositions," *SBL Seminar Papers, 1985* (SBLSP 24; Chico, Calif.: Scholars Press, 1985), 205–16. However, this claim is problematic in light of the source-critical analysis that has been done on the Temple Scroll. See, for example, Andrew M. Wilson and Lawrence Wills, "Literary Sources of the *Temple Scroll*," *HTR* 75 (1982): 275–88, which has been widely accepted among scholars. See also the comments by Solomon Zeitlin, "The Book of 'Jubilees' and the Pentateuch," *JQR* 48 (1957): 218–35; Philip Callaway, "Source Criticism of the Temple Scroll: The Purity Laws," *RevQ* 12 (1986): 213–22; and Menahem Kister, "על שני מטבעות לשון בספר היובלים," *Tarbiz* 70 (2001): 289–300. These source-critical arguments complicate and undermine any attempt to consider the Temple Scroll and *Jubilees* as belonging to the same original work.

[7] On the term and concept of Rewritten Bible see notes 13, 14 and 33 in chapter 1. In his recent essay, J. C. VanderKam has suggested that is it better to refer to texts such as *Jubilees* or the Temple Scroll with the "more general, less suggestive" term of "Rewritten Scripture" rather than Rewritten Bible ("Questions of Canon," 292).

[8] In recent scholarship there is a general consensus among scholars who work on Second Temple literature that the essential function of Rewritten Bible is interpretive. It is also important to consider the way Reworked Pentateuch has been influential in this development in scholarship. On this last point, I am indebted to

If one is to speak of "rewriting the Bible," then one must be clear
about the status of the Bible in the period in question, and also
about the motivation and significance of the act of rewriting in its
historical context.[9] It is important to consider the implications of the
fact that, although some sacred written traditions were recognized
as authoritative Torah from the very beginning of the Second Temple
period, canonization did not occur until later.[10] In such a climate,
it was entirely possible to aspire, not to replace, but rather to *accompany* traditions already regarded as authoritative, and thus to provide those traditions with their proper interpretive context. Of course,
this is exactly what happened in the case of Deuteronomy and the
earlier Covenant Code. And it may be what happened in the library
at Qumran, where multiple copies of *Jubilees* and 11QT were preserved alongside the Pentateuch. If this was indeed the aspiration of
works like *Jubilees* and 11QT, then the goal of rewriting was not to
replace but rather to honor the past, while re-presenting it to their
distinctive audience(s).[11]

---

a conversation with Moshe Bernstein, May 2002. See footnote 33 in chapter 1 for
more on this point. For a recent study that supports such an exegetical understanding of Rewritten Bible with an emphasis on Philo of Alexandria, see Peder
Borgen, *Philo of Alexandria: An Exegete for His Time* (NovTSup 86; Leiden: Brill, 1997),
esp. "Chapter 3: Reviewing and Rewriting Biblical Material," 46–62; "Chapter 4:
Rewritten Bible," 63–79; and his "Concluding Summary," 282–87.

[9] Craig A. Evans states: "Apparent discrepancies, lacunae, and embarrassing
behavior on the part of an Old Testament worthy provide, it would appear, much
of the motivation behind the retelling . . . There seems to be a consistent tendency
to illustrate and exaggerate the piety or wickedness of Old Testament characters.
How this is done varies, but that it is done remains constant. Similarly, certain
doctrines, such as the exaltation of Torah . . . are underscored and are usually placed
on the lips of the patriarchs, often by incorporating other scriptural materials. What
is common to most of this rewriting is the desire to update the biblical narrative,
to bring it more closely into alignment with the theological orientation of the Judaism
of late antiquity" ("The Genesis Apocryphon and the Rewritten Bible," *RevQ* 13
[1988], 153–65, citation 162).

[10] See J. C. VanderKam, "Authoritative Literature in the Dead Sea Scrolls."
For an earlier view, see S. Z. Leiman, *The Canonization of Hebrew Scripture*. See also
the forthcoming discussions by E. Ulrich, "From Literature to Scripture," and
G. J. Brooke, "Between Authority and Canon."
See the work of E. Ulrich on the significance of the state of the Pentateuch at
Qumran and the importance of the evidence from the LXX apart from Qumran in
his collection of essays, *The Dead Sea Scrolls and the Origins of the Bible.*

[11] This is in opposition to the view held by Ben Zion Wacholder that *Jubilees*
and the Temple Scroll were more authoritative than the Pentateuch in his essay,
"*Jubilees* as the Super Canon: Torah-Admonition versus Torah-Commandment," in
Legal Texts and Legal Issues: Proceedings of the Second Meeting of the International Organization

Texts that "rewrote the Bible," like *Jubilees* and the Temple Scroll, responded to both the demand for interpretation and the demand for a demonstration of authority. On the one hand, they retold biblical stories in ways that resolved apparent inconsistencies or solved puzzles for their readers. On the other hand, they wove their own versions of law, temple ritual, calendrical system[12] and covenant, along with the very words of already authoritative traditions, into a single seamless whole. Thus they claimed, for their interpretations of authoritative texts, the already established authority of the texts themselves. Unlike, say, the genre of commentary,[13] which acknowledges the distinction between an interpretation and what it interprets, the sort of rewriting in which the Temple Scroll and *Jubilees* engage has the effect of denying any such distinction. Although Deuteronomy is—as I will argue—a precedent of particular importance for *Jubilees* and the Temple Scroll, it is by no means the only one.[14]

If we try to avoid anachronism, then I think that the following characterization of the rewriting strategy is consistent with all the evidence. Works like *Jubilees* and the Temple Scroll, not unlike the

---

for Qumran Studies, Cambridge 1995 (ed. M. Bernstein, F. García Martínez, and J. Kampen; STDJ 23; Leiden: Brill, 1997), 195–211. See also the criticisms by Wayne O. McCready, "A second Torah at Qumran?" *SR* 14 (1985): 5–15; and the nuanced view of Hans-Aage Mink, "The Use of Scripture in the Temple Scroll and the Status of the Scroll as Law," *SJOT* 1 (1987): 20–50.

[12] On the calendar in *Jubilees* and in the Temple Scroll see A. Jaubert, "Le calendrier des Jubilés et de la secte de Qumrân. Ses origins bibliques," *VT* 3 (1953): 250–64; idem, "Le calendrier des Jubilés et les jours liturgiques de la semaine," *VT* 7 (1957): 35–61; Joseph M. Baumgarten, "The Calendar of the Book of Jubilees and the Bible," *Tarbiz* 32 (1962): 317–28 [Hebrew]; repr. in *Studies in Qumran Law* (SJLA 24; Leiden: Brill, 1977), 101–14; idem, "The Calendars of the Book of Jubilees and the Temple Scroll," *VT* 37 (1987): 71–78; J. C. VanderKam, "The Temple Scroll and the Book of Jubilees," 211–36; idem, "The Origins and Purposes of the *Book of Jubilees*," 3–24; "Das chronologische Konzept des Jubiläenbuches," *ZAW* 107 (1995): 80–100; repr. and trans. "Studies in the Chronology of the Book of Jubilees," in *From Revelation to Canon: Studies in the Hebrew Bible and Second Temple Literature* (JSJSup 62; Leiden: Brill, 2000), 522–44; idem, *Calendars in the Dead Sea Scrolls: Measuring Time* (The Literature of the Dead Sea Scrolls; London: Routledge, 1998).

[13] On the concept of *pesher* as a form of proto-commentary and for a review of recent scholarship on the genre of *pesher*, see the essay by Shani Berrin, "Qumran Pesharim," in *Biblical Interpretation at Qumran* (ed. M. Henze; Grand Rapids: Eerdmans, forthcoming). See also the analysis of the interpretive methodology of the Temple Scroll by Dwight D. Swanson, *The Temple Scroll and the Bible: The Methodology of 11QT* (STDJ 14; Leiden: Brill, 1995).

[14] See J. D. Levenson, "The Sources of Torah," 559–74. See also the works of G. N. Knoppers, S. Japhet, and S. J. Schweitzer on Chronicles as noted in footnote 58 in chapter 1.

earlier work of Deuteronomy, seek to provide the interpretive context within which scriptural traditions already acknowledged as authoritative can be properly understood. This is neither a fraudulent
attempt at replacement, nor an act of impiety.[15] It is rather, we may
charitably assume, a pious effort to convey what is taken to be the
essence of earlier traditions, an essence that the rewriters think is in
danger of being missed. At the same time, the interpretations con-
veyed in works like Deuteronomy, *Jubilees* and the Temple Scroll
acquire authority through their intermingling with the well-known
words of traditions whose authority is already acknowledged. Thus
such works may acquire scriptural status without displacing the scriptural status of the traditions they rewrite.[16] Thus with respect to
rewriting we can speak of the goal of *Jubilees* and the Temple Scroll
as trying to provide an interpretive context for received revealed literature, a context whose absence might engender dangerous misin-
terpretations. In this clarified sense, then, *Jubilees* and the Temple
Scroll do "rewrite the Bible," both in order to solve interpretive
problems and in order to appropriate the authority of Mosaic Torah
for its preferred calendar and temple practices.

However, as in the case of Deuteronomy, discussed above, it has
been suggested that *Jubilees* and the Temple Scroll are intended to
replace the traditions they rewrite.[17] On this view, the fact that ear-

---

[15] See, again, B. M. Levinson, *Deuteronomy and the Hermeneutics of Legal Innovation*,
150 and my comments in chapter 1, pages 5–7.

[16] In "Retelling the Old Testament," P. S. Alexander claims: "Jubilees puts itself
on a par with Scripture; it carries its own origins back to the same supreme moment
of revelation that gave birth to the canonical Pentateuch. *Jubilees* did not, however,
intend to supplant the Pentateuch, but rather to supplement and to explain it"
(100). See the compelling arguments that have fleshed out this claim by the following: M. J. Bernstein, "4Q252," 2–27; F. García Martínez, "Temple Scroll,"
Encyclopedia of the Dead Sea Scrolls 2:927–33; G. J. Brooke, "Rewritten Bible," *Encyclopedia
of the Dead Sea Scrolls* 2:777–81; Lawrence H. Schiffman, "The Theology of the
Temple Scroll," *JQR* 85 (1994): 109–28; James C. VanderKam, "The Theology of
the Temple Scroll: A Response to Lawrence H. Schiffman," *JQR* 85 (1994): 129–35;
idem, "Questions of Canon," 269–92; Moshe Weinfeld, "God versus Moses in the
Temple Scroll: 'I do not speak on my own but on God's authority' (*Sifrei Deut.* Sec.
5; *John* 12, 48 f.)," *RevQ* 15 (1992): 175–80.

[17] E.g., Ben Zion Wacholder, "The Relationship between 11QTorah (The Temple
Scroll) and the Book of Jubilees," 205–16. Also, note the insistence by Gabriele
Boccaccini that the Temple Scroll and *Jubilees* are part of Enochic Judaism and not
Zadokite Judaism (*Beyond the Essene Hypothesis: The Parting of Ways between Qumran and
Enochic Judaism* [Grand Rapids: Eerdmans, 1998], 86–103). Although Boccaccini
does not explicitly speak of the Temple Scroll as a replacement, I believe that ultimately he does conceive of the Temple Scroll as reflective of a replacement theology. See my review in *AJSR*, forthcoming and J. C. VanderKam's review in *RivB*,
forthcoming.

lier traditions were in fact preserved alongside their rewritings shows only that the intention to replace those earlier traditions was not fulfilled.

However, as I argued in the case of Deuteronomy, the fact that a text constantly invokes and recasts the language of earlier traditions cannot be the *sole* evidence for the thesis that the text is intended to replace those earlier traditions. In the absence of further evidence, what motivates the replacement thesis, I suggest, is the difficulty *we* have making sense of rewriting as an act of reverence, given our contemporary conceptions of textual integrity and authorial property rights.[18]

More specifically, Schiffman points out that the Temple Scroll fails to mention undeniably important laws found in the traditions it rewrites—such as the prohibitions of adultery and murder.

> The redactor [of the Temple Scroll] did not really intend his Torah to eliminate the need for the canonical one or he would certainly have prohibited such transgressions as murder and adultery, which are never mentioned in the Temple Scroll.[19]

Therefore the Temple Scroll cannot have been intended to stand on its own as a complete work, independent of, say, Deuteronomy. Similar arguments can be made in the case of *Jubilees* which reworks and retells Genesis through the middle of Exodus.

In addition, *Jubilees* refers at least twice to an already existing, authoritative Torah.[20] First, let us consider the much discussed passage

---

[18] See the arguments by J. C. VanderKam, "Questions of Canon," 269–92; Liora Ravid, "Issues in the Book of Jubilees" (Ph.D. diss., Bar-Ilan University, 2001 [Hebrew]), 184; and the numerous essays regarding the now famous lawsuit over the reconstructed text of 4QMMT in T. H. Lim, H. L. MacQueen, and C. M. Carmichael, eds., *On Scrolls, Artefacts and Intellectual Property*.

[19] L. H. Schiffman, "The Theology of the Temple Scroll," 110. See also Schiffman's further discussion of this point in "The Temple Scroll and the Halakhic Pseudepigrapha of the Second Temple Period," in *Pseudepigraphic Perspectives: The Apocrypha and Pseudepigrapha in Light of the Dead Sea Scrolls. Proceedings of the International Symposium of the Orion Center for the Study of the Dead Sea Scrolls and Associated Literature, 12–14 January, 1997* (ed. E. G. Chazon and M. E. Stone; STDJ 31; Leiden: Brill, 1999): "We should note that Yadin never really considered this text [the Temple Scroll] as a substitute for the canonical Torah, no doubt because so many issues were omitted completely, for example, the prohibition of murder. This was a selective work which was never intended to replace the original on which it was based" (121–31, citation 124).

[20] See Cana Werman, "'The תורה and the תעודה' engraved on the Tablets," *DSD* 9 (2002): 75–103; trans. from "התורה והתעודה' הכתובה על הלוחות," *Tarbiz* 68

from *Jub.* 6:20–22 where *Jubilees* refers to a "first Torah," in which the laws of Shabuoth are written:

> (20) Now you command the Israelites to keep this festival during all their generations as a commandment for them: one day in the year, during this month, they are to celebrate the festival (21) because it is the festival of weeks and it is the festival of firstfruits. This festival is twofold and of two kinds. Celebrate it as it is written and inscribed regarding it. (22) For I have written (this) in the book of the first law, in which I wrote for you that you should celebrate it at each of its times one day in a year. I have told you about its sacrifice so that the Israelites may continue to remember and celebrate it throughout their generations during this month—one day each year.[21]

Here *Jubilees* refers to the first law that is part of the larger corpus of heavenly writing that was revealed to Israel. A second, less explicit reference to an earlier Torah is in *Jubilees'* retelling of Genesis 34, where the reader is referred to another text (*Jub.* 30:12):

> For this reason I have written for you in the words of the law everything that the Shechemites did to Dinah and how Jacob's sons said: "We will not give our daughter to a man who has a foreskin because for us that would be a disgraceful thing."

Thus in *Jubilees* 6, an authoritative text is invoked as prior to *Jubilees*, while in *Jubilees* 30, an authoritative text is invoked as existing along-side *Jubilees*. The words of the law are part of the heavenly tablets, but not all those words are repeated in *Jubilees*. This further supports the argument that *Jubilees* is not intended to replace the authoritative Torah, but rather to accompany it as its authoritative interpretation and supplement, in much the way that Deuteronomy came to accompany earlier traditions.[22]

(1999): 473–92; and J. L. Kugel, on this passage and on *Jub.* 30:12, in *The Bible as It Was*, 238–39 and 412–14.

[21] English quotations from the book of Jubilees are from the translation of James C. VanderKam, *The Book of Jubilees* (2 vols.; CSCO 510–11, SAe 87–88; Leuven: Peeters, 1989). For the Hebrew fragments of Jubilees and the reconstructed Hebrew text based upon a retroverted Ethiopic text see James C. VanderKam and Josef T. Milik," Jubilees," in *Qumran Cave 4. VIII Parabiblical Texts Part I* (DJD 13; Oxford: Clarendon, 1994), 1–140.

[22] P. S. Alexander writes: "The canonical Pentateuch is 'the first law', Jubilees (by implication) the 'second law'. Both are divine in origin, both given to Moses on Sinai: the latter contains the authoritative interpretation of the former (cf. Jub. 1:1; 6:11; 30:12; 50:6). Jubilees, then does not present itself as a self-sufficient statement of the law. Throughout it presupposes and alludes to Scripture; it was meant to be read side by side with Scripture" ("Retelling the Old Testament," 100).

Further evidence that the author of *Jubilees* does not intend to replace the Torah can be seen in the way it responds to difficulties in biblical narratives. Consider, to take one example from many, *Jubilees'* interpretation of Genesis 38. Like other Second Temple interpreters, as well as later biblical interpreters, the author of *Jubilees* is bothered by a narrative in which Judah, the ancestor of David, has sexual relations with his daughter-in-law, Tamar.[23] To make matters even worse, the line of David springs from that illicit union! If *Jubilees* intended to replace the existing Genesis narrative, then it should have erased the problem by reworking the Judah and Tamar narrative. Instead, *Jubilees* offers an exegetically ingenious solution to the problem. In its version of the story, neither of Judah's sons, Er and Onan, *consummated* marriage with Tamar (*Jub.* 41:2–5):

> (2) He hated (her) and did not lie with her because his mother was a Canaanite woman and he wanted to marry someone from his mother's tribe. But his father Judah did not allow him. (3) That Er, Judah's firstborn, was evil, and the Lord killed him. (4) Then Judah said to his brother Onan: 'Go in to your brother's wife, perform the levirate duty for her, and produce descendants for your brother'. (5) Onan knew that that the descendants would not be his but his brother's, so he entered the house of his brother's wife and poured out the semen on the ground. In the Lord's estimation it was an evil act, and he killed him.

Consequently, although Judah transgressed, his transgression was not, strictly speaking, adulterous union with his daughter-in-law. He did not deserve the death penalty, and achieved atonement through his remorse, as well as his commitment to the law, even if it should turn out to require death (*Jub.* 41:27–28):

> (27) We told Judah that his two sons had not lain with her. For this reason his descendants were established for another generation and would not be uprooted. (28) For in his integrity he had gone and demanded punishment because Judah had wanted to burn her on the basis of the law which Abraham had commanded his children.[24]

---

[23] See, e.g., the treatment of this passage in the *Testament of Judah* 8–17; *L.A.B.* 9:5–6; *Mekhilta* Bešallaḥ par 6. See also Esther Marie Menn, *Judah and Tamar (Genesis 38) in Ancient Jewish Exegesis: Studies in Literary Form and Hermeneutics* (JSJSup 51; Leiden: Brill, 1997); and Kenneth E. Pomykala, *The Davidic Dynasty Tradition in Early Judaism: Its History and Significance for Messianism* (SBLEJL 7; Atlanta: Scholars Press, 1995), 246–55.

[24] See the discussion of this passage by G. A. Anderson, "The Status of the Torah Before Sinai," 1–29, esp. 19–29.

A text genuinely intended to replace Genesis would have had no
need for the exegetical creativity exhibited here, and indeed in almost
every section of *Jubilees*. It would simply have given its own "correct" and unproblematic versions of biblical narratives.

Jubilees *and* 11QTemple *as* This Torah

Both *Jubilees* and the Temple Scroll describe themselves as Torah,
using the deictic in a way that is reminiscent of Deuteronomy.[25]
Thus each book claims to be an authentic expression of divinely
revealed Torah, and claims the authority of Torah for laws, festivals and calendrical rules that are not found explicitly in the Pentateuch.
As we will see below, each book exhibits this feature of Mosaic
Discourse in a distinctive manner.

First, I will begin with *Jubilees*' complex and multi-layered argument for ascribing to itself Torah status. *Jubilees* purports to describe
the occasion on which the Torah was written at Sinai. Making extensive use of Deuteronomy 31,[26] where Moses is instructed to write
down "the words of this Torah," the opening verse of *Jubilees* authorizes the work as a whole. While Deuteronomy portrays Moses re-
presenting Sinai at Moab,[27] *Jubilees* goes one bold step further,
re-presenting the Sinai event itself. Indeed, whereas Deuteronomy
repeatedly refers to the divine command to transcribe the revealed
law, *Jubilees* claims to be that transcription, carried out by Moses
himself. Thus *Jubilees* employs Deuteronomy as a model for its self-
authorization, but goes even further than Deuteronomy in claiming
the authority of Moses' revelation at Sinai.[28]

The final columns of the Temple Scroll make repeated use of the
deictic particle, in order to emphasize the Torah status of the Temple

---

[25] See my discussion of this grammatical issue in chapter 1, pages 30–32.

[26] See Liora Ravid's the influence of Deuteronomy in Jubilees, "Issues in the
Book of Jubilees," 138–41.

[27] See, e.g., Deut 1:1–5; 3:29–4:1; 4:44–49; 28:68; 34:1–9.

[28] Of course I am not arguing that Jubilees is operating with modern critical
assumptions about the production of the Deuteronomic law code. Rather, I am
suggesting that the concept of authoritative, even inspired, rewriting as exposition
and as Scripture shaped and perhaps even inspired the author of *Jubilees* and, very
possibly, the author of the Temple Scroll. They both explicitly use and re-use the
language of Deuteronomy to authorize their own rewriting and to attach to themselves the status and authority of Scripture.

Scroll itself. For example, both 11QT 50:5–9 and 50:17 refer to the regulation of this law, כחוק משפט הזה:

(5) וכול איש אשר ינע על פני השדה בעצם אדם מת ובחלל חרב (6) או
במת או בדם מת או בקבר וטהר כחוק המשפט (7) הזה ואם לוא יטהר
כמשפט התורה הזואת טמא הוא עוד (8) טמאתו בו וכול האדם אשר ינע בו
יכבס בגדו ורחץ וטהר (9) לערב ... (17) ... מעשה עזים כמשפט התורה
הזואת תעשו להמה

> And every (5) man who in an open field should come into contact
> with the bones of a dead person, or one slain by a sword, (6) or a
> corpse, or the blood of a dead person, or a grave, shall purify him-
> self according to the precept of this stipulation (7) and if he does not
> purify himself according to the regulation of this law, he will be impure,
> (8) his impurity will stick to him; and everyone who comes into con-
> tact with him shall wash his clothes and bathe and become pure (9)
> by the evening.... (17) the objects of goatskin, you shall deal with
> them according to the regulation of this law.[29]

In 11QT 57:1, we are told:

הכוהנים [...] וזואת התורה

> And this is the law [...] the priests.

And it is again this torah that is to be written for the king in
56:20–21:

(20) והיה בשבתו על כסא ממלכתו וכתבו (21) לו את התורה הזואת על ספר
מלפני הכוהנים

> (20) And when he [the king] sits upon the throne of his kingdom they
> shall write (21) for him this law according to the book which is before
> the priests.

---

[29] English quotations from the Temple Scroll are from the translation of Florentino
García Martínez and Eibert J. C. Tigchelaar, eds., "11Q19, 11Q20," in *The Dead
Sea Scrolls Study Edition. Volume 2: 4Q274–11Q31* (2 vols.; Leiden: Brill and Grand
Rapids: Eerdmans, 1997–98), 1228–1304. The Hebrew text of the Temple Scroll
is based on that of Yigael Yadin, *The Temple Scroll* (3 vols.; Jerusalem: IES and The
Shrine of the Book, 1977, 1983), supplemented by that of Elisha Qimron, *The Temple
Scroll: A Critical Edition with Extensive Reconstructions* (Judean Desert Studies; Beer-Sheva
and Jerusalem: Ben-Gurion University of the Negev Press and IES, 1996); and with
the suggestions of Michael O. Wise, *A Critical Study of the Temple Scroll from Qumran
Cave 11* (SAOC 49; Chicago: Oriental Institute of the University of Chicago, 1990).
See also the additional comments in Elisha Qimron, "New Readings in the Temple
Scroll," *IEJ* 28 (1978): 161–72; and idem, "Further New Readings in the Temple
Scroll," *IEJ* 37 (1987): 31–35.

Similarly, the people's return to God is characterized as being in accordance with this Torah (again using the deictic התורה הזאת) in 59:7–10:

(7) ואסתיר פני מהמה והיו לאוכלה (8) ולבז ולמשוסה
ואין מושיע מפני רעתמה אשר הפרו בריתי (9) ואת תורתי נעלה נפשמה עד
יאשמו כול אשמה אחר ישובו (10) אלי בכול לבבמה ובכול נפשמה ככול
דברי התורה הזואת

. . . And I will hide my face from them; and they shall be fodder (8) and prey and spoil, and no-one will save them because of their wicked-ness—for they broke my covenant (9) and their soul loathed my law, so that they became guilty of all wrong-doing. Afterwards they shall come back (10) to me with all their heart and with all their soul, in agreement with all the words of this law. . . .

In addition to repeating the deictic particle to refer to the Temple Scroll as Torah itself, the Temple Scroll also applies to itself the Deuteronomic prohibition against altering the law commanded "today" (11QT 54:5–7):

כול הדברים אשר (6) אנוכי מזו{כ}ה היום אזהכה תשמור לעשות לוא תוסיף
עליהמה ולוא (7) תנרע מהמה

. . . All the things which I (6) order /you/ today, take care to carry them out; you shall not add to them nor (7) shall you remove any-thing from them.

The prohibition against alteration of sacred texts is similarly re-invoked in the narratives that describe the production of the Septua-gint.[30] In both cases, the effect is to claim authority on the model of Deuteronomy.

Noting its self-ascription of the status of Torah, the earliest schol-arly studies of the Temple Scroll already called it the "new Torah." However, this phrase can misleadingly suggest that the Temple Scroll is intended to replace pentateuchal texts—a thesis against which I have already argued. A better construal is given by Michael Fishbane, who acknowledges the Temple Scroll's claim to Torah status, while emphasizing that it continues to presuppose earlier biblical texts as authoritative:

---

[30] See, e.g., the *Let. Aris.* 301–17 and Philo's description of the holiness and pro-duction of the LXX in *Mos.* 2.25–44. See also my discussion in chapter 3, pages 114–16.

In 11QTemp it is not Moses who reports God's instructions, but God Himself who is the speaker. Through this reauthorization (of old laws and new interpretations) it is a rewritten book: a new Tora ... In the Temple Scroll, therefore, the reader confronts the text as a new Tora, even while perceiving the biblical base around which the sources and innovations were integrated. One may confidently surmise that this was the very hope and intent of the author.[31]

The visibility of "the biblical base" can only enhance the authority of the Torah and, by association, the "new Torah," if that authority is not intended to displace the authority of biblical traditions.

Re-Presentation of Sinai in Second Temple Interpretation

Both *Jubilees* and the Temple Scroll claim that their text is part of the original and authoritative Sinaitic revelation. By implication, both claim that the materials revealed at Sinai amount to far more than the Decalogue or the Pentateuch. Again, Deuteronomy serves as a model, but *Jubilees* and the Temple Scroll go still further. Whereas Deuteronomy re-presents Sinai at Moab, these texts portray Sinai as itself a re-presentation of the covenant (*Jubilees* and the Temple Scroll) and laws (*Jubilees* only) revealed long before Sinai. The suggestion is that the Pentateuch contains only part of what was revealed at Sinai, and that it can be properly understood only by those who have access to even more ancient traditions. The more ancient the tradition, of course, the more it is to be revered.[32]

Sinai Revisited

Jubilees begins with a reference to the revelation at Sinai. This is said to be the context for the production of the book of *Jubilees*, which is identified as the Torah that Moses transcribed on Sinai (*Jub.* 1:1–4a):

---

[31] Michael Fishbane, "Chapter 10: Use, Authority and Interpretation of Mikra at Qumran," in *Mikra: Text, Translation, Reading and Interpretation of the Hebrew Bible in Ancient Judaism and Early Christianity* (ed. M. J. Mulder; CRINT 2.1; Assen: Van Gorcum and Minneapolis: Fortress, 1990), 339–77, citation 351.

[32] See my discussion of authorizing strategies in the book of *Jubilees* in "Interpretation as Primordial Writing," 379–410. In contrast, see Heb 2:2–3 where it is post-Mosaic revelation that is said to be superior to that of Moses.

(1) During the first year of the Israelites' exodus from Egypt, in the third month—on the sixteenth of the month—the Lord said to Moses: "Come up to me on the mountain. I will give you the two stone tablets of the law and the commandments which I have written so that you may teach them." (2) So Moses went up the mountain of the Lord. The glory of the Lord took up residence on Mt. Sinai, and a cloud covered it for six days. (3) When he summoned Moses into the cloud on the seventh day, he saw the glory of the Lord like a fire blazing on the summit of the mountain. (4) Moses remained on the mountain for forty days and forty nights . . .

Jubilees also ends with an implicit reference to Sinai. Towards the end of chapter 49 and the beginning of chapter 50, the author re-presents pre-Sinaitic laws that were given to Israel (e.g., the laws of Passover in Egypt and the laws of the Sabbath in the wilderness of Sin). The author of *Jubilees* then elaborates upon the Sabbath law and upon the importance of faithful adherence to it (*Jub.* 50:6–13). Since observance of the Sabbath is part of the Decalogue, the text returns implicitly to the idea that *Jubilees* is the transcription of the revelation to Moses at Sinai:

(6) I have now written for you the sabbath commandments and all the statutes of its laws. (7) You will work for six days, but on the seventh day is the sabbath of the Lord your God. Do not do any work on it—you, your children, your male and female servants, all your cattle or the foreigner who is with you. (8) The man who does any work on it is to die. . . . (12) Any man who does work; who goes on a trip; who works farmland whether at his home or in any (other) place; who lights a fire; who rides any animal; who travels the sea by ship; any man who beats or kills anything; who slits the throat of an animal or bird; who catches either a wild animal, a bird, or a fish; who fasts and makes war on the sabbath day—(13) a man who does any of these things on the sabbath day is to die, so that the Israelites may continue observing the sabbath in accord with the commandments for the sabbaths of the land as it was written in the tablets which he placed in my hands so that I could write for you the laws of each specific time in every division of its times. Here the words regarding the divisions of the times are completed.

Nor is it without design that *Jubilees* ends with the only one of the ten commandments whose concern is calendrical. For the proper interpretation and implementation of calendrical law is *Jubilees*' primary objective.

Jubilees describes a long line of pre-Sinaitic tradents who receive the revelation of the heavenly tablets, e.g., Enoch, Noah, Abraham,

Jacob, Levi, Amram and Moses. These tradents are responsible for the observance of the Law and for its faithful transmission to select individuals. Only Moses, however, is also responsible for teaching the content of revelation to the entire people of Israel. And only at Sinai does the entire people become obliged to obey the Law. Thus Sinai remains unique. Indeed, through its repeated emphasis on pre-Sinaitic revelation *Jubilees* does not downplay the authority of Sinai. Instead, *Jubilees* bolsters its own authority as the context in which Sinai should be viewed.

Of course, the author of *Jubilees* is well aware that his interpretations are not universally accepted. But Deuteronomy also provides the author of *Jubilees* with a model for dealing with this problem. In what is generally considered an exilic stratum of Deuteronomy, the people are warned that, if they disregard the revelation at Sinai, they will suffer disgrace and exile.[33] *Jubilees* follows Deuteronomy's lead (*Jub.* 1:7–11):

> (7) Now you write this entire message which I am telling you today, because I know their defiance and their stubbornness (even) before I bring them into the land which I promised by oath to Abraham, Isaac, and Jacob: 'To your posterity I will give the land which flows with milk and honey.' When they eat and are full, (8) they will turn to foreign gods—to one which will not save them from any of their afflictions. Then this testimony will serve as evidence. (9) For they will forget all my commandments—everything that I command them—and will follow the nations, their impurities, and their shame. They will serve their gods, and (this) will prove an obstacle for them—an affliction, a pain, and a trap. (10) Many will be destroyed. They will be captured and will fall into the enemy's control because they abandoned my statutes, my commandments, my covenantal festivals, my sabbaths, my holy things which I hallowed for myself among them, my tabernacle, and my temple which I sanctified for myself in the middle of the land so that I could set my name on it and that it could live (there). (11) They made for themselves high places, (sacred) groves, and carved images; each of them prostrated himself before his own in order to go astray. They will sacrifice their children to demons and to every product (conceived by) their erring minds.

Since exile has already occurred by the time of the promulgation of *Jubilees*, these prophecies have been fulfilled, which further enhances its authority. The fact that others follow a calendar different from

---

[33] Deut 27:1–10; 30:1–20; 31:24–29.

the one advocated by *Jubilees* is easily accommodated: the Sinaitic calendar has been forgotten, just as the prophecy in *Jubilees* predicts.

The Temple Scroll also situates itself and its readers at Sinai (11QT 51:6–7):

ולוא יטמאו בהמה אשר (7) אני מגיד לכה בהר הזה

> . . . And they shall not defile themselves with those things which (7) I tell you on this mountain. . . .

Indeed, the first section of the preserved text of the Temple Scroll rewrites Exodus 34, which describes the covenant renewal ceremony that takes place at Sinai. So there is good reason to think that the entire text of the Temple Scroll, not only specific purity laws, should be understood as revealed at Sinai.[34]

Appeals to Pre-Sinaitic Authority

In addition to re-presenting Sinai, both *Jubilees* and the Temple Scroll appeal to pre-Sinaitic tradition, specifically to a pre-Sinaitic covenant. Once again, there is some precedent in Deuteronomy. For in the final stratum of Deuteronomy, dated to the final years of the Babylonian exile or to the early years of the return to Judah, there are not only ambiguous references to the "fathers," which could refer either to the Exodus generation or to the patriarchal generations prior to Egypt, but also unequivocal references to a patriarchal covenant.[35] The patriarchs are also invoked repeatedly in Ezra-Nehemiah. As Thomas Römer has argued, these appeals should be seen in light of post-exilic restoration theology.[36] The point is not to downplay the authority of Sinai. Instead, the point is that, after the exile had fulfilled the Deuteronomic warnings, the returning exiles were reas-

---

[34] The point that all of *Jubilees* was considered to be "divine" for the author/redactor of the text is claimed by L. H. Schiffman, "The Theology of the Temple Scroll," 111. J. C. VanderKam notes that both *Jubilees* and the Temple Scroll are "presented as Sinaitic revelations from God to Moses" but that it "does not seem very likely that *Jubilees* and the Temple Scroll were meant to form a new or rival Pentateuch" ("The Theology of the Temple Scroll," 131–32).

[35] See the discussion of the patriarchal narratives by T. Römer, "Deuteronomy in Search of Origins," 112–38; T. Römer and M. Brettler, "Deuteronomy 34 and the Case for a Persian Hexateuch," 401–19; M. Weinfeld, *Deuteronomy and the Deuteronomic School*, 74–81; J. D. Levenson, *Sinai and Zion*, 10–11.

[36] T. Römer, "Deuteronomy in Search of Origins," 156–57.

sured by the recollection of a time prior to Israelite transgression, a time of unconditional covenant and promise.

The theme of the pre-Sinaitic covenant is greatly elaborated in both *Jubilees* and the Temple Scroll. This is evident in both of our later participants in Mosaic Discourse. As we have seen, *Jubilees* reworks pre-Sinaitic narratives to include divine revelations of law and ritual. It thereby renders Sinai one of a series of revelations, so that, although it is unique in its address to the entire people, Sinai becomes a reaffirmation of earlier patriarchal revelations.[37] Although the Temple Scroll does not invoke a patriarchal covenant many times, as *Jubilees* does, there is such an invocation in column 29, in a passage which is perhaps the most revealing with respect to the Temple Scroll's own self-understanding. Specifically, Column 29 invokes "the covenant which I have made with Jacob at Bethel," a covenant that founds the priesthood and that is ultimately to be fulfilled through the creation or recreation of the temple.[38]

ואקדשה [את מ]קדשי בכבודי אשר אשכין (9) עליו את כבודי עד יום הבריה
אשר אברא אני את מקדשי (10) להכינו לי כול הימים כברית אשר כרתי
עם יעקוב בבית אל

. . . I shall sanctify my [te]mple with my glory, for I shall make my glory reside (9) over it until the day of creation, when I shall create my temple, (10) establishing it for myself for all days, according to the covenant which I made with Jacob at Bethel.[39]

---

[37] See my discussion of this point in "Interpretation as Primordial Writing," 381–88.

[38] On issues surrounding how to understand the construction of this future temple see the following: Lawrence H. Schiffman, "The Construction of the Temple according to the *Temple Scroll*," *RevQ* 17 (1996): 555–71; Michael O. Wise, "The Covenant of Temple Scroll XXIX, 3–10," *RevQ* 14 (1989): 49–60; idem, "The Eschatological Vision of the Temple Scroll," *JNES* 49 (1990): 155–73; Judith L. Wentling, "Unraveling the Relationship between 11QT, the Eschatological Temple, and the Qumran Community," *RevQ* 14 (1989): 61–73; John A. Davies, "The *Temple Scroll* from Qumran and the Ultimate Temple," *RTR* 57 (1998): 1–21, esp. 15–16; Magen Broshi, "The Gigantic Dimensions of the Visionary Temple in the Temple Scroll," *BAR* 13, no. 6 (November/December 1987): 36–37.

[39] The reading "day of creation" given by F. García Martínez is based on the suggestion made by Elisha Qimron, "לנוסחה של מגילת המקדש" *Leš* 42 (1978): 136–45. Yadin's reading of "day of blessing" (הברכה) has not been accepted as correct. Yadin himself noted that Qimron's suggested reading was a possible alternative to his own (*The Temple Scroll*, 2:129).

The similarity to *Jubilees* in this respect has often been noted.[40] In *Jubilees* 32 Jacob returns to Bethel, where he had previously experienced a dream-vision and had taken an oath. On this occasion, it is Levi, Jacob's son, who dreams that he has been appointed priest and that his sons will inherit the priesthood forever. Jacob then inaugurates Levi's priestly service. God appears to Jacob, changing his name to Israel, and speaks to him in language that reworks the covenantal language between God and Abraham (*Jub.* 32:16–26).[41]

> (16) During the next night, on the twenty-second day of this month, Jacob decided to build up that place and to surround the courtyard with a wall, to sanctify it, and make it eternally holy for himself and for his children after him forever. (17) The Lord appeared to him during the night. He blessed him and said to him: 'You are not to be called Jacob only but you will (also) be named Israel'. (18) He said to him a second time: 'I am the Lord who created heaven and earth. I will increase your numbers and multiply you very much. Kings will come from you, and they will rule wherever mankind has set foot. (19) I will give your descendants all of the land that is beneath the sky. They will rule over all the nations just as they wish. Afterwards, they will gain the entire earth, and they will possess it forever'. (20) When he had finished speaking with him, he went up from him, and Jacob kept watching until he had gone up into heaven. (21) In a night vision he saw an angel coming down from heaven with seven tablets in his hands. He gave (them) to Jacob, and he read them. He read everything that was written in them—what would happen to him and his sons throughout all ages. (22) After he had shown him everything that was written on the tablets, he said to him: 'Do not build up this place, and do not make it an eternal temple. Do not live here because this is not the place. Go to the house of your father Abraham and live where your father Isaac is until the day of your father's death. (23)

---

[40] E.g., Baruch A. Levine, "The Temple Scroll: Aspects of its Historical Provenance and Literary Character," *BASOR* 232 (1978): 5–23; and L. H. Schiffman, "The Theology of the Temple Scroll," 109–28.

[41] See the parallels drawn between these narratives by J. L. Kugel, *The Bible as It Was*, 211–13, 224–26. See also my article, "Interpretation as Primordial Writing," 385–87; James L. Kugel, "Levi's Elevation to the Priesthood in Second Temple Writings," *HTR* 86 (1993): 1–64; idem, "The Ladder of Jacob," *HTR* 88 (1995): 209–28; Joshua Schwartz, "Jubilees, Bethel and the Temple of Jacob," *HUCA* 56 (1985): 63–85; Dwight D. Swanson, "A Covenant Just like Jacob's: the Covenant of 11QT 29 and Jeremiah's New Covenant," in *New Qumran Texts and Studies: Proceedings of the First Meeting of the International Organization for Qumran Studies, Paris 1992* (ed. G. J. Brooke with F. García Martínez; Leiden: Brill, 1994), 273–86; James C. VanderKam, "*Jubilees'* Exegetical Creation of Levi the Priest," *RevQ* 17 (1996): 359–73; repr. in *From Revelation to Canon*, 545–61.

For you will die peacefully in Egypt and be buried honorably in this land in the grave of your fathers—with Abraham and Isaac. (24) Do not be afraid because everything will happen just as you have seen and read. Now write down everything just as you have seen and read'. (25) Then Jacob said: 'Lord, how shall I remember everything just as I have read and seen'? He said to him: 'I will remind you of everything'. (26) When he had gone from him, he awakened and remembered everything that he had read and seen. He wrote down all the things that he had read and seen.

However, there are significant differences between *Jubilees* and the Temple Scroll, which also deserve to be noted. Most importantly, for *Jubilees*, Bethel—like Sinai—is associated with heavenly tablets, angelic transmission and earthly transcription, but not with the temple site, as *Jubilees* takes pains to make clear.[42] Jacob is given seven tablets by an angel descending from heaven and, after reading in them everything that will happen to him and to his sons, he is instructed to "write down everything just as you have seen and read."[43] In the Temple Scroll, however, there seems to be no trace of *Jubilees'* scribal preoccupation with the authority of writing and the need for accurate transcription and transmission. Instead, the covenant with Jacob at Bethel is invoked by God in his first-person speech. No angel intervenes. No transcription is commanded. The reader is placed in the immediate presence of the divine voice. Here, not only the deep affinity between *Jubilees* and the Temple Scroll, but also their significant differences begin to emerge.

Although the eventual construction of the temple is important to *Jubilees*, it is of course the calendrical system that is paramount. In contrast, although calendrical matters are significant for the Temple Scroll, it focuses on the concentration of the divine presence, not in

---

[42] It should be noted that the LXX (οἶκος θεοῦ) and *Targum Onqelos* (בית אל) agree with the Temple Scroll and understand Bethel to be the future site of the house of God. See also *Sifre Deb. para.* 452 for further discussion of Jacob's vision in Gen 28:17. In addition, see the comments on this motif by Esther Eshel, "Hermeneutical Approaches to Genesis in the Dead Sea Scrolls," in *The Book of Genesis in Jewish and Oriental Christian Interpretation: A Collection of Essays* (ed. J. Frishman and L. Van Rompay; Leuven: Peeters, 1997), 1–12, esp. 2–5.

[43] In addition, in the book of *Jubilees*, the covenant is always granted in the third month, whereas Jacob's return to Bethel and his vision occurs in the seventh month. Note also that *Jubilees* recounts that Levi already received the covenant of the priesthood in *Jubilees* 30, and shortly thereafter Jacob receives the tradition of the heavenly tablets in his angelic vision (*Jubilees* 32). I am indebted to a conversation with James VanderKam on this point, November 2001.

time, but in space—in the temple itself,[44] which, unlike *Jubilees*, the
Temple Scroll locates at Bethel—literally, in the "house of God."

But the similarity is nevertheless noteworthy. Both *Jubilees* and the
Temple Scroll establish their origin and foundation long before Sinai,
in the time of the patriarchs. They have a shared notion of pre-
patriarchal covenant that is explicitly linked to the continuation of
Jewish people in their land. Furthermore, both *Jubilees* and the Temple
Scroll understand their own vision for the future of the Jewish people as linked to a divine promise for a renewed covenant.[45] Perhaps
in response to the exile and perhaps in celebration of the independence under the Maccabean dynasty, both *Jubilees* and the Temple
Scroll understand the existence and future of the Jewish people as
deeply rooted in a patriarchal covenant that remains in effect, despite
the people's transgression and exile.

Mediated versus Unmediated Revelation

Although both *Jubilees* and the Temple Scroll situate themselves and
their readers at Sinai, they conceive the revelation at Sinai in radically different ways. First, as mentioned above, the contents of *Jubilees*
are dictated by an angel to Moses,[46] who transcribes what is revealed
and who remains the initial addressee. From the Temple Scroll, however, Moses has been all but erased.[47]

Angelic mediation is one mode of authoritative revelation.[48] Indeed,
Jubilees is said to be dictated, not by just any angel, but by the angel

---

[44] See, e.g., Baruch M. Bokser, "Approaching Sacred Space," *HTR* 78 (1985):
279–99, esp. 281–87; Aharon Shemesh, "The Origins of the Laws of Separatism:
Qumran Literature and Rabbinic Halacha," *RevQ* 18 (1997): 223–41.

[45] E.g., Jer 31:31; Ezek 37:26; Isa 59:21.

[46] See L. Ravid, "Issues in the Book of Jubilees," 21–25, 35–36; and L. H.
Schiffman, "The Temple Scroll and the Halakhic Pseudepigrapha of the Second
Temple Period," 121–31; idem, "The Theology of the Temple Scroll," 109–28;
and Y. Yadin, *The Temple Scroll*, 1:71–73.

[47] L. H. Schiffman, however, characterizes both the Temple Scroll and *Jubilees*
as essentially divine pseudepigrapha. See his comments in "The Temple Scroll and
the Halakhic Pseudepigrapha of the Second Temple Period," 121–31; idem, "The
Temple Scroll and the Nature of Its Law: The Status of the Question," in *The
Community of the Renewed Covenant* (ed. E. Ulrich and J. C. VanderKam; CJAS 10;
Notre Dame: University of Notre Dame Press, 1994), 37–55.

[48] See my discussion of the significance of angelic meditation in my articles:
"Interpretation as Primordial Writing," 379–410, and "Angels at Sinai," 313–33.

of the presence,[49] who enjoys a special intimacy with God. Here is a passage from *Jub.* 1:27–29:

> (27) Then he said to an angel of the presence: "Dictate to Moses (starting) from the beginning of the creation until the time when my temple is built among them throughout the ages of eternity. . . ." (29) The angel of the presence, who was going along in front of the Israelite camp, took the tablets (which told) of the divisions of the years from the time the law and the testimony were created—for the weeks of their jubilees, year by year in their full number, and their jubilees from [the time of creation until] the time of the new creation when the heavens, the earth, and all their creatures will be renewed like the powers of the sky and like all the creatures of the earth, until the time when the temple of the Lord will be created in Jerusalem on Mt. Zion.

Again, in the opening lines of the second chapter (*Jub.* 2:1), the angel of the presence is told to instruct Moses to write[50] "all the words about the creation." *Jubilees* here conceives the authority of Mosaic Torah as deriving from its origin in an angelic intermediary, whose authority results in turn from his elevated status and from his acting at God's command.[51] The angel of the presence makes

---

[49] See the insightful treatment of the angel of the presence by James C. VanderKam, "The Angel of the Presence in the Book of Jubilees," *DSD* 7 (2000): 378–93.

[50] James C. VanderKam, "The Putative Author of the Book of Jubilees," in *From Revelation to Canon: Studies in the Hebrew Bible and Second Temple Literature* (JSJSup 62; Leiden: Brill, 2000), 439–47; repr. from *JSS* 26 (1981): 209–17.

[51] The Book of *Jubilees* is structured by an *inclusio* concerning Sinai. On this point in its final chapter regarding the Sabbath and Sinai, see my article, "Interpretation as Primordial Writing," 389–95. Compare also the following texts from *Jubilees*:

> (Prologue) These are the words regarding the divisions of the times of the law and of the testimony, of the events of the years, of the weeks of their jubilees throughout all the years of eternity as he related (them) to Moses on Mt. Sinai when he went up to receive the stone tablets—the law and the commandments—on the Lord's orders as he had told him that he should come up to the summit of the mountain.

> (1:1) During the first year of the Israelites' exodus from Egypt, in the third month—on the sixteenth of the month—the Lord said to Moses: "Come up to me on the mountain. I will give you the two stone tablets of the law and the commandments which I have written so that you may teach them."

> (1:4) Moses remained on the mountain for forty days and forty nights while the Lord showed him what (had happened) beforehand as well as what was to come. He related to him the divisions of all the times—both of the law and of the testimony. (5) He said to him: "Pay attention to all the words which I tell you on this mountain. Write (them) in a book so that their offspring may see that I have not abandoned them because of all the evil they have done in *straying from* the covenant between me and you which I am making today on Mt. Sinai for their offspring.

occasional appearances throughout the book of *Jubilees*. Interestingly, although this angel is never mentioned in the Pentateuch, his appearance in *Jubilees* is often occasioned by a reference to angels in the relevant biblical narratives.[52] This association enables the angel to acquire the status of the pentateuchal angels. Of course, reinforcing the authority of the angel also strengthens the authority of what he dictates, hence that of *Jubilees* itself. For the angel is the messenger who links the heavenly realm of the tablets with the earthly realm of the scribe. Acting on divine instruction, the angel insures the accuracy of the scribe's copy, thus transmitting heavenly authority to the product of an otherwise fallible process of human writing. In the Temple Scroll, however, it is God himself who speaks, in the first person as direct, unmediated revelation.[53]

Second, *Jubilees* conceives authority as bound up with *writtenness*.[54] Thus the laws detailed in *Jubilees* are said to be written on heavenly tablets; they are said to have been transcribed in earthly records since antiquity; and they are said to be dictated by an angel so that Moses can write them down once again.[55] A concern with books—

(50:13) ... a man who does any of these things on the sabbath day is to die, so that the Israelites may continue observing the sabbath in accord with the commandments for the sabbaths of the land as it was written in the tablets which he placed in my hands so that I could write for you the laws of each specific time in every division of its times."

[52] There are four such examples in *Jubilees*: 16:1–4; 16:15–19; 18:9; 48:13. However, the angel of the presence does not appear on *every* occasion when angels are mentioned in the Pentateuch. For example, when Jacob dreams of the ladder of angels (*Jub.* 32:21–26), *Jubilees* reports the presence of angels but the angel of the presence *does not* claim to have been present. In addition, when Hagar is expelled from Abraham's household, an angel appears to her. Here too, in *Jub.* 17:11, the angel of the presence does not claim to have been that angel (cf. *Jub.* 5:6 concerning the "bad angels"). On one important occasion, the angel of the presence appears when there is no reference to an angel in the biblical text. This addition to the biblical text provides the divinely authorized forgiveness of Judah, which is nowhere mentioned in the Hebrew Bible. When *Jubilees* recounts the narrative of Genesis 38, it inserts a reference to a dream that Judah had in which the angels ("we", thus including the angel of the presence) spoke to him in a dream. See *Jub.* 41:23–24.

[53] On the distinction between Priestly (immediate) and Deuteronomic (mediated) conceptions of revelation see B. A. Levine, "The Temple Scroll: Aspects of its Historical Provenance and Literary Character," 17–21; Lawrence H. Schiffman, "The Deuteronomic Paraphrase of the Temple Scroll," *RevQ* 15 (1992): 543–67.

[54] See my article "Angels at Sinai," 314–19.

[55] See my article, "Interpretation as Primordial Writing," 379–410. See also Andrei A. Orlov, "Overshadowed by Enoch's Greatness: 'Two Tablets' Traditions from the *Book of Giants* to *Palaea Historica*," *JSJ* 32 (2001): 137–58, on similar motifs

mentions of which are inserted into numerous scriptural narratives—and with the art of writing is evident throughout *Jubilees*. In striking contrast, the Temple Scroll mentions the writing of the law only once, when it repeats the Deuteronomic command to write the ספר תורה for the King. To be sure, the Temple Scroll identifies itself as "this" ספר תורה. But its sense of its own authority is not bound up with writtenness. Instead, as we see in 11QT 51:6–7, the Temple Scroll conceives authority as bound up with *the immediate presence of the divine voice at Sinai*: "which I tell you on this mountain."[56]

This point alone, I believe, would be sufficient to refute Wacholder's suggestion that *Jubilees* and the Temple Scroll are parts of a single work.[57] Despite their similarities—despite the fact that both participate in Mosaic Discourse—they have different conceptions of their own authority and, indeed, of the authority of revelation as such.

Divine Pseudepigraphon

Finally we turn to the fourth feature of Mosaic Discourse: attribution of the Torah to—or association of the Torah with—Moses, the founding figure.

Jubilees' rewritings and interpretations of biblical traditions are authorized both as angelic revelation from the angel of the presence[58]

---

of pre-Sinaitic authoritative writing in the form of tablets, in Enoch and related traditions. On the heavenly tablets tradition, see esp.: Robert Eppel, "Les tables de la Loi et les tables célestes," *RHPR* 17 (1937): 401–12; Shalom M. Paul, "Heavenly Tablets and the Book of Life," *JANESCU* 5 (1973): 345–53; and Florentino García Martínez, "The Heavenly Tablets in the Book of Jubilees," in *Studies in the Book of Jubilees* (ed. M. Albani, J. Frey, and A. Lange; Tübingen: Mohr Siebeck, 1997), 243–60; trans. by M. T. Davis from "Las Tablas Celestes en el Libro de los Jubileos," in *Palabra y Vida: Homenaje a José Alonso Díaz en su 70 cumpleaños* (ed. A. Vargas Machuca and G. Ruiz; Publicationes de la Universidad Pontifica Comillias Madrid, Series I, Estudios 58; Madrid: Ediciones Universidad de Comillias, 1984), 333–49.

[56] There are related passages in the Temple Scroll that emphasize "this day" as the time when the Temple Scroll is revealed to the people; e.g., 54:6; 55:11–14; 62:15.

[57] See Ben Zion Wacholder, *The Dawn of Qumran: The Sectarian Torah and the Teacher of Righteousness* (Cincinnati: Hebrew Union College Press, 1983). See also the recent discussions by S. White Crawford in which she argues against Wacholder's view of the unity of *Jubilees* and the Temple Scroll (*The Temple Scroll and Related Texts*; "The 'Rewritten Bible' at Qumran: A Look at Three Texts," *ErIsr* 26 [1999]: 1–8; "Three Fragments from Qumran Cave 4 and Their Relationship to the Temple Scroll," *JQR* 85 [1994]: 259–73).

[58] The angel of the presence is also referred to in the Qumran literature. See,

from a divinely produced set of heavenly tablets and as the faithful
record of Moses, the paradigmatic amanuensis.

Thus, after Moses is instructed to "write all these words" (*Jub.*
1:26), God speaks to an angel of the presence in *Jub.* 1:27–29:

> (27) Then he said to an angel of the presence: "Dictate to Moses (start-
> ing) from the beginning of the creation until the time when my tem-
> ple is built among them throughout the ages of eternity. (28) The Lord
> will appear in the sight of all, and all will know that I am the God
> of Israel, the father of all Jacob's children, and the king on Mt. Zion
> for the ages of eternity. Then Zion and Jerusalem will become holy."
> (29) The angel of the presence, who was going along in front of the
> Israelite camp, took the tablets (which told) of the divisions of the years
> from the time the law and the testimony were created—for the weeks
> of their jubilees, year by year in their full number, and their jubilees
> from [the time of creation until] the time of the new creation when
> the heavens, the earth, and all their creatures will be renewed like the
> powers of the sky and like all the creatures of the earth, until the time
> when the temple of the Lord will be created in Jerusalem on Mt. Zion.

In *Jub.* 2:1, the angel of the presence once again instructs Moses to
write:

> On the Lord's orders the angel of the presence said to Moses: "Write
> all the words about the creation—how in six days the Lord God com-
> pleted all his works, everything that he had created, and kept sabbath
> on the seventh day. He sanctified it for all ages and set it as a sign
> for all his works."

Why should angelic dictation be necessary, in addition to Mosaic
transcription of the heavenly tablets? Some scholars have argued that
the apparent contradiction reveals a complex redactional history of
Jubilees. However, these suggestions have been decisively refuted by
VanderKam. He argues that there is no contradiction: while the

---

e.g., 3Q7, column 5; 1QH^a, column 6; 1QS^b, column 3. For further discussion of
the role of angels in Second Temple and Rabbinic literature, see Maxwell J. Davidson, *Angels at Qumran: A Comparative Study of 1Enoch 1–36, 72–108 and Sectarian Writings
from Qumran* (JSPSup 11; Sheffield: JSOT Press, 1992); Michael Mach, *Entwicklungsstadien
des jüdischen Engelglaubens in vorrabbinischer Zeit* (TSAJ 34; Tübingen: J. C. B. Mohr
[Paul Siebeck], 1992); Saul M. Olyan, *A Thousand Thousands Served Him: Exegesis and
the Naming of Angels in Ancient Judaism* (TSAJ 36; Tübingen: J. C. B. Mohr [Paul
Siebeck], 1993); Moshe J. Bernstein, "Angels at the Aqedah: A Study in the
Development of a Midrashic Motif," *DSD* 7 (2000): 263–91; J. C. VanderKam,
"The Angel of the Presence in the Book of Jubilees," 378–93; and my article,
"Angels at Sinai," 313–33.

instructions given to the angel of the presence and Moses are certainly related, insofar as they both use the same verbal root כ.ת.ב., nevertheless, Moses is said to write in the *qal* while the angel of the presence is instructed to dictate, i.e., to cause Moses to write, in the *hiphil*.[59] Thus, the narrative of the first chapter of *Jubilees* does not betray a complex redactional history but instead portrays a complex series of actions, involving: an already existing collection of heavenly tablets; an angel of the presence who is instructed to dictate the contents of these tablets to Moses; and Moses himself, who assiduously records all that is dictated to him by the angel.

Thus, in addition to claiming that *Jubilees* is angelic dictation from heavenly tablets, *Jubilees* insists on Moses' role in its production. Moses is the *writer* of this text, although he is not its *author*. For Moses is the scribe who transcribes what is read to him from the heavenly tablets by the angel of the presence, and he is the person to whom the revealed traditions are, in the first place, addressed (*Jub.* 1:26):

> Now you write all these words which I will tell you on this mountain: what is first and what is last and what is to come during all the divisions of time which are in the law and which are in the testimony and in the weeks of their jubilees until eternity—until the time when I descend and live with them throughout all the ages of eternity.

The role of Moses is reinforced for the reader in the following way: into pentateuchal narratives are inserted either laws that occur elsewhere in the Pentateuch (such as the prohibition of sexual relations with one's father's wife, unmentioned in the episode of Reuben and Bilhah) or laws that are nowhere to be found in the Pentateuch (such as the prohibition of intermarriage on pain of death). On these occasions, the angel of the presence speaks directly to Moses and

---

[59] See J. C. VanderKam, "The Putative Author of the Book of Jubilees," 439–47. VanderKam argues convincingly that *Jubilees* presents a single account of divine dictation by the angel of the presence to Moses who then *writes* the tradition down. I am convinced by VanderKam's argument that there is a single author of the book of *Jubilees*. However, a number of scholars have posited a variety of schemes for the redactional stages in the book of *Jubilees*. See, e.g., Gene L. Davenport, *The Eschatology of the Book of Jubilees* (StPB 20; Leiden: Brill, 1971); Ed P. Sanders, *Paul and Palestinian Judaism: A Comparison of Patterns of Religion* (Philadelphia: Fortress, 1977), 287; Ernest Wiesenberg, "The Jubilee of Jubilees," *RevQ* 3 (1961–62): 3–40; Michel Testuz, *Les Idées Religieuses du Livre des Jubilés* (Geneva: Librarie E. Droz and Paris: Librairie Minard, 1960), 39–42.

tells him to record such a law.[60] It is clear why *Jubilees* employs this method of emphasizing that the text before the reader was transcribed by Moses: the pre-Sinaitic history of Genesis through the beginning of Exodus is thereby shown to have legal implications, and the laws endorsed by *Jubilees* are shown to have the authority of Mosaic Torah, while the authority of Mosaic Torah is at the same time shown to be rooted in a heavenly tradition ascribed to God and known to select individuals since the beginnings of history.[61] All of this underscores the peculiarly authoritative status of *Jubilees* itself, its calendrical system and its chronology—an authority that, if taken at face value, would be hard to outweigh.[62]

It is important to distinguish between rewriting the Bible and insisting on Moses' scribal role, as distinct but connected features of Mosaic Discourse. The former is a way of claiming the authority of *Mosaic Torah*, a sacred written tradition whose authority was long established, while the latter is a way of claiming the authority of *Moses the figure*. In *Jubilees*, Moses' sole function is that of the amanu-

---

[60] For references to Moses in the book of *Jubilees*: see *Jub*. Prologue; 1:1–28; 2:1; 6:19–22, 32; 15:28, 33; 23:32; 30:11–12, 17, 21; 33:13–14, 18–19; 41:26; 46:10; 47:1–49:2; 49:7, 11, 15–17; 49:22–50:2; 50:4, 6, 13.

[61] This claim to heavenly or divine ascription is not unique to *Jubilees*. For example, the Temple Scroll rewrites selections of the Pentateuch in such a way that it is God who is speaking in the first person. By rewriting and appropriating the Mosaic Torah, the Temple Scroll assumes a position of divine authority. In the context of rewriting Mosaic Torah, the Temple Scroll supplements the biblical tradition with laws and holidays. But in the case of both *Jubilees* and the Temple Scroll, in addition to affirming divine ascription, the authors employ additional strategies to claim their authority as interpreters of Mosaic Torah. For an extensive discussion of the laws (both biblical and extra-biblical) cited in the Temple Scroll, see Y. Yadin, "Chapter Two: The Festivals," in *The Temple Scroll*, 1:89–142.

[62] James L. Kugel has noted that *Jubilees* incorporates passages from Psalm 90, a psalm which was already attributed to Moses. In each case, *Jubilees* attaches to these passages themes that are distinctive of its interpretive and legal positions. Thus the incorporation of passages from Psalm 90 serves as yet another device to confirm the Mosaic authority of the "law and testimony" to be found in *Jubilees*. For a discussion of the integration of this psalm into *Jubilees*, see Kugel, "The Jubilees Apocalypse," *DSD* 1 (1994): 322–37. Kugel writes: "By weaving these other themes in with a few obvious references to Psalm 90, the author of Jubilees could provide the whole chapter with a certain legitimacy: the echoes of Psalm 90 in the angel's speech would serve to 'prove' that Moses had indeed heard this whole speech on Mt. Sinai (since he later incorporated at least some parts of it into his famous psalm), and this would allow the other elements to, as it were, ride in on biblical coattails. Thus, the author of Jubilees sought to incorporate a few key verses from this psalm into this chapter, radically reinterpreting them in such a way as to fit his own vision of the present and future" (336).

ensis:[63] he must accurately transcribe what is dictated to him from the heavenly tablets by the angel of the presence. Of his life before Sinai, we are told principally that he learned the art of writing from his father, Amram the Levite, and thus that he stands in the authentic line of Enochic and Abrahamic inheritance. For *Jubilees*, Moses the figure is important only as an appropriate, authoritative transmitter of heavenly tradition, not unlike Noah or Abraham. Thus, for *Jubilees*, the authority of Moses the figure is subordinate to the authority of the Torah of Moses.

Already in the earlier part of the Second Temple period, the Torah of Moses had assumed a position of special authority, so that laws or interpretations could be authorized by being connected to it.[64]

As I have mentioned, the Temple Scroll is written in the first-person voice of God, and lacks the elaborate dictation scene portrayed in *Jubilees*, as well as, more generally, *Jubilees*' scribal preoccupation with writing. As Schiffman has argued, the Temple Scroll is not a Moses pseudepigraphon[65] but rather a divine pseudepigraphon.[66] Like

---

[63] John Strugnell points out that Moses functions as amanuensis in only two Second Temple texts. In *Jubilees* he is the amanuensis for the angels, and in the Temple Scroll he is the amanuensis for God himself. See John Strugnell, "Moses-Pseudepigrapha at Qumran," 221–56, esp. 249. See also the discussion of several Qumran fragments labeled as "Pseudo-Ezekiel," "Pseudo-Jeremiah," and (no longer) "Pseudo-Moses" texts by Devorah Dimant, *Qumran Cave 4. Parabiblical Texts, Part 4: Pseudo-Prophetic Texts* (DJD 21; Oxford: Clarendon, 2001); see esp. her comments regarding the decision to abandon the label "Pseudo-Moses" on pages 2–3. Also, see Monica Walsh Brady's incisive critique of Dimant's position in "Prophetic Traditions at Qumran: A Study of 4Q383–391" (2 vols.; Ph.D. diss., The University of Notre Dame, 2000); see esp. her conclusions on 2:535–61.

[64] See my essay, "Torah of Moses," 202–16; and E. Ulrich, "From Literature to Scripture," forthcoming.

[65] While there has been much discussion of Moses pseudepigrapha, M. Brady has demonstrated beyond question that the material from Qumran has been misnamed ("Prophetic Traditions at Qumran: A Study of 4Q383–391," 2:543–55).

[66] As noted previously, L. H. Schiffman distinguishes between Moses pseudepigrapha and divine pseudepigrapha. He argues that both *Jubilees* and the Temple Scroll constitute divine pseudepigrapha. He writes: "Certainly, the scroll is not a Moses pseudepigraphon as it does not allow Moses his own voice anywhere in the scroll. If he appears at all, it is in the second person, as the oblique addressee. It is possible that in the complete scroll, he appeared in the third person as the bearer of the divine message in the introduction (or prologue) and perhaps in a concluding section. If so, then the scroll would constitute a divine pseudepigraphon with Moses acting as an intermediary. While this is the case in *Jubilees*, where Moses' role is sprinkled throughout the text, in the Temple Scroll he does not appear in the body of the document except obliquely" ("The Temple Scroll and the Halakhic Pseudepigrapha of the Second Temple Period," 131).

Jubilees, Moses' only role—at most—is that of amanuensis. However, Moses remains implicitly present in two passages.

In 44:5, the Temple Scroll addresses Moses in the second person:

לבני אהרון אחיכה תח[ן]לק]

You shall al[lot] to the sons of Aaron, your brother . . .

Here, while Moses' name is nowhere mentioned, he is nevertheless referred to as Aaron's brother.[67] And again, in 11QT 51:6–7 there is a reference to Moses:[68]

ולוא יטמאו בהמה אשר (7) אני מגיד לכה בהר הזה

And they shall not defile themselves with those things which (7) I tell you on this mountain . . .

By means of the second person singular pronoun, the reader is placed in the position of Moses, as the direct addressee of divine revelation on Mount Sinai. Given the incompleteness of the text, it is impossible to know whether these are Moses' only appearances.[69] It seems, however, that, in the Temple Scroll, the subordination of the authority of the figure of Moses to the authority of the Torah of Moses, also seen in *Jubilees*, has taken a further turn: Moses is nothing but the implicit, initial addressee and the implicit teacher of a Torah whose authority rests primarily on its direct revelation by God.

Conclusion

I have argued, then, that *Jubilees* and the Temple Scroll both participate in the Mosaic Discourse initiated by Deuteronomy. But this deep affinity does not imply that, as some have suggested, they could once have been parts of a single work. For there is a fundamental difference in the way they conceive the authority they both seek to appropriate from the biblical traditions they rework. *Jubilees* is inescap-

---

[67] See B. A. Levine, "The Temple Scroll: Aspects of its Historical Provenance and Literary Character," 5–23; and L. H. Schiffman, "The Theology of the Temple Scroll," 109–28.

[68] Again, see the discussion of this passage by L. H. Schiffman, "The Theology of the Temple Scroll," 110.

[69] On this point, see A. M. Wilson and L. Wills, "Literary Sources of the *Temple Scroll*," 275–88.

ably aware of its own writtenness, and seeks to authorize itself as the product of angelic dictation. In contrast, although the Temple Scroll also rewrites the rewriting of Deuteronomy, it does not seek to account for its own origin *as a piece of writing.* Indeed, it calls no attention to the fact that it is written, or rather rewritten. Instead, with disarming directness, it authorizes itself as divine speech.[70]

---

[70] L. H. Schiffman concludes: "Indeed, we may say that much of the literary activity of the author/redactor was directed at converting the deuteronomic material to this priestly form, in order to present the entire text as direct revelation, possibly with Moses as a mouthpiece" ("The Temple Scroll and the Halakhic Pseudepigrapha of the Second Temple Period," 131).

CHAPTER THREE

COPYING NATURE, COPYING MOSES

> Jewgreek is greekjew. Extremes meet.
>
> James Joyce, *Ulysses*

Does Philo Participate in Mosaic Discourse?

Under what conditions was Mosaic Discourse possible? Or: of what transformations was Mosaic Discourse capable under varying conditions?

The works of Philo of Alexandria provide a fascinating test-case for the exploration of these questions. While unquestionably a Second Temple Jew, both chronologically and in many aspects of his religious consciousness, Philo was also one of the most striking representatives of a Hellenistic Judaism that can seem worlds apart from the Second Temple Judaisms of Palestine. In the cultural competition of Ptolemaic Egypt, and in a community that relied upon the Septuagint rather than Hebrew versions of biblical texts, was Mosaic Discourse still possible? If so, what transformations did it undergo?

The Authority of the Figure and Law of Moses in a Hellenistic Context

Philo's challenge was different from the challenge confronting the authors of *Jubilees* and the Temple Scroll. They had to authorize, to an exclusively Jewish audience, what they took to be authentic Judaism, in the face of rival practices and interpretations. Philo had to authorize Judaism itself to both Jews and non-Jews, within the relatively new context of the Hellenistic competition of cultures, a competition that was at the same time political, especially in light of the even newer Roman Empire's quest to authorize itself through the appropriation of the Greek philosophical and literary heritage.[1]

---

[1] See the recent volume edited by John J. Collins and Gregory E. Sterling, *Hellenism in the Land of Israel* (CJAS 13; Notre Dame: University of Notre Dame

The place of Judaism within this new Roman world was far from clear. On the one hand, the significance of the Greek heritage was now as universal as the empire itself sought to be. Near eastern cultures, which enjoyed the mystique of antiquity and exoticism, could legitimize themselves by identifying their gods with Greek gods and their teachings with Greek teachings. On the other hand, religious syncretism did not cohere easily with Jewish monotheism, and the Mosaic Law, which seemed primarily to address Jews alone, was in danger of appearing parochial, thus rendering it potentially threatening to Rome and potentially insignificant to Hellenized Jews.

The issue took a violent turn within Philo's lifetime. Philo reports that under Augustus' reign, the Jews had the right to live according to their ancient laws.[2] *Legat.* 155–158 (Colson, LCL):

Πῶς οὖν ἀπεδέχετο τὴν πέραν τοῦ Τιβέρεως ποταμοῦ μεγάλην τῆς ʽΡώμης ἀποτομήν, [ἣν] οὐκ ἠγνόει κατεχομένην καὶ οἰκουμένην πρὸς Ἰουδαίων; ʽΡωμαῖοι δὲ ἦσαν οἱ πλείους ἀπελευθερωθέντες· αἰχμάλωτοι γὰρ ἀχθέντες εἰς Ἰταλίαν ὑπὸ τῶν κτησαμένων ἠλευθερώθησαν, οὐδὲν τῶν πατρίων παραχαράξαι βιασθέντες. ἠπίστατο οὖν καὶ προσευχὰς ἔχοντας καὶ συνιόντας εἰς αὐτάς, καὶ μάλιστα ταῖς ἱεραῖς ἑβδόμαις, ὅτε δημοσίᾳ τὴν πάτριον παιδεύονται φιλοσοφίαν. ἠπίστατο καί χρήματα συνάγοντας ἀπὸ τῶν ἀπαρχῶν ἱερὰ καὶ πέμποντας εἰς Ἱεροσόλυμα διὰ τῶν τὰς θυσίας ἀναξόντων. ἀλλ᾽ ὅμως οὔτε ἐξῴκισε τῆς ʽΡώμης ἐκείνους οὔτε τὴν ʽΡωμαϊκὴν αὐτῶν ἀφείλετο πολιτείαν, ὅτι καὶ τῆς Ἰουδαϊκῆς ἐφρόντιζον, οὔτε ἐνεωτέρισεν εἰς τὰς προσευχὰς οὔτε ἐκώλυσε συνάγεσθαι πρὸς τὰς τῶν νόμων ὑφηγήσεις οὔτε ἠναντιώθη τοῖς ἀπαρχομένοις, ἀλλ᾽ οὕτως ὡσίωτο περὶ τὰ ἡμέτερα, ὥστε μόνον οὐ πανοίκιος ἀναθημάτων πολυτελείαις τὸ ἱερὸν ἡμῶν ἐκόσμησε, προστάξας καὶ διαιωνίους ἀνάγεσθαι θυσίας ἐντελεχεῖς ὁλοκαύτους καθ᾽ ἑκάστην ἡμέραν ἐκ τῶν ἰδίων προσόδων ἀπαρχὴν τῷ ὑψίστῳ θεῷ, αἵ καὶ μέχρι νῦν ἐπιτελοῦνται καὶ εἰς ἅπαν ἐπιτελεσθήσονται, μήνυμα τρόπων ὄντως αὐτοκρατορικῶν. οὐ μὴν ἀλλὰ κἀν ταῖς μηνιαίοις τῆς πατρίδος διανομαῖς, ἀργύριον ἢ σῖτον ἐν μέρει παντός τοῦ δήμου λαμβάνοντος, οὐδέποτε τοὺς Ἰουδαίους ἠλάττωσε τῆς χάριτος, ἀλλ᾽ εἰ καὶ συνέβη τῆς ἱερᾶς ἑβδόμης ἐνεστώσης γενέσθαι τὴν διανομήν, ὅτε οὔτε λαμβάνειν οὔτε διδόναι ἢ συνόλως τι πράττειν τῶν κατὰ βίον καὶ μάλιστα τὸν ποριστὴν ἐφεῖται, προσετέτακτο τοῖς διανέμουσι ταμιεύειν τοῖς Ἰουδαίοις εἰς τὴν ὑστεραίαν τὴν κοινὴν φιλανθρωπίαν.

How then did he [Augustus] show his approval? He was aware that the great section of Rome on the other side of the Tiber is occupied

---

Press, 2001). In particular see the essays by John J. Collins, "Cult and Culture: The Limits of Hellenization in Judea," 38–61 and by Gregory E. Sterling, "Judaism Between Jerusalem and Athens," 263–301.

[2] P. Borgen, *Philo of Alexandria: An Exegete For His Time*, 14–45.

and inhabited by Jews, most of whom were Roman citizens emanci-
pated. For having been brought as captives to Italy they were liber-
ated by their owners and were not forced to violate any of their native
institutions. He knew therefore that they have houses of prayer and
meet together in them, particularly on the sacred Sabbaths when they
receive as a body a training in their ancestral philosophy. He knew
too that they collect money for sacred purposes from their first fruits
and send them to Jerusalem by persons who would offer the sacrifices.
Yet nevertheless he neither ejected them from Rome nor deprived
them of their Roman citizenship because they were careful to preserve
their Jewish citizenship also, nor took any violent measures against the
houses of prayer, nor prevented them from meeting to receive instructions in the laws, nor opposed their offerings of the firstfruits. Indeed
so religiously did he respect our interests that supported by wellnigh
his whole household he adorned our temple through the costliness of
his dedications, and ordered that for all time continuous sacrifices of
whole burnt offerings should be carried out every day at his own
expense as a tribute to the most high God. And these sacrifices are
maintained to the present day and will be maintained for ever to tell
the story of a character truly imperial. Yet more, in the monthly doles
in his own city when all the people each in turn receive money or
corn, he never put the Jews at a disadvantage in sharing the bounty,
but even if the distributions happened to come during the Sabbath
when no one is permitted to receive or give anything or to transact
any part of the business of ordinary life, particularly of a lucrative
kind, he ordered the dispensers to reserve for the Jews till the mor-
row the charity which fell to all.[3]

However, the Greeks were given the right to rule over other peoples
in Alexandria.[4] While the Greeks resented the religious separatism
of the Jews, which they regarded as misanthropic, the Jews resented
the political privileges of the Greeks, to which they regarded themselves as having equal right in light of their ancient culture.[5] Tensions
came to a head when, under Gaius Caligula, the Jews were forced
to worship the Roman emperor. A violent attack against the Jewish
community in Alexandria ensued between 38–41 c.e. Places of Jewish
worship, homes, and shops were destroyed and many Jews were left
destitute. During these difficult years, Philo was a member of an un-

---

[3] See also *Flacc.* 50.
[4] On the Jewish community in Alexandria, see John J. Collins, "Chapter 8: The
Diaspora Setting," in *Jewish Wisdom in the Hellenistic Age* (OTL; Louisville: Westminster/
John Knox, 1997), 135–57; Peter Marshall Fraser, "Chapter 5: The Cults of
Alexandria," in *Ptolemaic Alexandria* (3 vols.; Oxford: Clarendon, 1972), 1:189–301.
[5] J. J. Collins, "Chapter 8: The Diaspora Setting," 135–57.

successful Jewish embassy sent to Gaius Caligula to defend Jewish ancestral rights. When Gaius Caligula was assassinated in 41 c.e., the Jews reacquired the rights previously granted to them by Augustus. But tensions in Alexandria did not cease.

Thus, in Philo's world, the authority of Mosaic Law itself is a live issue. Of course, Philo interprets that law in a particular way that may not have been accepted by all Jews, even in Alexandria. Thus Philo claims to have the correct interpretations and, on occasion, challenges other interpretive methods and conclusions that are prevalent in the Alexandrian Jewish community.[6] But the question of authority arises for him primarily as a question about how to authorize the law of Moses against competing non-Jewish traditions.[7]

In response, Philo claims that the law of Moses is *superior* to the laws of all other nations, arguing (*Mos.* 2.12 [Colson, LCL]):

῞Οτι δ᾽ αὐτός τε νομοθετῶν ἄριστος τῶν πανταχοῦ πάντων, ὅσοι παρ᾽ ῞Ελλησιν ἢ βαρβάροις ἐγένοντο, καὶ οἱ νόμοι κάλλιστοι καὶ ὡς ἀληθῶς θεῖοι . . .

That Moses himself was the best of all lawgivers in all countries, better in fact than any that have ever arisen among either the Greeks or the barbarians, and that his laws are most excellent and truly come from God . . .

To be sure, Mosaic Law is particular in the sense that it is binding in all its details only for the particular people of Israel. However, the Law of Moses has a special relation to Natural Law that gives it universal significance. *Mos.* 2.14:

τὰ δὲ τούτου μόνου βέβαια, ἀσάλευτα, ἀκράδαντα, καθάπερ σφραγῖσι φύσεως αὐτῆς σεσημασμένα, μένει παγίως ἀφ᾽ ἧς ἡμέρας ἐγράφη μέχρι

---

[6] On Philo's challenges to other contemporaneous interpreters, see Peder Borgen, "Philo of Alexandria: A Critical and Synthetical Survey of Research Since World War II," *ANRW* 21.1:126–28; David M. Hay, "References to Other Exegetes in Philo's *Quaestiones*," in *Both Literal and Allegorical: Studies in Philo of Alexandria's Questions and Answers on Genesis and Exodus* (ed. D. M. Hay; BJS 232; Atlanta: Scholars Press, 1991), 81–97; idem, "Philo's References to Other Allegorists," *StPh* 6 (1979–80): 41–76; idem, "Defining Allegory in Philo's Exegetical World," *SBL Seminar Papers, 1994* (SBLSP 33; Atlanta: Scholars Press, 1994), 55–68.

[7] Other Hellenistic Jewish writers addressed the problem by claiming that Greek culture originates in Jewish tradition. See the insightful discussion by Eric S. Gruen, "Jewish Perspectives on Greek Culture," in *Hellenism in the Land of Israel* (ed. J. J. Collins and G. E. Sterling; CJAS 13; Notre Dame: University of Notre Dame Press, 2001), 62–93, esp. 71–83.

νῦν καὶ πρὸς τὸν ἔπειτα πάντα διαμενεῖν ἐλπὶς αὐτὰ αἰῶνα ὥσπερ ἀθά-
νατα, ἕως ἂν ἥλιος καὶ σελήνη καὶ ὁ σύμπας οὐρανός τε καὶ κόσμος ᾖ.

But Moses is alone in this, that his laws—firm unshaken, immovable,
stamped, as it were, with the seals of nature herself—remain secure
from the day when they were first enacted to now, and we may hope
that they will remain for all future ages as though immortal, so long
as the sun and moon and the whole heaven and universe exist.

Now, in his account of creation, Philo uses the metaphor of stamp-
ing with a seal to express the relationship between original and copy
(*Leg.* 1.22):

ὥσπερ τοῦ ἐπὶ μέρους καὶ ἀτόμου νοῦ προϋπάρχει τις ἰδέα ὡς ἂν ἀρχέτυπος
καὶ παράδειγμα τούτου, καὶ πάλιν τῆς κατὰ μέρος αἰσθήσεως (ἰδέα τις
αἰσθήσεως) σφραγῖδος λόγον ἔχουσα εἴδη τυπούσης, . . .

As before the particular and individual mind there subsists a certain
original as an archetype and pattern of it, and again before the particular sense-perception, a certain original of sense perception related
to the particular as a seal-making impression is to the form which it
makes; . . .

Philo's claim, then, is that the laws of Moses are *copies* of the Laws
of Nature. Indeed, he says elsewhere that they are "likenesses and
copies of the patterns enshrined in the soul" (*Mos.* 2.11), and that "the
laws [are] the most faithful copy of the world-polity" (*Mos.* 2.51–52).
In light of this special relation to Natural Law, both Jews and non-
Jews alike should recognize the excellence of Mosaic Law and the
perfection of Moses the lawgiver, and the charge of misanthropy
may be refuted.

As has long been noted, Philo hereby undertakes to authorize
Judaism by identifying various Greek philosophical ideas in the Torah
of Moses. He is drawing specifically on both Stoic ethics, which is
based on a conception of the wise man as following the Law of
Nature,[8] and Middle Platonic metaphysics, which views the world as

---

[8] See J. J. Collins, "Cult and Culture: The Limits of Hellenization in Judea,"
38–61. For discussions of earlier Greek foundations for the Stoic concept of Natural
Law see Paul A. Vander Waerdt, "Zeno's Republic and the Origins of Natural
Law," in *The Socratic Movement* (ed. P. A. Vander Waerdt; Ithaca: Cornell University
Press, 1994), 272–308; Joseph G. DeFilippo and Phillip T. Mitsis, "Socrates and
Stoic Natural Law," in *The Socratic Movement* (ed. P. A. Vander Waerdt; Ithaca:
Cornell University Press, 1994), 252–71; David Sedley, "The nomothêtes in Plato's
Cratylus," in *The Law of Nature: Ancient Origins and Contemporary Transformations* (ed.
H. Najman, D. K. O'Connor, and G. E. Sterling, forthcoming).

created in accordance with ideas in the divine mind.[9] While this authority-conferring strategy was clearly drawn from surrounding Hellenistic culture, Philo seems to have been on the cutting edge of philosophical thought.[10] As various scholars have demonstrated, the idea of Nature as a divinely created cosmic order providing normative guidance for human action was absent from early Greek thought,[11]

---

[9] For some helpful discussions on the relationship between Middle Platonism and Philo of Alexandria, see David T. Runia, "Was Philo a Middle Platonist? a Difficult Question Revisited," *StPhA* 5 (1993): 112–40; Gregory E. Sterling, "Platonizing Moses: Philo and Middle Platonism," *StPhA* 5 (1993): 96–111; John M. Dillon, *The Middle Platonists: 80 B.C. to A.D. 220* (Ithaca: Cornell University Press, 1996); idem, "A Response to Runia and Sterling," *StPhA* 5 (1993): 151–55; Thomas H. Tobin, "Was Philo a Middle Platonist? Some Suggestions," *StPhA* 5 (1993): 147–50; David Winston, "Response to Runia and Sterling," *StPhA* 5 (1993): 141–46.

It is a matter of speculation whether Philo and Cicero shared a common Middle Platonic source, perhaps Antiochus, Panaetius or Posidonius. Richard A. Horsley states: "Antiochus, Cicero, and Philo conceive of a transcendent grounding for the law of nature: (1) they connected political affairs closely with the more contemplative quest for higher, divine truth and honors; they viewed the true, universal reason or law as the mind of the divine Creator and Lawgiver—a divine mind which transcended the sense-perceptible creation and worldly affairs; and (3) they understood the human mind, divinely given and partaking in the divine essence, as the means of ascending to knowledge of this transcendent truth" ("The Law of Nature in Philo and Cicero," *HTR* 71 [1978]: 35–59, citation 57). For discussion of the role of Middle Platonism in the writings of Philo, see John Dillon, "Chapter 3, Platonism at Alexandria: Eudorus and Philo," in *The Middle Platonists*, 114–83. Although Philo was operating with pre-existing conceptual elements and must be situated within the relevant context, nevertheless my argument shows that he had to make significant adjustments to the concept of the law of the nature if it was to serve his purpose by grounding the authority of the written law of Moses.

[10] Helmut Koester is surely incorrect when he suggests that Philo originated the notion of Natural Law. See his article, "'ΝΟΜΟΣ ΦΥΣΕΩΣ': The Concept of Natural Law in Greek Thought," in *Religions in Antiquity: Essays in Memory of Erwin Ramsdell Goodenough* (ed. J. Neusner; SHR 14; Leiden: Brill, 1968), 521–41, 540. For a refutation of Koester's view, see R. A. Horsley, "The Law of Nature in Philo and Cicero," 35–59, esp. 56 ff.

See also Gisela Striker, "Origins of the Concept of Natural Law," in *Essays on Hellenistic Epistemology and Ethics* (ed. S. Engstrom and J. Whiting; New York: Cambridge University Press, 1996), 209–20. On page 217, she states: "According to the Stoics, the universe—Nature as a whole—must be considered to be organized and ruled by a divine reason, which produces the harmony and order we can observe. Since Nature is the best thing there is, its goodness—perfect rational order—is the only thing that can be called good without qualification.... Knowledge of the good thus turns out to be, more precisely, knowledge of the rational order of nature. And since this order was assumed to have been created by a divine reason, its rules could also be conceived of as laws given by a divine legislator."

[11] In early Greek philosophy, Nature and Law were contrasting terms, whose competing merits were the subject of an important controversy. For an excellent discussion of this debate with extensive primary sources see Richard D. McKirahan

but must have emerged shortly before the time of Philo, perhaps in some fusion of Stoic ethics and Middle Platonic metaphysics.

However, it would be hard to underestimate the formidable obstacles facing Philo in his employment of this strategy. Far from simply helping himself to a Hellenistic idea, Philo is employing that idea in a way that is bound to seem incoherent and paradoxical to his contemporaries who are schooled in Hellenistic philosophy. To put the problem in its general form: the Law of Nature is surely of universal significance for all peoples, but the Law of Moses appears to be concerned, for the most part, with the obligations of a particular people arising from its particular history and relationship with God. How, then, could the particular Law of Moses be, as Philo claims, the perfect copy of the universal Law of Nature?

More specifically, if Philo is to authorize the Law of Moses, he must overcome the fact that Hellenistic appreciation for the Law of Nature is inseparably connected to a denigration of *written* law. Here we see a sharp distinction between Hellenistic culture and the Israelite valorization of sacred writing. For the Hellenistic thinkers who developed the concept of the Law of Nature, no written civil law could be more than a shadow and appearance of the original.[12] Although

---

Jr., "Chapter 19: The NOMOS-PHYSIS Debate," in *Philosophy Before Socrates: An Introduction with Texts and Commentary* (Indianapolis: Hackett, 1994), 390–413. There is one reference to Natural Law in Plato: *Gorg.* 483A7–484C3; see G. Striker, "Origins of the Concept of Natural Law," 212. However, as Striker argues, Gorgias uses the term as a deliberate paradox, on the assumption that nature itself, of course, has no normative import for human actions whatsoever. H. A. Wolfson claims that Philo borrows Aristotle's concept of nature; see his discussion in *Philo*, 1:332–47. However, it seems quite clear that Philo's concept of Nature and of Natural Law is derived from later Stoic philosophers, who derived their concept of the Law of Nature from the ancient Greeks. On this point, see P. A. Vander Waerdt, "Zeno's Republic and the Origins of Natural Law," 272–308; J. G. DeFilippo and P. T. Mitsis, "Socrates and Stoic Natural Law," 252–71.

[12] E.g., Cicero, *Off.* 3.69: "I see that because custom is so corrupted such behavior is neither thought dishonorable nor forbidden by statute and civil law. It is, however, forbidden by the law of nature. For there is a fellowship that is extremely widespread, shared by all with all (even if this has often been said, it ought to be said still more often); a closer one exists among those of the same nation, and one more intimate still among those of the same city. For this reason our ancestors wanted the law of nations and the civil law to be different: everything in the civil law need not be in the law of nations, but everything in the law of nations ought also to be a part of civil law. We, however, do not have the firm and lifelike figure of true law and genuine justice: we make use of shadows and sketches. I wish we would follow even those! For they are drawn from the best examples of nature and truth." The above passage is cited from the translation of Miriam T. Griffin and

the Law of Nature was a relatively new construct, it was identified with the universally shared "unwritten law" of which Socrates, among others, had spoken. This claim to ancient authority was plausible only insofar as the Law of Nature *contrasted* with the written laws of particular polities. This was already evident in much earlier classical traditions. For example, Antigone had insisted on unwritten law in her resistance to the written, and later Hellenistic writers would have characterized the written law of the city as unnatural for just that reason.[13] Furthermore, *if* there could be *any* adequate copy of the Law of Nature, it would not be a written law, but rather the life of a perfect sage or king, who would be nothing less than ensouled law. Again, this notion *contrasts* with that of a written law. So Philo must show—*in opposition to Greek thought on the topic*—that the perfect and authoritative copy of the Law of Nature is to be found, not only in the unwritten law exhibited by the life of the sage, but also in the written Law of Moses, despite its writtenness and despite its apparent particularity. At the same time, Philo must show that the Greek concept of *Nature* is central to the authority of Mosaic Law, despite the general absence from Scripture of that concept, for which no Hebrew word existed.[14]

E. Margaret Atkins, eds., *Cicero: On Duties* (CTHPT; Cambridge: Cambridge University Press, 1991), 125–26.

[13] See Sophocles, *Ant.* 450–460. See also Aristotle's discussion of Natural Law in *Eth. Nic.* 5.7; and Plutarch, *Lyc.* 13.1–2 (Perrin, LCL): "None of his laws were put into writing by Lycurgus, indeed, one of the so-called 'rhetras' forbid it. For he thought that if the most important and binding principles which conduce to the prosperity and virtue of a city were implanted in the habits and training of its citizens, they would remain unchanged and secure, having a stronger bond than compulsion in the fixed purposes imparted to the young by education, which performs the office of a law-giver for every one of them. . . . Indeed, he assigned the function of law-making wholly and entirely to education." On rhetras, see *Lyc.* 13.6, where Plutarch says that Lycurgus understood them to be divine oracles.

[14] Markus Bockmuehl states: "Strictly speaking, there is no 'natural' law in the Second Temple Judaism. That is to say . . . neither the Hebrew Bible nor post-biblical Jewish literature allows for a moral authority in nature which is somehow distinct from that of God himself. Law, inasmuch as it carries any real authority, is never 'natural' in the sense of being anything other than divine" ("Natural Law in Second Temple Judaism," *VT* 45 [1995]: 17–44, citation 43). In his article, Bockmuehl also discusses the role of nature in Hellenistic Jewish works such as 4 Maccabees. However, it is notable that it is only in the thirteenth century c.e. that an actual term for *nature* (טבע) is used in Hebrew. This innovation in the Hebrew language was occasioned by Ibn Tibbon's translation of Moses Maimonides' *Guide of the Perplexed.*

Indeed, some passages in Philo might suggest that he too would contrast the unwritten laws of nature on the one hand and written laws on the other. Thus Philo emphasizes that the intelligible originals, through which God created the material world, can never be adequately represented in language (*Opif.* 4–5a):[15]

τὸ μὲν οὖν κάλλος τῶν νοημάτων τῆς κοσμοποιίας οὐδεὶς οὔτε ποιητὴς οὔτε λογογράφος ἀξίως ἂν ὑμνῆσαι δύναιτο· καὶ γὰρ λόγον καὶ ἀκοὴν ὑπερβάλλει, μείζω καὶ σεμνότερα ὄντα ἢ ὡς θνητοῦ τινος ὀργάνοις ἐναρμοσθῆναι. οὐ μὴν διὰ τοῦθ᾽ ἡσυχαστέον, ἀλλ᾽ ἕνεκα τοῦ θεοφιλοῦς καὶ ὑπὲρ δύναμιν ἐπιτολμητέον λέγειν, . . .

In celebrating the beauty of thoughts contained in this creation account, no one, whether writing poetry or prose, can do them true justice. They transcend both speech and hearing, for they are greater and more august than what can be adapted to the instruments of a mortal being. This does not mean, however, that we must keep our peace. No, on behalf of the God-beloved (author) we must dare to speak, even if this goes beyond our ability, . . .

If the originals cannot be adequately represented in language, then of course they cannot be adequately represented in writing. So it is no surprise to find that Philo says of the patriarchs, whom he portrays as living in accordance with nature, that they "followed the unwritten law" (*Abr.* 5 [Colson, LCL]). For it would seem that, if a life of virtue is a life in accordance with nature, and if the originals of nature cannot be adequately represented in writing, then the law followed by the virtuous is of necessity unwritten.

In what follows, I will show how Philo adapted and transformed the Hellenistic concepts of Law of Nature, ensouled law and unwritten law, in his attempt to employ universal terms for the authorization of the written and apparently particular law of Moses.[16]

The result is a strikingly original fusion. Two scholarly debates—one concerning the synthesis of universality and particularity in Philo's thought, the other concerning the extent to which the idea of Natural

---

[15] All translations of *De Opificio Mundi* are taken from David T. Runia, *Philo of Alexandria*: On the Creation of the Cosmos according to Moses. *Introduction, Translation and Commentary* (PACS 1; Leiden: Brill, 2001).

[16] On the question of whether or not ensouled law is embodied in general principles, see P. A. Vander Waerdt, "Zeno's Republic and the Origins of Natural Law," 272–308; J. G. DeFilippo and P. T. Mitsis, "Socrates and Stoic Natural Law," 252–71. See also the earlier formulation of Leo Strauss in *Natural Right and History* (Chicago: University of Chicago Press, 1953), 146–61.

Law is transformed within post-Philonic thought—arise in part from
the difficulty of appreciating just how original and revolutionary Philo
is. First, although Philo is using universal terms, he is neither subordinating the Law of Moses to a higher, universal law, as E. R.
Goodenough claimed,[17] nor is he basing his claims for the authority of his version of doctrine and law on a proto-rabbinic oral law,
as Naomi Cohen has suggested, although he is indeed employing
traditions that stem from the particular history of the Jewish people.[18] To take either Goodenough's position or Cohen's is to miss
the specificity of Philo's Hellenistic Judaism, to ignore the specific
ways in which he argues for the universal significance of Judaism
without compromising its particular relation to the Jewish people.
Philo is, in fact, making the revolutionary claim that a universal
norm may have a perfect particular copy or instance.[19]

The difficulty of finding conceptual room for Philo's position seems
to be one factor underlying a debate between Phillip Mitsis and Paul
Vander Waerdt. According to Joseph DeFilippo and Mitsis, "The
Stoic theory of natural law . . . assumes . . . that the divine order of
nature legislates a system of moral laws that provides a normative
structure for human conduct."[20] However, Vander Waerdt sees here
the risk of anachronism. He argues that

> the early Stoics clearly do not conceive of natural law as being con-
> stituted by a code of moral rules comparable, for instance, to Aquinas'
> code of primary and secondary precepts. To the contrary, they advance
> a dispositional rather than a rule-following model of natural law, and
> a correspondingly different account of the content of the moral con-
> duct prescribed by it: in their theory, it prescribes not a determinate
> class of actions but a certain rational disposition with which one is to
> act, namely, the perfectly rational and consistent disposition which

---

[17] Erwin Ramsdell Goodenough, *By Light, Light: The Mystic Gospel of Hellenistic
Judaism* (New Haven, Conn.: Yale University Press, 1935).

[18] Naomi G. Cohen, "The Jewish Dimension of Philo's Judaism—An Elucidation
of de Spec. Leg. IV 132–150," *JJS* 38 (1987): 165–86.

[19] John W. Martens states: "Philo seems to be arguing against the Graeco-Roman
view that there is no true representation here on earth of the law of nature" ("Philo
and the 'Higher' Law," *SBL Seminar Papers, 1991* [SBLSP 30; Atlanta: Scholars Press,
1991], 309–22, citation 317). On this point see Plato's *Republic* V, 449–480. On
Philo and the higher law, see Valentin Nikiprowetsky, *Le Commentaire De L'Ecriture
Chez Philon D'Alexandrie* (Leiden: Brill, 1977), 122 ff.

[20] J. G. DeFilippo and P. T. Mitsis, "Socrates and Stoic Natural Law," 265.

enables the sage to apprehend and act in accordance with the provident order of nature.[21]

Underlying Vander Waerdt's argument is the question: How could the early Stoic conception of the Law of Nature be expressed by a code of precepts, since the early Stoics conceive the Law of Nature as unwritten and as embodied in the life of the sage? The question is not, I suggest, only interpretive. It is also conceptual. For early Stoic texts seem to leave no room for the idea of a code of precepts, a code that could be enshrined in a written text, which has the authoritative status of a copy of the Law of Nature. Underlying the debate between Mitsis and Vander Waerdt, then, is the question of how to make sense of Philo's revolutionary move.

An initial answer to the question is that—for Philo—the Law of Nature and the Law of Moses have the same source. Both are legislated by God. Thus, for example, John Martens contrasts Philo's position with Cicero's:

> Philo could not admit that the Mosaic law was only a shadowy sketch of true law. God gave the law to Moses; God also created the world and with it the law of nature. The law of Moses, divinely given, could in no way contradict the law of nature, divinely implanted in the world at creation.[22]

Now, this answer certainly has some validity. It is clearly important to Philo to emphasize that God is the source of both the Law of Nature and the Law of Moses. He makes this point in two main ways. First, he sees it as one of the main reasons why Moses prefaces the law with an account of creation that might otherwise be out of place:

Opif. 3:

ἡ δ᾽ ἀρχή, καθάπερ ἔφην, ἐστὶ θαυμασιωτάτη κοσμοποιίαν περιέχουσα, ὡς καὶ τοῦ κόσμου τῷ νόμῳ καὶ τοῦ νόμου τῷ κόσμῳ συνᾴδοντος καὶ τοῦ νομίμου ἀνδρὸς εὐθὺς ὄντος κοσμοπολίτου πρὸς τὸ βούλημα τῆς φύσεως τὰς πράξεις ἀπευθύνοντος, καθ᾽ ἣν καὶ ὁ σύμπας κόσμος διοικεῖται.

The beginning is, as I just said, quite marvelous. It contains an account of the making of the cosmos, the reasoning for this being that the cos-

---

[21] P. A. Vander Waerdt, "Zeno's Republic and the Origins of Natural Law," 275–76.

[22] J. W. Martens, "Philo and the 'Higher' Law," 317.

mos is in harmony with the law and the law with the cosmos, and the man who observes the law is at once a citizen of the cosmos, directing his actions in relation to the rational purpose of nature, in accordance with which the entire cosmos also is administered.

Mos. 2.48:

οὐ γὰρ οἷά τις συγγραφεὺς ἐπετήδευσε παλαιῶν πράξεων καταλιπεῖν ὑπομνήματα τοῖς ἔπειτα τοῦ ψυχαγωγῆσαι χάριν ἀνωφελῶς, ἀλλ᾽ ἠρχαιολόγησεν
ἄνωθεν ἀρξάμενος ἀπὸ τῆς τοῦ παντὸς γενέσεως, ἵν᾽ ἐπιδείξῃ δύο τὰ
ἀναγκαιότατα· ἓν μὲν τὸν αὐτὸν πατέρα καὶ ποιητὴν τοῦ κόσμου καὶ ἀληθείᾳ νομοθέτην, ἕτερον δὲ τὸν χρησόμενον τοῖς νόμοις ἀκολουθίαν φύσεως
ἀσπασόμενον καὶ βιωσόμενον κατὰ τὴν τοῦ ὅλου διάταξιν ἁρμονίᾳ καὶ
συμφωνίᾳ πρὸς ἔργα λόγων καὶ πρὸς λόγους ἔργων.

He did not, like any historian, make it his business to leave behind for posterity records of ancient deeds for the pleasant but unimproving entertainment which they give; but, in relating the history of early times, and going for its beginning right to the creation of the universe, he wished to show two most essential things: first, that the Father and Maker of the world was in the truest sense also its Lawgiver; secondly, that he who would observe the laws will accept gladly the duty of following nature and live in accordance with the ordering of the universe, so that his deeds are attuned to harmony with his words and his words with his deeds.

Second, Philo takes pains to show, not only that the laws of Moses have a moral purpose even when that purpose is not obvious, but also that the laws of Moses are structurally similar to the created cosmos. Hence, for example, the importance of numerological analyses, such as Philo's account of the role of the decad in both natural and Mosaic Law.

However, it is simply not enough to say, with Martens, that God is the source of both natural and Mosaic Law. Martens himself is careful to infer from this common origin only that "the Law of Moses . . . could in no way contradict the natural law."[23] But what needs to be clarified is how the Law of Moses could be a *copy* of the natural law, so that fulfilling the former is at the same time fulfilling the latter! We might say, perhaps, that the omnipotent creator can make it the case that the Law of Moses is a copy of the Law of Nature. But this is to say that God can do even what is— or seems to be—conceptually impossible. If we can say no more

---

[23] Ibid.

than this, then it would seem that we have located a point where
communication simply breaks down between, on the one hand, Philo
and those who believe in an omnipotent creator, and, on the other
hand, those who do not believe in an omnipotent creator. Those on
one side of the Philonic revolution have no standard of intelligibil-
ity in common with those on the other side.

But I think that we can say more than this. One might think that
there are two exclusive alternatives: either conceive the Law of Nature
as a code of rules which can be written down, or else conceive it
as exemplified by the disposition of the sage. But, for Philo, these
are not exclusive alternatives. In three ways, the Law of Moses is
more than a code of rules. First, it includes an account of the divine
creation of nature. Second, it includes the lives of the patriarchs.
Third, it is the Law *of Moses*, an expression of the *life* of Moses. Both
the patriarchs and Moses are portrayed by Philo as sages living in
accordance with Nature. Thus, although to be sure the Law of Moses
is written, it is not reducible to a code of precepts. For the precepts
it contains must be understood in the context of the exemplary lives
they express.

First, Philo emphasizes that Moses, whom he takes to be the author
of the Pentateuch, not only of the speeches explicitly attributed to
him, begins "his lawbook" with an account of creation. The non-
legal character of Genesis and the first part of Exodus has been
problematic for Jewish interpreters. While *Jubilees* responds to the
difficulty by construing these pre-Sinaitic narratives as having crypto-
legal content, Philo interprets them as having crypto-philosophical
content. In both cases, the true significance of the narratives can
emerge only when they are read, not on their own, but rather within
the proper context, which needs to be supplied (*Mos.* 2.47–48):

οὗ δὲ χάριν ἐνθένδε τῆς νομοθεσίας ἤρξατο τὰ περὶ τὰς προστάξεις καὶ
ἀπαγορεύσεις ἐν δευτέρῳ θείς, λεκτέον.... ἵν᾿ ἐπιδείξῃ δύο τὰ ἀναγκαιότατα·
ἓν μὲν τὸν αὐτὸν πατέρα καὶ ποιητὴν τοῦ κόσμου καὶ ἀληθείᾳ νομοθέτην,
ἕτερον δὲ τὸν χρησόμενον τοῖς νόμοις ἀκολουθίαν φύσεως ἀσπασόμενον
καὶ βιωσόμενον κατὰ τὴν τοῦ ὅλου διάταξιν ἁρμονίᾳ καὶ συμφωνίᾳ πρὸς
ἔργα λόγων καὶ πρὸς λόγους ἔργων.

We must now give the reason why he began his lawbook with the history, and put the commands and prohibitions in the second place....
[H]e wished to show two most essential things: first that the Father
and Maker of the world was in the truest sense also its Lawgiver, secondly that he who would observe the laws will accept gladly the duty

of following nature and live in accordance with the ordering of the universe, so that his deeds are attuned to harmony with his words and his words with his deeds.

As this passage makes clear, Philo's interest in creation is never merely an exercise in theoretical cosmology, but is always also practical. To understand Moses' account of creation is at the same time to see that God cares for the world and deserves to be obeyed in the way that parents deserve obedience (*Opif.* 171d–172):

... ἐπιμελεῖσθαι γὰρ ἀεὶ τὸ πεποιηκὸς τοῦ γενομένου φύσεως νόμοις καὶ θεσμοῖς ἀναγκαῖον, καθ᾽ οὓς καὶ γονεῖς τέκνων προμηθοῦνται. ὁ δὴ ταῦτα μὴ ἀκοῇ μᾶλλον ἢ διανοίᾳ προμαθὼν καὶ ἐν τῇ αὑτοῦ ψυχῇ σφραγισά- μενος θαυμάσια καὶ περιμάχητα εἴδη, καὶ ὅτι ἔστι καὶ ὑπάρχει θεὸς καὶ ὅτι εἷς ὁ ὢν ὄντος ἐστὶ καὶ ὅτι πεποίηκε τὸν κόσμον καὶ πεποίηκεν ἕνα, ὡς ἐλέχθη, κατὰ τὴν μόνωσιν ἐξομοιώσας ἑαυτῷ καὶ ὅτι ἀεὶ προνοεῖ τοῦ γεγονότος, μακαρίαν καὶ εὐδαίμονα ζωὴν βιώσεται δόγμασιν εὐσεβείας καὶ ὁσιότητος χαραχθείς.

... for that the maker always takes care of what has come into existence is a necessity by the laws and ordinances of nature, in accordance with which parents too take care of their children. He, then, who first has learnt these things not so much with his hearing as with his understanding, and has imprinted their marvellous and priceless forms on his own soul, namely that God is and exists, and that he who truly exists is one, and that he made the cosmos and made it unique, making it, as was said, similar to himself in respect to its being one, and that he always takes thought for what has come into being, this person will lead a blessed life of well-being, marked as he is by the doctrines of piety and holiness.

To understand Moses' account of creation is also to grasp that the Law of Nature is identical with *right reason*, which is the law of divine creation and governance and thus the proper law of human action. Philo reproaches those who adhere to laws of particular republics, yet deny right reason, which is the law of the republic of the wise (*Prob.* 46–47 [Colson, LCL]):

νόμος δὲ ἀψευδὴς ὁ ὀρθὸς λόγος, οὐχ ὑπὸ τοῦ δεῖνος ἢ τοῦ δεῖνος, θνητοῦ φθαρτός, ἐν χαρτιδίοις ἢ στήλαις, ἄψυχος ἀψύχοις, ἀλλ᾽ ὑπ᾽ ἀθανάτου φύσεως ἄφθαρτος ἐν ἀθανάτῳ διανοίᾳ τυπωθείς. διὸ καὶ θαυμάσαι ἄν τις τῆς ἀμβλυωπίας τοὺς τρανὰς οὕτω πραγμάτων ἰδιότητας μὴ συνορῶντας, οἳ μεγίστοις μὲν δήμοις Ἀθήναις καὶ Λακεδαίμονι πρὸς ἐλευθερίαν αὐταρκεστάτους εἶναί φασι τοὺς Σόλωνος καὶ Λυκούργου νόμους κρατοῦντάς τε καὶ ἄρχοντας, πειθαρχούντων αὐτοῖς τῶν πολιτευομένων, σοφοῖς δὲ ἀνδράσι τὸν ὀρθὸν λόγον, ὃς καὶ τοῖς ἄλλοις ἐστὶ πηγὴ νόμοις, οὐχ ἱκανὸν

εἶναι πρὸς μετουσίαν ἐλευθερίας ὑπακούουσι πάντων, ἅττ᾽ ἂν ἢ προστάττῃ
ἢ ἀπαγορεύῃ.

Right reason is an infallible law engraved not by this mortal or that
and, therefore, perishable as he; nor on parchment or slabs, and therefore, soulless as they, but by immortal nature on the immortal mind,
never to perish. So, one may well wonder at the short-sightedness of
those who ignore the characteristics which so clearly distinguish different
things and declare that the laws of Solon and Lycurgus are all-sufficient
to secure the greatest of republics, Athens and Sparta, because their
sovereign authority is loyally accepted by those who enjoy that citizenship, yet deny that right reason, which is the fountain head of all
other law, can impart freedom to the wise, who obey all that it pre-
scribes or forbids.

Since the law of the cosmos is at the same time the law of reason,
and since human beings are capable of reason, it follows that human
beings are capable of grasping and living according to the Law of
Nature.[24]

Furthermore, because right reason is the perfection of human beings, it also follows that the transgression of a Law of Nature is at
the same time contrary to human nature.[25] To show this for specific
moral duties is of course one of the most difficult tasks undertaken
by Stoic ethics. Philo explains how certain laws of Moses reflect human nature.[26] Helmut Koester discusses some specific instances in
Philo's writings:

Philo relates Moses' and nature's law in a very characteristic way
which, again, expresses the harmony of his understanding of law, nature
and man: For those who keep the divine writing of the law, God

---

[24] R. A. Horsley notes: "This same twofold conception of law as the right reason of universal nature and as the mature reason in the human mind is the basic
assumption and structure of Philo's thought in *De opificio* as in much of his writing" ("The Law of Nature in Philo and Cicero," 47). On the universal relevance
of Mosaic Law see Peder Borgen, "Chapter Eight: *Proclamatio Graeca*—Hermeneutical
Key," in *Philo of Alexandria: An Exegete For His Time*, 140–57; in particular see Borgen's
section entitled "The Mosaic Law and cosmic law," 144–53.
[25] For a very helpful and detailed discussion of the way Philo applies the concept of natural law, see H. Koester, "'ΝΟΜΟΣ ΦΥΣΕΩΣ': The Concept of Natural
Law in Greek Thought," 532–40.
[26] For a very clear and insightful discussion of the Stoics' appeal to nature, see
John M. Cooper, "Eudaimonism, Nature, and 'Moral Duty' in Stoicism," in *Aristotle,
Kant, and the Stoics: Rethinking Happiness and Duty* (ed. S. Engstrom and J. Whiting;
New York: Cambridge University Press, 1996), 261–84; in particular see "II: Appeal
to Nature," 267–75.

grants as a prize the more ancient law of immortal nature (παρέχει τὸν ἀρχαιότερον νόμον τῆς ἀθανάτου φύσεως), i.e. the begetting of sons and the perpetuity of the race (*Quaest. Ex. II* 19). At the same time, the injunction to produce children is called a "law of nature" . . . Other laws that are based on the law of nature in a similar way are: the law of inheritance, from parents to children, . . . the law against killing infants at birth . . . since to do this would tear down what nature builds up. . . . A general law against killing (*Decal.* 132).[27]

So far, what has been said should seem familiarly Stoic. However, Philo arguably departs from Stoicism when he explains that, since God is both the creator and the lawgiver, the transgressor is punished by the forces of nature themselves (*Mos.* 2.52–53):

τῶν γοῦν ἐν μέρει διατεταγμένων τὰς δυνάμεις εἴ τις ἀκριβῶς ἐξετάζειν ἐθελήσειεν, εὑρήσει τῆς τοῦ παντὸς ἁρμονίας ἐφειμένας καὶ τῷ λόγῳ τῆς ἀιδίου φύσεως συνᾳδούσας. διὸ καὶ τοὺς ἀφθόνων μὲν ἀγαθῶν ἀξιωθέντας ὅσα κατ᾽ εὐεξίαν σωμάτων καὶ τὰς περὶ πλοῦτον καὶ δόξαν καὶ τὰ ἄλλα ἐκτὸς εὐτυχίας, ἀρετῆς δ᾽ ἀφηνιάσαντας καὶ οὐκ ἀνάγκῃ γνώμῃ δ᾽ ἑκουσίῳ πανουργίαν καὶ ἀδικίαν καὶ τὰς ἄλλας κακίας, ὡς μέγα ὄφελος τὴν μεγίστην ζημίαν, ἐπιτηδεύσαντας καθάπερ οὐκ ἀνθρώπων ἐχθροὺς ἀλλὰ τοῦ σύμπαντος οὐρανοῦ τε καὶ κόσμου τὰς ἐν ἔθει τιμωρίας οὔ φησιν ὑπομεῖναι, ἀλλὰ καινοτάτας καὶ παρηλλαγμένας, ἃς ἐμεγαλούργησεν ἡ πάρεδρος τῷ θεῷ μισοπόνηρος δίκη, τῶν τοῦ παντὸς δραστικωτάτων στοιχείων ἐπιθεμένων ὕδατος καὶ πυρός, ὡς καιρῶν περιόδοις τοὺς μὲν κατακλυσμοῖς φθαρῆναι, τοὺς δὲ καταφλεχθέντας ἀπολέσθαι.

Thus whoever will carefully examine the nature of the particular enactments will find that they seek to attain to the harmony of the universe and are in agreement with the principles of eternal nature. Therefore all those to whom God thought fit to grant abundance of the good gifts of bodily well-being and of good fortune in the shape of wealth and other externals—who then rebelled against virtue, and, freely and intentionally under no compulsion, practiced knavery, injustice and the other vices, thinking to gain much by losing all, were counted, Moses tells us, as enemies not of men but of the whole heaven and universe, and suffered not the ordinary, but strange and unexampled punishments wrought by the might of justice, the hater of evil and assessor of God. For the most forceful of elements of the universe, fire and water, fell upon them, so that, as the times revolved, some perished by deluge, others were consumed by conflagration.

---

[27] H. Koester, "'ΝΟΜΟΣ ΦΥΣΕΩΣ': The Concept of Natural Law in Greek Thought," 538.

He sometimes seems to use this Mosaic point to emphasize the superiority of the Jewish conception of natural law over its non-Jewish rivals: according to other conceptions, transgressions must be punished by human courts, which are notoriously liable to be swayed by bribery and rhetoric, but the Mosaic conception allows no such escape, for it is ultimately God Himself, acting through nature, who ensures that punishment is exacted (*Hypoth.* 7.9):

> ... ὁ θεὸς αὐτὸς ἐπόπτης τῶν τοιούτων καὶ τιμωρὸς ἀπανταχοῦ.

> ... God is himself the guardian of such matters and the omnipresent avenger.

At this point, it is helpful to consider the extent to which Philo is drawing upon Second Temple interpretive tradition as well as upon Hellenistic philosophy. Both *Jubilees* and Philo inherit the Jewish interpretive tradition that a system of law was established at the time of creation. Both claim that this pre-Sinaitic law is identical with (at least a large part of) the Law of Moses revealed at Sinai, and that the original law is therefore still binding upon Israel. Yet, beyond this consensus these two Second Temple texts could hardly be more different. For *Jubilees*, pre-Sinaitic law may be known only through divine revelation. Such revelation is given only to a select few, who transmit their tradition through a particular line of descent to the Jewish people, for whom alone the law is normative. For Philo, however, *the pre-Sinaitic law is the Law of Nature*, which may be known through the use of reason and which is incumbent on all human beings.[28]

---

[28] For *Jubilees* and related Second Temple traditions, the revelation at Sinai was merely the national version of an earlier revelation that had already occurred for worthy individuals who had practiced and transmitted the law for generations since Enoch. Furthermore, the correct interpretation of the Mosaic Law was only available to those who had access to pre-Sinaitic traditions. Sinai itself was not sufficient, and its authoritative interpretation depended upon a more ancient tradition.

Similarly, the law *before* Sinai has a great deal of significance for Philo. This is not because Philo claims a pre-Sinaitic tradition in the manner of *Jubilees*, but rather because Philo takes the Mosaic Law to be *that* Law which agrees with the pre-existent Law (what Philo calls the Natural Law) available to the *virtuous* since the creation of the cosmos. Thus the patriarchs, as virtuous people, could be exemplary law-observers, even *ensouled laws*, long before the Law was revealed to Moses on Sinai. The fulfillment of pre-Sinaitic law requires that these pre-Sinaitic figures attain access to what Philo calls the "unwritten law." For the origin of this term and its function in Philo's writings see my discussion in "The Law of Nature and the Authority of Mosaic Law," 55–73.

In Philo's view, then, it is possible to lead a virtuous life even if one does not have access to the written Law of Moses. Indeed, Moses himself emphasizes this point by recording the lives of the patriarchs (*Abr.* 16):

πολλὰ μὲν οὖν οἱ νομοθέται, πολλὰ δὲ οἱ πανταχοῦ νόμοι πραγματεύονται περὶ τοῦ τὰς ψυχὰς τῶν ἐλευθέρων ἐλπίδων χρηστῶν ἀναπλῆσαι· ὁ δ' ἄνευ παραινέσεως δίχα τοῦ κελευσθῆναι γενόμενος εὔελπις ἀγράφῳ μὲν νόμῳ δὲ πάλιν αὐτομαθεῖ τὴν ἀρετὴν ταύτην πεπαίδευται, ὃν ἡ φύσις ἔθηκε.

Great indeed are the efforts expended both by lawgivers and by laws in every nation in filling the souls of free men with comfortable hopes; but he who gains this virtue of hopefulness without being led to it by exhortation or command has been educated into it by a law which nature has laid down, a law unwritten yet intuitively learnt.

In a striking phrase, Philo says that the patriarchs were not merely obedient to law; they were "laws endowed with life and reason" (*Abr.* 5). Similarly, Philo says that Abraham was "himself a law and an unwritten statute" (*Abr.* 276). The point is that the patriarchs are sages, who have fully internalized the disposition to live in accordance with nature. So the lives of the patriarchs are copies of the Law of Nature and have the normative force of law.[29]

Moses had two reasons, according to Philo, for including the lives of these living laws in the Pentateuch (*Abr.* 5):

ἑνὸς μὲν βουλόμενος ἐπιδεῖξαι, ὅτι τὰ τεθειμένα διατάγματα τῆς φύσεως οὐκ ἀπάδει, δευτέρου δὲ ὅτι οὐ πολὺς πόνος τοῖς ἐθέλουσι κατὰ τοὺς κειμένους νόμους ζῆν, ὁπότε καὶ ἀγράφῳ τῇ νομοθεσίᾳ, πρίν τι τὴν ἀρχὴν ἀναγραφῆναι τῶν ἐν μέρει, ῥᾳδίως καὶ εὐπετῶς ἐχρήσαντο οἱ πρῶτοι· ὡς δεόντως ἄν τινα φάναι, τοὺς τεθέντας νόμους μηδὲν ἄλλ' ἢ ὑπομνήματα εἶναι βίου τῶν παλαιῶν, ἀρχαιολογοῦντας ἔργα καὶ λόγους, οἷς ἐχρήσαντο.

First he wished to show that the enacted ordinances are not inconsistent with nature; and secondly that those who wish to live in accordance with the laws as they stand have no difficult task, seeing that the first generations before any at all of the particular statutes was set

---

[29] This phrase should be compared with Plutarch's later interpretation of a verse from Pindar. When Pindar describes law as "the king of all," Plutarch explains that law rules even a king: "not law written outside him in books or on wooden tablets or the like, but reason endowed with life within him, always abiding with him and watching over him and never leaving his soul without its leadership." See *Princ. iner.* 780C (Fowler, LCL). In *Mos.* 2.4, Philo also says that, "the king is a living law and the law is a just king."

in writing followed the unwritten law with perfect ease, so that one might properly say that the enacted laws are nothing else than memorials of the life of the ancients, preserving to a later generation their actual words and deeds.

This last phrase is of great importance for my argument. Philo says that the enacted laws—that is to say, the laws given by God to Israel through Moses—may be properly regarded as memorials of the lives of the patriarchs, indeed as nothing else. In other words, if read in accordance with Philo's instruction, the lives of the patriarchs and the laws of Moses turn out to be equivalent. Now, since the lives of the patriarchs embody the Law of Nature, it follows that the enacted laws of Moses also embody the Law of Nature.[30] But this implies that the status of the laws of Moses, as copies of the laws of nature, would have remained unclear if not for the fact that the laws of Moses are situated within the context of the lives of the patriarchs and their descendants. Thus, the laws of Moses cannot be reduced to a code. They are expressions of the "actual words and deeds" of sages.

But this is not all. It is also of the utmost importance to Philo that God gave the laws to Israel through Moses, whose own life is also included in the Pentateuch. Indeed, Philo wrote not one but two treatises on the life of Moses,[31] and he clearly thought that the

---

[30] See Sidney G. Sowers, *The Hermeneutics of Philo and Hebrews: A Comparison of the Interpretation in Philo Judaeus and the Epistle to the Hebrews* (Basel Studies of Theology 1; Richmond, Va.: John Knox, 1965), 44–49; David Winston, "Philo's Ethical Theory," *ANRW* 21.1:381–88; E. R. Goodenough, *By Light, Light*, 48–94; Maren Niehoff, *Philo on Jewish Identity and Culture* (TSAJ 86; Tübingen: J. C. B. Mohr, 2001), 247–66; David M. Hay, "Philo of Alexandria," in *The Complexities of Second Temple Judaism* (ed. D. A. Carson, P. T. O'Brien, M. A. Seifrid; vol. 1 of *Justification and Variegated Nomism*; WUNT Reihe 2:140; Tübingen: J. C. B. Mohr, 2001), 357–79, esp. 373–78; H. Najman, "The Law of Nature and the Authority of Mosaic Law," 55–73; idem, "A Written Copy of the Law of Nature: An Unthinkable Paradox," in *The Law of Nature: Ancient Origins and Contemporary Transformations* (ed. H. Najman, D. K. O'Connor, G. E. Sterling; forthcoming); Francesca Calabi, *The Language and the Law of God: Interpretation and Politics in Philo of Alexandria* (ed. J. Neusner; USFSHJ 188; Atlanta: Scholars Press, 1998), 31–78, esp. 36–43.

[31] Erwin R. Goodenough discusses the question of the intended audience for Philo's two essays on Moses in "Philo's Exposition of the Law and His De Vita Mosis," *HTR* 26 (1933): 109–25. Although I disagree with Goodenough's claim that *De vita Mosis* is written for a gentile audience, I do agree that these two essays on Moses should be considered as part of Philo's exposition of the Pentateuch. See also Gregory E. Sterling, "Philo and the Logic of Apologetics: An Analysis of the *Hypothetica*," *SBL Seminar Papers, 1990* (SBLSP 29; Atlanta: Scholars Press, 1990), 412–30.

laws of Moses could not be fully appreciated without a proper understanding of the figure of Moses.[32] As Philo sets out to show, Moses
is the philosopher-king called for in Plato's *Republic* (*Mos.* 2.2; *Resp.*
V, 473D). Indeed, using the very terminology applied to the patriarchs, Philo describes Moses as "a law endowed with life and reason"
(*Mos.* 1.162). Again, the point is that Moses is a sage. So his life, as
a copy of the Law of Nature, has the normative force of law.

Greek literature had long exhibited a tendency to produce idealized
biographies[33] of philosophers and rulers, members of a genre that
some scholars have called aretalogy.[34] These *bioi* had a variety of
authority-related functions: they sought to dispel false images of the
hero, to establish a normative pattern for the reader to follow, and
sometimes to establish a line of legitimate succession that authorized
the writer's viewpoint against other competing claims to succession.[35]
We lack many of the aretalogies that must have been prior to or
contemporaneous with Philo's lives of Moses, but much of their flavor
has been preserved in third century versions and collections drawing
explicitly upon earlier sources, such as Diogenes Laertius' *Lives of the
Eminent Philosophers*, Philostratus' *Life of Apollonius of Tyana*,[36] and numerous versions of the *Life of Pythagoras*. Dillon writes of Philo's time:

---

[32] B. Mack, "Moses on the Mountain Top," 23. See also Mack's excellent essay
on the rise of attribution to specific authors in Hellenistic Judaism: "Under the
Shadow of Moses," 299–318; D. C. Allison Jr., *The New Moses*, esp. 23–134; D. L.
Tiede, "The Figure of Moses in *The Testament of Moses*," 86–92.

[33] Abraham C. Geljon has argued that *De Vita Mosis* 1 and 2 should be understood as an introductory *bios* to Philo's exposition of the Law of Moses. Relying on
the work of Burridge and Mansfeld, Geljon convincingly demonstrates that Philo's
work belongs in the long history of Graeco-Roman *bioi*. See his recent dissertation,
"Moses as Example: The Philonic Background of Gregory of Nyssa's *De Vita Moysis*"
(Ph.D. diss., University of Leiden, 2000), 16–46, esp. 36.

[34] On the origin and various uses of this term see Morton Smith, "Prolegomena
to a Discussion of Aretalogies, Divine Men, the Gospels and Jesus," *JBL* 90 (1971):
174–99. See also Duane Reed Stuart, "Chapter V: Aristoxenus and the Early Perpa-
tetics," and "Chapter VI: The Alexandrian Continuators," in *Epochs of Greek and Roman
Biography* (SCL 4; Berkeley, Calif.: University of California Press, 1928), 119–88;
Simon Swain, "Biography and Biographic in the Literature of the Roman Empire,"
in *Portraits: Biographical Representation in the Greek and Latin Literature of the Roman Empire*
(ed. M. J. Edwards and S. Swain; Oxford: Clarendon, 1997), 1–37; Charles H. Talbert, "Biographies of Philosophers and Rulers as Instruments of Religious Propaganda in Mediterranean Antiquity," *ANRW* 16.2:1619–51; idem, "The Myth of the
Immortals in Mediterranean Antiquity," *JBL* 94 (1975): 419–36. For a general discussion of Greek biography, see A. Momigliano, *The Development of Greek Biography*.

[35] C. H. Talbert, "Biographies of Philosophers and Rulers," 1620–25.

[36] For an excellent discussion of Philostratus' *Life of Apollonius of Tyana*, see Ewen
Lyall Bowie, "Apollonius of Tyana: Tradition and Reality," *ANRW* 16.2:1652–99.

It is in this period also, presumably, that the myth of Pythagoras' life
took the shape which we find reflected later in the Lives of Pythagoras
by Diogenes Laertius, Porphyry and Iamblichus, since this image of
Pythagoras serves as an inspiration to Apollonius of Tyana in the first
part of the first century A.D. and indeed as a stimulus to Philo in com-
posing his portrait of Moses.[37]

Three typical features of these aretalogies are especially worthy of
mention because of their relevance to Philo's lives of Moses. First,
the hero is portrayed as undergoing an education that includes voyage
from his homeland and initiation into mysteries, especially the mysteries of Egypt.[38] Second, his exemplary treatment of others and his

---

[37] J. Dillon, *The Middle Platonists*, 119.
[38] Since the Exodus narrative suggests that Moses grew up in Pharaoh's palace,
the claim that he was educated in the palace and that this education consisted of
a training in the tradition of the Egyptian mysteries was not a difficult connection
for Philo to make. The Greek fascination with Egyptian antiquity and wisdom can
be found, for example, in Plato, *Tim.* 21b–23c which purports to represent the
ancient Egyptian understanding of creation, as told to Timaeus and Solon, legislator to Athens, on a trip to Egypt. On the importance of Plato's *Timaeus* in Philo
see, e.g., David T. Runia, "The Language of Excellence in Plato's *Timaeus* and
Later Platonism," in *Platonism in Late Antiquity* (ed. S. Gersh and C. Kannengiesser;
Notre Dame: University of Notre Dame Press, 1992), 11–37; idem, *Philo of Alexandria
and the Timaeus of Plato* (2 vols.; Alblasserdam: Boekhandel, 1983).
Pythagoras is also said to have traveled in quest of wisdom. See, e.g., Diogenes
Laertius' (third century C.E.), "*Book VIII, The Life of Pythagoras*": "While still young,
so eager was he for knowledge, he left his own country and had himself initiated
into all the mysteries and rites not only of Greece but also of foreign countries"
(line 2, 323 [Hicks, LCL]). According to Iamblicus of Chalcis' (250 C.E.–325 C.E.)
Life of Pythagoras: "Pythagoras . . . sailed to Sidon, both because it was his native
country, and because it was on his way to Egypt. In Phoenicia he conversed with
the prophets who were the descendents of Moschus the physiologist, and with many
others, as well as with the local hierophants. He was also initiated into all the mysteries of Byblos and Tyre, and in the sacred function performed in many parts of
Syria. He was led to all this not from any hankering after superstition, as might
easily be supposed, but rather from a desire and love for contemplation, and from
an anxiety to miss nothing of the mysteries of the divinities which deserved to be
learned.
After gaining all he could from the Phoenician mysteries, he found that they had
originated from the sacred rites of Egypt, forming as it were an Egyptian colony.
This led him to hope that in Egypt itself he might find monuments of erudition
still more genuine, beautiful and divine. Therefore following the advice of his teacher,
Thales, he left as soon as possible, through the agency of some Egyptian sailors,
who very opportunely happened to land on the Phoenician coast under Mount
Carmel where, in the temple on the peak, Pythagoras for the most part had dwelt
in solitude" (in *The Pythagorean Sourcebook and Library* [ed. D. Fideler; trans. K. S.
Guthrie; Grand Rapids: Phanes, 1988], 60).
For another example, see Flavius Philostratus' "*Book I, chapter 2*," in *Life of Apollonius
of Tyana*: "For quite akin to theirs was the ideal which Apollonius pursued, and

foundation or legislation of a way of life is emphasized.[39] Third, the hero is said to be superior to other humans, to be or become divine, sometimes even to be or become a god worthy of worship.[40]

The tendency towards authorization through biographical idealization—even divinization—seems to have intensified during the crisis of authority attending the rise of Rome, and the new rulers were also authorized aretalogically. There had long been an Alexander

---

more divinely than Pythagoras he wooed wisdom and soared above tyrants; and he lived in times not long gone by nor again quite of our own day, yet men know him not because of the true wisdom, which he practised as a sage and sanely; but one man singles out one feature for praise in him ... while some, because he had interviews with the wizards of Babylon and with the Brahmins of India, and with the nude ascetics of Egypt, put him down as a wizard, and spread the calumny that he was a sage of an illegitimate kind, judging of him ill" (7 [Conybeare, LCL]) Philostratus wrote in the third century C.E. about a hero born at the beginning of the Christian era—who would thus, if historical, have lived at the same time as Philo—and claimed to base his biography on the record of Apollonius' disciple, Damis, whose historicity has been hotly disputed.

[39] Pythagoras was, of course, regarded as the founder and legislator of a community of philosophers leading a distinctive way of life. See, for example, Diogenes Laertius' *Book VIII, The Life of Pythagoras*: "He is said to have advised his disciples as follows: ... Not to call gods to witness, man's duty being rather to strive to make his own word carry conviction. To honor their elders, on the principle that precedence in time gives a greater title to respect.... To support the law, to wage war on lawlessness ... To avoid excess of flesh, on a journey let exertion and slackening alternate, to train the memory, in wrath to restrain hand and tongue, to respect all divination, to sing to the lyre and by hymns to show due gratitude to gods and to good men" (lines 22–23, 339–341). According to Iamblichus' *Life of Pythagoras*: "Pythagoras is generally acknowledged to have been the inventor and legislator of friendship, under its many various forms, such as universal amity of all towards all, of God towards men through their piety and scientific theories, or of the mutual interrelation of teachings, or universally of the soul towards the body, and of the rational to the irrational part, through philosophy and its underlying theories; or whether it be that of men towards each other, of citizens indeed through sound legislation ... In short, Pythagoras procured his disciples the most appropriate converse with the Gods, both waking and sleeping—something which never occurs in a soul disturbed by anger, pain, or pleasure, and all the more by any base desire, or defiled by ignorance" (*The Pythagorean Sourcebook and Library*, 73).

[40] I will discuss Philo's characterization of Moses as divine below. Pythagoras was regarded, at least by some, as an incarnation of the god Apollo. See Diogenes Laertius' *Book VIII, The Life of Pythagoras*: "Indeed, his bearing is said to have been most dignified, and his disciples held the opinion about him that he was Apollo come down from the far North" (line 11, 331). According to Iamblichus' *Life of Pythagoras*: "This Hyperborean Abaris was elderly, and most wise in sacred concerns, being a priest of the Apollo there worshipped. At that time he was returning from Greece to his country, in order to consecrate the gold which he had collected to the God in his temple among the Hyperboreans. As therefore he was passing through Italy, he saw Pythagoras, and identified him as the God of whom he was the priest.

cult at Alexandria, with which the Ptolemies too were associated
and, as we have seen, the divinization of the Roman emperor had
direct implications for the life of Philo and his fellow Alexandrian
Jews.[41] Like Xenophon's seminal *Memorabilia*, Philo's lives of Moses
were also written to dispel false images of the hero—notably those
disseminated by authors such as Manetho (third century B.C.E.) and
Apion (a contemporary of Philo), who had contributed to anti-Judaism
in Egypt. In the context of a Hellenistic culture where authoritative
figures had to have led heroic lives and, more specifically, in the
context of a culture where the significance of Moses and the rights
of the Jews were already contested, the authority of Mosaic Law had
to rest on more than Moses' role as God's own scribe.[42]

Although Philo is undoubtedly employing a Hellenistic strategy of
authorization, he nevertheless draws upon Jewish tradition. Reproaching
Greek writers who did not pay sufficient attention to Moses when
they were writing biographies of great heroes, Philo writes (*Mos.* 1.4):

ἀλλ' ἔγωγε τὴν τούτων βασκανίαν ὑπερβὰς τὰ περὶ τὸν ἄνδρα μηνύσω
μαθὼν αὐτὰ κἀκ βίβλων τῶν ἱερῶν, ἃς θαυμάσια μνημεῖα τῆς αὐτοῦ
σοφίας ἀπολέλοιπε, καὶ παρά τινων ἀπὸ τοῦ ἔθνους πρεσβυτέρων· τὰ γὰρ

Believing that Pythagoras resembled no man, but was none other than the God
himself, Apollo, both from the venerable indications he saw around him, and from
those the priest already knew, he paid him homage by giving him a sacred dart"
(*The Pythagorean Sourcebook and Library*, 80). The divinization of the Hellenistic sage
may have reached its apogee in Philostratus' *Life of Apollonius of Tyana*, which begins
by emphatically repeating the story of Pythagoras' divinity and which culminates
with the apotheosis of Apollonius, prophesied long in advance. See, for example,
Book III, 50.335: "But when he (Apollonius) was minded to go on his way, they
persuaded him to send back to Phraotes with a letter his guide and the camels;
and they themselves gave him another guide and camels, and sent him forth on
his way, congratulating both themselves and him. And having embraced Apollonius
and declared that he would be esteemed a god by the many, not merely after his
death, but while he was still alive, they turned back to their place of meditation"
(Conybeare, LCL).

[41] For a discussion of various cults in Alexandria see P. M. Fraser, "Chapter 5:
The Cults of Alexandria," in *Ptolemaic Alexandria*, 1:189–301.

[42] B. Mack states: "During the Hellenistic period, the Greek notions of authorship as an accomplishment and of a text as a memorial to its author became common coin. It was just during this period that Moses came to be imagined as a
figure of imposing authority and that his books came to be regarded as texts that
established epic precedence. So the Greek notions of authorship and authority must
have been at work. But the authority of an author, even the author of an epic literature, could hardly become the central figure around which a substitute model
for the people of Israel could easily be constructed. The profile of the scribe was
simply not sufficient to incorporate the powers, privileges, and executive functions
of the offices that organized the archaic model" ("Moses on the Mountaintop," 23).

λεγόμενα τοῖς ἀναγινωσκομένοις ἀεὶ συνύφαινον καὶ διὰ τοῦτ᾽ ἔδοξα μᾶλλον ἑτέρων τὰ περὶ τὸν βίον ἀκριβῶσαι.

But I will disregard their malice and tell the story of Moses as I have learned it, both from sacred books, the wonderful monuments of his wisdom which he has left behind him, and from some of the elders of the nation; for I always interwove what I was told with what I read, and thus believed myself to have a closer knowledge than others of his life's history.

Thus, Philo claims as his sources the Pentateuch itself, in the form of the Septuagint, along with ancient interpretation inherited through the elders of the nation (*Spec.* 1.8 [Colson, LCL]):

Ταῦτα μὲν οὖν εἰς ἀκοὰς ἦλθε τὰς ἡμετέρας, ἀρχαιολογούμενα παρὰ θεσπεσίοις ἀνδράσιν, οἳ τὰ Μωυσέως οὐ παρέργως διηρεύνησαν.

These are the explanations handed down to us from the old-time studies of divinely gifted men who made deep research into the writings of Moses.

Yet, at the same time, Philo incorporates concepts from Greek culture—even from idolatrous Greek religion—when he is recounting biblical stories elaborated by Jewish tradition. For example, the life of a shepherd is an appropriate preparation in the Bible for both Moses and David, and the relevance of shepherding to rulership is elaborated in later rabbinic traditions. Here is Philo's explanation of Moses' shepherding career, which might have seemed to a Hellenistic sensibility to be unbecoming of a ruler (*Mos.* 1.62):[43]

καί μοι δοκεῖ μὴ πρὸς δόξας τῶν πολλῶν ἀλλὰ πρὸς ἀλήθειαν ἐρευνωμένῳ τὸ πρᾶγμα—γελάτω δ᾽ ὁ βουλόμενος—μόνος ἂν γενέσθαι βασιλεὺς τέλειος ὁ τὴν ποιμενικὴν ἐπιστήμην ἀγαθός, ἐν ἐλάττοσι ζῴοις παιδευθεὶς τὰ τῶν κρειττόνων· ἀμήχανον γὰρ τὰ μελάλα πρὸ τῶν μικρῶν τελεσθῆναι.

And my opinion, based not on the opinions of the multitude but on my own inquiry into the truth of the matter, is that the only perfect king (let him laugh who will) is one who is skilled in the knowledge of shepherding, one who has been trained by management of the inferior creatures to manage the superior. For initiation in the lesser mysteries must precede initiation in the greater.

---

[43] For a detailed discussion of Philo's conception of Moses the Mystic, see E. R. Goodenough, "Chapter 8: The Mystic Moses," in *By Light, Light*, 199–234.

Moses' experience in governing sheep was a fit preparation for the governance of humans, just as, in the rites of Eleusis, initiation into the lesser mysteries is the only appropriate preparation for initiation into the greater mysteries.[44] To be sure, by the first century c.e., the language of initiation into the mysteries—especially into the Eleusinian mysteries—had become common cultural currency, and could be used to signify transformative education into elevated regions of philosophy, without any ritualistic connotation.[45] Nevertheless, Philo's guileless combination of Jewish tradition with Greek religious concepts is striking.

No less striking is Philo's unparalleled combination of *all* the aretalogical ideals in the single person of Moses, who is at once not only prophet and lawgiver, but also philosopher, king and priest (*Mos.* 2.2–7):[46]

φασὶ γάρ τινες οὐκ ἀπὸ σκοποῦ, μόνως ἂν οὕτω τὰς πόλεις ἐπιδοῦναι πρὸς τὸ βέλτιον, ἐὰν (ἢ) οἱ βασιλεῖς φιλοσοφήσωσιν ἢ οἱ φιλόσοφοι βασιλεύσωσιν. ὁ δ᾽ ἐκ περιττοῦ φανεῖται μὴ μόνον ταύτας ἐπιδεδειγμένος τὰς δυνάμεις ἐν ταὐτῷ, τήν τε βασιλικὴν καὶ φιλόσοφον, ἀλλὰ καὶ τρεῖς ἑτέρας, ὧν ἡ μὲν πραγματεύεται περὶ νομοθεσίαν, ἡ δὲ περὶ ἀρχιερωσύνην, ἡ δὲ τελευταία περὶ προφητείαν ... ἀλλ᾽ ἐπειδὴ μυρία καὶ βασιλεῖ καὶ νομοθέτῃ καὶ ἀρχιερεῖ τῶν ἀνθρωπείων καὶ θείων ἄδηλα—γενητὸς γὰρ οὐδὲν ἧττον καὶ θνητός ἐστιν, εἰ καὶ τοσοῦτον καὶ οὕτως ἄφθονον περιβέβληται κλῆρον εὐπραγιῶν—, ἀναγκαίως καὶ προφητείας ἔτυχεν, ἵν᾽ ὅσα μὴ λογισμῷ δύναται καταλαμβάνειν, ταῦτα προνοίᾳ θεοῦ εὕροι· ὧν γὰρ ὁ νοῦς ἀπολείπεται, πρὸς ταῦθ᾽ ἡ προφητεία φθάνει. καλή γε ἡ συζυγία καὶ παναρμόνιος τῶν τεττάρων δυνάμεων·

For it has been said, not without good reason, that states can only make progress in well-being if either kings are philosophers or philosophers are kings. But Moses will be found to have displayed, and more than displayed, combined in his single person, not only these two fac-

---

[44] For discussion of these mysteries in Alexandria see P. M. Fraser, "Chapter 5: The Cults of Alexandria," in *Ptolemaic Alexandria*, 1:189–301; E. R. Goodenough, "Chapter 9: The Mystery," in *By Light, Light*, 235–64; Walter Burkert, *Greek Religion: Archaic and Classical* (trans. J. Raffan; Cambridge, Mass.: Harvard University Press, 1985), 285–90.

[45] For philosophical use of language from Eleusis, see, e.g., Plato, *Symp.* 209e–f; *Phaedr.* 250b–c. On the philosophical use of mysteries see Paul W. Franks, "Kant and Hegel on the Esotericism of Philosophy" (Ph.D. diss., Harvard University, 1993), 1–19.

[46] See also *Ios.* 125–127, where Philo discusses the role of a statesman. For a discussion of the relationship between the various roles played by Moses, see H. A. Wolfson, *Philo*, 2:20 ff.

ulties—the kingly and the philosophical—but also three others, one of which is concerned with law-giving, the second with the high priest's office, and the last with prophecy. . . . Since to this king, lawgiver and high priest who, though possessed of so generous a heritage of fortune's gifts, is after all but a mortal creature, countless things both human and divine are wrapped in obscurity, Moses necessarily obtained so, in order that through the providence of God he might discover what by reasoning he could not grasp. For prophecy finds its way to what the mind fails to reach. Beautiful and all-harmonious is the union of these four faculties.

This hyperbolic description seems designed to trump any competing claim. While the Greeks had dreamt of a philosopher-king,[47] the Jews had actually had one. Indeed, they still lived under his legislation.

Indeed, Philo goes so far as to describe Moses as a god, or sometimes as a divine human (*Mos.* 1.158–159):

οὐχὶ καὶ μείζονος τῆς πρὸς τὸν πατέρα τῶν ὅλων καὶ ποιητὴν κοινωνίας ἀπέλαυσε προσρήσεως τῆς αὐτῆς ἀξιωθείς; ὠνομάσθη γὰρ ὅλου τοῦ ἔθνους θεὸς καὶ βασιλεύς· εἴς τε τὸν γνόφον, ἔνθα ἦν ὁ θεός, εἰσελθεῖν λέγεται (Exodus 20, 21), τουτέστιν εἰς τὴν ἀειδῆ καὶ ἀόρατον καὶ ἀσώματον τῶν ὄντων παραδειγματικὴν οὐσίαν, τὰ ἀθέατα φύσει θνητῇ κατανοῶν· καθάπερ τε γραφὴν εὖ δεδημιουργημένην ἑαυτὸν καὶ τὸν ἑαυτοῦ βίον εἰς μέσον προαγαγὼν πάγκαλον καὶ θεοειδὲς ἔργον ἔστησε παράδειγμα τοῖς ἐθέλουσι μιμεῖσθαι. εὐδαίμονες δ᾽ ὅσοι τὸν τύπον ταῖς ἑαυτῶν ψυχαῖς ἐναπεμάξαντο ἢ ἐσπούδασαν ἐναπομάξασθαι· φερέτω γὰρ ἡ διάνοια μάλιστα μὲν τὸ εἶδος τέλειον ἀρετῆς, εἰ δὲ μή, τὸν γοῦν ὑπὲρ τοῦ κτήσασθαι τὸ εἶδος ἀνενδοίαστον πόθον.

Again, was not the joy of his partnership with the Father and Maker of all magnified also by the honor of being deemed worthy to bear the same title? For he was named god and king of the whole nation, and entered, we are told, into the darkness where God was, that is into the unseen, invisible, incorporeal and archetypal essence of existing things. Thus he beheld what is hidden[48] from the sight of mortal nature, and in himself and his life displayed for all to see, he has set before us, like some well-wrought picture, a piece of work beautiful and godlike, a model for those who are willing to copy it. Happy are those who imprint, or strive to imprint, that image in their souls. For

---

[47] Plato, *Resp.* V, 473d.
[48] On this passage from Philo, A. C. Geljon notes: "Philo too presents Moses' life as an example in *Mos.* 1.158, writing that Moses puts forward his own life as a paradeigma for those who are willing to imitate it. The Jewish exegete refers here to Ex. 20:21, where it is written that Moses entered into the darkness where God was" ("Moses as Example," 43).

it were best that the mind should carry the form of virtue in perfection, but, failing this, let it at least have the unflinching desire to possess that form.

Divinization is also a characteristic of Hellenistic aretalogy, with roots in Pythagorean tradition.[49] This may sound surprising, but Philo has biblical support for the divinity of Moses.[50] Nor is he alone: Josephus also calls Moses a *theios aner*.[51] Besides, Philo does not make Moses into a god worthy of worship, which would sound idolatrous. Hellenistic biographers had several options: some figures were said to have actually become immortal gods, like Apollonius of Tyana,[52] while others were said to be divine human beings.[53] Philo carefully chooses the

---

[49] According to Iamblichus, Aristotle related in his treatise *On the Pythagoric Philosophy* that the Pythagoreans made a tripartite distinction between gods, men, and beings like Pythagoras. See Iamblichus, *The Life of Pythagoras*, in *The Pythagorean Sourcebook and Library*, 63.

[50] See Exod 7:1. For further discussion of biblical sources and interpretive traditions surrounding the claim that Moses is a king and a god, see Wayne Meeks, "Moses as God and King," in *Religions in Antiquity: Essays in Memory of Erwin Ramsdell Goodenough* (ed. J. Neusner; Leiden: Brill, 1968), 354–71; Carl R. Holladay, *Theios Aner in Hellenistic Judaism: A Critique of the Use of This Category in the New Testament Christology* (SBLDS 40; Missoula, Mont.: Scholars Press, 1977); David S. du Toit, *Theios Anthropos: Zur Verwendung von* θεῖος ἄνθρωπος *und sinnverwandten Ausdrücken in der Literatur der Kaiserzeit* (ed. M. Hengel and O. Hofius; WUNT Reihe 2:91; Tübingen: J. C. B. Mohr, 1997); David L. Tiede, *The Charismatic Figure As Miracle Worker* (SBLDS 1; Missoula, Mont.: University of Montana Press, 1972); David T. Runia, "God and Man in Philo of Alexandria," *JTS* 39 (1988): 48–75; repr. in *Studia Patristica: Papers of the 1983 Oxford Patristics Conference* (ed. E. A. Livingston; StPatr 18.2; Leuven: Peeters, 1989), 48–74; Erkki Koskenniemi, "Apollonius of Tyana: A Typical ΘΕΙΟΣ ΑΝΗΡ?" *JBL* 117 (1998): 455–67.

[51] *Ant.* III 180 (Thackeray, LCL): "For if one reflects on the construction of the tabernacle and looks at the vestments of the priest and the vessels which we use for the sacred ministry, he will discover that our lawgiver was a man of God (θεῖον ἄνδρα) and that these blasphemous charges brought against us by the rest of men are idle."

[52] For an excellent discussion of Philostratus' *Life of Apollonius of Tyana* see E. L. Bowie, "Apollonius of Tyana: Tradition and Reality," 1653–99. For more general discussion of various trends among Hellenistic biographers, see Moses Hadas and Morton Smith, *Heroes and Gods: Spiritual Biographies in Antiquity* (ed. R. N. Anshen; RP 13; New York: Harper & Row, 1965); M. Smith, "Prolegomena to a Discussion of Aretalogies," 174–99; Charles H. Talbert, "Biographies of Philosophers and Rulers," 1619–51; idem, "The Myth of the Immortals," 419–36.

[53] C. H. Talbert states: "Not every *theios aner* was believed to have become an immortal. Porphyry's 'Life of Pythagoras', for example, describes Pythagoras as a divine man but not as immortal. There were, furthermore, attempts in some circles to keep the two conceptions separate . . . Philo, in addition to the categories 'eternals/immortals', knew of the concept *theios aner*" ("Biographies of Philosophers and Rulers," 1637).

latter option, taking pains, for instance, not to portray Moses as undergoing apotheosis like Apollonius, but rather as dispassionately confronting his own death like Socrates. As evidence of the latter, Philo cites the fact, troubling to some later readers, that Moses describes his own death (*Mos.* 2.290–292):

θαυμασιώτατον δὲ καὶ τὸ τέλος τῶν ἱερῶν γραμμάτων, ὃ καθάπερ ἐν τῷ ζῴῳ κεφαλὴ τῆς ὅλης νομοθεσίας ἐστίν. ἤδη γὰρ ἀναλαμβανόμενος καὶ ἐπ᾿ αὐτῆς βαλβῖδος ἑστώς, ἵνα τὸν εἰς οὐρανὸν δρόμον διιπτάμενος εὐθύνῃ, καταπνευσθεὶς καὶ ἐπιθειάσας ζῶν ἔτι τὰ ὡς ἐπὶ θανόντι ἑαυτῷ προφητεύει δεξιῶς, ὡς ἐτελεύτησε μήπω τελευτήσας, ὡς ἐτάφη μηδενὸς παρόντος, δηλονότι χερσὶν οὐ θνηταῖς ἀλλ᾿ ἀθανάτοις δυνάμεσιν, ὡς οὐδ᾿ ἐν τάφῳ τῶν προπατόρων ἐκηδεύθη τυχὸν ἐξαιρέτου μνήματος, ὃ μηδεὶς εἶδεν ἀνθρώπων, ὡς σύμπαν τὸ ἔθνος αὐτὸν ὅλον μῆνα δακρυρροοῦν ἐπένθησεν ἴδιον καὶ κοινὸν πένθος ἐπιδειξάμενον ἕνεκα τῆς ἀλέκτου καὶ πρὸς ἕνα ἕκαστον καὶ πρὸς ἅπαντας εὐνοίας καὶ κηδεμονίας. τοιοῦτος μὲν ὁ βίος, τοιαύτη δὲ καὶ ἡ τελευτὴ τοῦ βασιλέως καὶ νομοθέτου καὶ ἀρχιερέως καὶ προφήτου Μωυσέως διὰ τῶν ἱερῶν γραμμάτων μνημονεύεται.

But most wonderful of all is the conclusion of the Holy Scriptures, which stands to the whole law-book as the head to the living creature; for when he was already being exalted and stood at the very barrier, ready at the signal to direct his upward flight to heaven, the divine spirit fell upon him and he prophesied with discernment while still alive the story of his own death; told ere the end how the end came; told how he was buried with none present, surely by no mortal hands but by immortal powers; how also he was not laid to rest in the tomb of his forefathers but was given a monument of special dignity which no man has ever seen; how all the nation wept and mourned for him a whole month and made open display, private and public, of their sorrow, in memory of his vast benevolence and watchful care for each one of them and for all.

Such as recorded in the Holy Scriptures, was the life and such the end of Moses, king, lawgiver, high priest, prophet.

Indeed, Philo's distinction between a divine man and a god worthy of worship is crucial to his response to the politics of emperor-divinization which, as we have seen, impacted heavily on the Jews during Philo's lifetime.[54] In Borgen's words:

Philo recognized that Augustus was venerated as God, and he refers explicitly to the worship of him in the temple Sebasteum in Alexandria.

---

[54] For discussion of this topic, see Colin Wells, *The Roman Empire* (Stanford, Calif.: Stanford University Press, 1984), 105 ff. The Jews were not alone in objecting to this innovation. See, e.g., Seneca, *The Apolocyntosis of the Divine Claudius.*

Philo stresses that Augustus did not directly claim to be a god. Although the Jews regarded emperor-worship with horror, Augustus still approved of them and permitted them to live in accordance with their Laws and worship only their one God. Philo interpreted this to mean that Augustus was never elated or puffed up by the vast honors given to him. The emperor Gaius Caligula, on the other hand, made a direct claim to divinity, and enforced the worship of himself. The Jews were not exempted. Philo makes it clear that the Jews opposed him on principle, since they acknowledged only one God, the creator. In Philo's judgment, Gaius Caligula overstepped the bounds of human nature in his eagerness to be thought a God (*Legat.* 75).[55]

Gaius Caligula, the imperfect king who demanded that he be worshiped, is contrasted with Moses, the perfect king who understood that worship is reserved for God.[56] For Moses aspires only to exhibit in his life a copy of nature, not to identify himself as the origin of nature.

Thus Philo reconfigures the relationship between the law and figure of Moses, a relationship already of great significance within Second Temple Judaism, in a way that allows him *both* to authorize the Law of Moses in Hellenistic, universal terms, *and* at the same time to transform those terms. To be sure, the Law of Moses includes rules

---

[55] P. Borgen, *Philo of Alexandria: An Exegete For His Time*, 22.

[56] P. Borgen states: "Philo expresses the view that Moses, as a result of his entry before God, was a living and reasonable law (νόμος ἔμψυχός τε καὶ λογικός) in anticipation of his coming role as the legislator appointed by God, *Mos.* 1.162. Moses' counterfeit, Gaius, regarded himself as a law (νόμος), and broke the laws of the lawgivers of every country, *Legat.* 119. In this way Philo gives two contrasting applications of the topos of Hellenistic kingship that the king's business was to articulate the divine realm and will into which he could penetrate: Moses was an authentic personification of the divine law, while Gaius illegitimately claimed that he was a law in himself.

Moses saw what is hidden for mortal nature and became a godlike work (θεοειδὲς ἔργον), like a well-wrought picture (γραφή), a model (παράδειγμα) for those who are willing to copy it, *Mos.* 1.158. Gaius, the counterfeit, went further in his claim of being god and regarded himself as a divine manifestation. He even 'introduced into Italy the barbarian practice of *proskynesis* of Gaius as a god', *Legat.* 116. Although Philo applies God's title to Moses, he does not see him as object of *proskynesis* or sacrifice" (*Philo of Alexandria: An Exegete For His Time*, 204–05).

Indeed, it is worth noting that Moses' authority depends on popular consent: "So, having received the authority which they willingly gave him, with the sanction and assent of God, he proposed to lead them to settle in Phoenicia and Coelesyria and Palestine, then called the land of the Canaanites, the boundaries of which were three days' journey from Egypt" (*Mos.* 1.163). This is a point that must have been made with reference to current debates about the authority of the emperor.

and precepts. But it cannot be *reduced* to a code. For the rules must be read as expressions of the virtuous lives of the patriarchs and of Moses. When they are read in this way, Philo claims, one will see that, just as the virtuous lives are copies of the Law of Nature, so are the rules. Indeed, one might argue that, if one were to abstract the rules from the lives of the sages, in order to form a code, then one would run the risk of obscuring the true significance of the rules.

At this point, one might say that only one aspect of the Philonic paradox has been addressed. The paradox is that Philo regards the Law of Moses as a written copy of the Law of Nature, but the Law of Nature is unwritten and so cannot be reduced to a code of rules that could be written down. I have argued that Philo does not regard the Law of Moses as reducible to a code of rules. Instead, the rules have weight insofar as they direct us towards the virtuous life of the sage who has internalized right reason. But it still remains the case, one might say, that the Law of Moses is supposed to be a *written* copy of the Law of Nature. Why does Philo think it is possible to have a written copy of a law that, as we have seen, he himself calls unwritten?

This paradox expresses the revolutionary character of Philo's conception of the law and nature. Consequently, the paradox cannot be entirely resolved. But something can be said to illuminate the inner logic of Philo's revolutionary move. Just as the Pentateuch contains rules but is not reducible to a code of rules, so too the Pentateuch is written but is not reducible to a piece of writing.[57] For it must be read within what we might call *an interpretive community*.[58] This is a community which inherits and transmits interpretive traditions—what Philo calls the "traditions of the fathers"—and which is also actively engaged in producing new interpretations. Thus Philo says that Scripture must be read along with the instruction of a priest or elder, and he says that he himself always combines his own ideas with the traditions he has heard. To abstract the Pentateuch from the life of the interpretive community of Israel, one might argue, would run

---

[57] Nevertheless, we see in Philo a characteristically ancient Greek preference for what is *inscribed in the soul* over what is *written* on stone, paper, or any physical surface. See, e.g., Plato, *Phaedr.* 276a.

[58] On the concept and development of "interpretive community" in Christian ethics see Jean Porter, *Natural and Divine Law: Reclaiming the Tradition for Christian Ethics* (Grand Rapids: Eerdmans, 1999), esp. 212–24, 187–244, 259–68, 303–18.

the risk of obscuring the true significance of the Pentateuch. Indeed, part of the motivation for Philo's authorial productivity may be precisely to make more widely available the interpretive context within which he thinks the Pentateuch should be read, while emphasizing the importance of the Jewish community that provides that context through its interpretive life. Here too, Philo's continuity with Second Temple Judaism in Palestine is clearly visible.

Philo of Alexandria and the Discourse of Moses

Having observed the revolutionary way in which Philo authorizes the law and figure of Moses by fusing Second Temple traditions with Hellenistic philosophy, we are now in a position to consider whether he may be regarded as participating in Mosaic Discourse.

Obstacles confront us as soon as we consider the first feature constitutive of Mosaic Discourse. For it would seem correct to exclude Philo from those who engage in rewriting the Bible. Thus Philip Alexander points out that, unlike the authors of, e.g., *Jubilees* and the Temple Scroll, Philo distinguishes explicitly between the scriptural text and his interpretations, and Philo is also self-conscious in discussions of his interpretive methodology:

> The limitations of the narrative form [in Rewritten Bible] also preclude making clear the exegetical reasoning. The rewritten Bible texts read the Bible with close attention, noting obscurities, inconsistencies and narrative lacunae. The methods by which they solve the problems of the original are essentially midrashic, i.e., similar to those found in the rabbinic midrashim. But unlike the midrashim (or Philo) they cannot make explicit their midrashic working.[59]

On the other hand, Peder Borgen has argued that Philo *should* be classed with those who engage in rewriting the Bible:

> In this *Exposition of the Laws of Moses* Philo basically follows the form also found in other Jewish books in which (parts of) the Pentateuch have been rewritten. Examples are the *Book of Jubilees*, the *Genesis Apocryphon*, the *Biblical Antiquities of Pseudo-Philo*, and Josephus' *Jewish Antiquities*. Philo covers the biblical story from creation to Joshua's succession of Moses. The *Book of Jubilees* narrates the story from creation

---

[59] P. S. Alexander, "Retelling the Old Testament," 117–18; see also the review of P. Borgen's book by Adam Kamesar in *JTS* 50 (1999): 753–58.

to the giving of the Laws on Mt. Sinai. The *Genesis Apocryphon* is only preserved in parts, covering Genesis from the birth of Noah to Genesis 15:4. The *Biblical Antiquities of Pseudo-Philo* contain an abstract of the biblical story from Gen 5 to the death of Saul. In his *Jewish Antiquities* Josephus begins with creation and relates the whole span of biblical history and goes beyond even to the beginning of the Jewish war in his own time.[60]

How should this dispute be adjudicated? One factor that must be considered at this point is the role of the Septuagint within the Greek-speaking, Jewish community of Philo. It is not only that reliance on a translation left Philo and others at a distance from the Hebrew language in which biblical traditions were originally written and continued to be rewritten. For this alone need not have prevented the development of Greek rewritings of the Bible. After all, Aramaic-speaking Jews were also dependent on translations, and this did not prevent the development of Aramaic rewritings of the Bible.[61] Indeed, the Deuteronomic project of rewriting traditional texts and ascribing those rewritings to Moses had parallels in Greek literature, where one finds Discourses tied to founders such as Pythagoras, Socrates and Aristotle that are contemporaneous with Philo. In Hellenistic Egypt itself, a parallel may be found in the body of literature ascribed to Hermes Trismegistus, which contains texts dating to the first century B.C.E. as well as much later texts, and which purports to be translated from Coptic into Greek.[62] So Philo could have chosen to rewrite the Bible in the style of Deuteronomy, *Jubilees* and the Temple Scroll. An appropriate conception of the authority of the tradition and of his own activity was available to him in Hellenistic Egypt.

However, Philo could not rewrite the Bible in the Deuteronomic style *and at the same time* accept the conception of the authority of the Septuagint employed by the Letter of Aristeas. According to the Letter, Ptolemy Philadelphus had commissioned a Greek translation of the Hebrew Scriptures, which was then produced by seventy Jewish elders who worked in isolation upon the island of Pharos, but miraculously produced a single text. Thus the Septuagint was authorized both by one of Alexander the Great's heirs and by God. Moreover,

---

[60] P. Borgen, *Philo of Alexandria: An Exegete for His Time*, 79.

[61] E.g., the Genesis Apocryphon.

[62] Garth Fowden, *The Egyptian Hermes: A Historical Approach to the Late Pagan Mind* (Cambridge: Cambridge University Press, 1986), 3 n. 11.

the Septuagint constituted the national epic of Israel, comparable
and even superior to the Odyssey, the national epic of Greece. Philo
repeats this account. But he could not thus compare Moses with
Homer and at the same time undertake to rewrite Mosaic texts in
the manner of the Deuteronomists. At Alexandria, scholiasts like
Aristarchus developed the methods of ancient textual criticism on
Homeric texts. These texts had to be restored to the authentic con-
dition in which, it was supposed, Homer had originally composed
them. Once this conception of the authority of texts and their author
had been invoked on behalf of the Septuagint, it was no longer possible to efface the distinction between text and interpretation.

Nevertheless, despite what has been said, I would still maintain
that Philo's interpretations rework biblical traditions in a way that
counts as a transformed version of the first feature of Mosaic Discourse.
For he does not merely put forward one among several possible
interpretations.[63] Rather, he claims to expose the latent, philosophical meaning of the text, to set the text in its proper interpretive context. Thus, although Philo distinguishes between text and interpretation,
he attributes both—the interpretation as well as the text—to Moses.
Consider the following passage, where Philo is discussing a philosophical idea that he claims to find in Genesis (*Opif.* 24–25):

> εἰ δέ τις ἐθελήσειε γυμνοτέροις χρήσασθαι τοῖς ὀνόμασιν, οὐδὲν ἂν ἕτερον
> εἴποι τὸν νοητὸν κόσμον εἶναι ἢ θεοῦ λόγον ἤδη κοσμοποιοῦντος· οὐδὲ
> γὰρ ἡ νοητὴ πόλις ἕτερόν τί ἐστιν ἢ ὁ τοῦ ἀρχιτέκτονος λογισμὸς ἤδη τὴν
> [νοητὴν] πόλιν κτίζειν διανοουμένου. τὸ δὲ δόγμα τοῦτο Μωυσέως ἐστίν,
> οὐκ ἐμόν· τὴν γοῦν ἀνθρώπου γένεσιν ἀναγράφων ἐν τοῖς ἔπειτα διαρρήδην
> ὁμολογεῖ, ὡς ἄρα κατ᾽ εἰκόνα θεοῦ διετυπώθη (Gen. 1,27). εἰ δὲ τὸ μέρος
> εἰκὼν εἰκόνος [δῆλον ὅτι] καὶ τὸ ὅλον εἶδος, σύμπας οὗτος ὁ αἰσθητὸς
> κόσμος, εἰ μείζων τῆς ἀνθρωπίνης ἐστίν, μίμημα θείας εἰκόνος, δῆλον ὅτι
> καὶ ἡ ἀρχέτυπος σφραγίς, ὅν φαμεν νοητὸν εἶναι κόσμον, αὐτὸς ἂν εἴη
> [τὸ παράδειγμα, ἀρχέτυπος ἰδέα τῶν ἰδεῶν] ὁ θεοῦ λόγος.

> If you would wish to use a formulation that has been stripped down
> to essentials, you might say that the intelligible cosmos is nothing else
> than the Logos of God as he is actually engaged in making the cosmos.

---

[63] Contra P. S. Alexander: "The narrative form of the texts means, in effect,
that they can impose only a single interpretation on the original. The original can
be treated only as monovalent. By way of contrast, the commentary form adopted
by the rabbis and by Philo allows them to offer multiple interpretations of the same
passage of Scripture, and to treat the underlying text as polyvalent" ("Retelling the
Old Testament," 117).

For the intelligible city too is nothing else than the reasoning of the architect as he is actually engaged in the planning of the foundation of the city. This is the doctrine of Moses, not my own. When describing the genesis of the human being in what follows, he explicitly declares that the human being was in fact formed after God's own image [Gen. 1:27]. Now if the part is image of an image, it is plain that this is also the case for the whole. But if this entire sense-perceptible cosmos, which is greater than the human image, is a representation of the divine image, it is plain that the archetypal seal, which we affirm to be the intelligible cosmos, would itself be the model and archetypal idea of the ideas, the Logos of God.

Here we see *both* why Alexander is right to say that Philo is not rewriting the Bible in the Deuteronomic manner, *and* why Borgen is right to say that Philo's enterprise is nonetheless continuous with the projects of *Jubilees* and the Temple Scroll.[64] Alexander is right, because Philo's self-conscious use of the first person pronoun exhibits his sense of his own independent activity as an interpreter. But Borgen is also right, because the point of Philo's statement is to efface that self-conscious self by attributing his philosophical interpretation to Moses, the founder who authored the text and who must be regarded as the source of all authentic practice and teaching.

However, the obstacles seem more formidable still when we consider whether Philo's interpretations exhibit the second and third features of Mosaic Discourse. As previously explained, participants in Mosaic Discourse claim Torah status for themselves, both by representing the revelation at Sinai, either allusively or explicitly, and by using deictic expressions to emphasize the reader's immediate presence at the revelatory scene. To be sure, we have just seen Philo use the deictic "this" to ascribe an interpretation to Moses. But, in one of Philo's most striking departures from much of Second Temple Judaism, the revelation at Sinai is of little importance to him. In *Mos.* 1 and 2, the Sinai event is not, as one might have expected, a climactic moment. Instead, it is alluded to only briefly. Indeed, both in that brief allusion and in the extended passage about Moses at Sinai in *QE* 2.27–49, Philo places emphasis, not on Moses' reception of the Law and his transmission of it to Israel, but rather on Moses'

---

[64] P. Borgen writes: "Philo should not be understood as an isolated individual outside the broad stream of Jewish outlooks, convictions and attitudes which existed in the history of the Alexandrian Jewish community" (*Philo of Alexandria: An Exegete for His Time*, 44).

spiritual transformation and, indeed, divinization. Thus the second and third features of Mosaic Discourse are absent. Philo does not seek to authorize his version of the Law of Moses by re-presenting Sinai and by telling his readers, "This is the Torah of Moses, given to you, here and now."

Still, I think that Philo compensates in two ways for the remarkable absence of Sinai. These compensations make sense when one considers that Sinai is the moment of national importance for Israel, whereas Philo's endeavor is to authorize the Law in universal terms. For what take the place of Sinai within Philo's works are, first, the moment of creation, at which the Law of Nature was established for all and, second, the miraculous translation at Pharos, where the perfect, written copy of the Law of Nature was made accessible to all. With respect to the first point, what happened at Sinai was not, as *Jubilees* recounts, that Moses received a set of laws peculiar to the Jewish people. What happened was rather that Moses was granted access to the mystery of creation, which he attempts to impart in Genesis. With respect to the second point, an association with Sinai is strongly suggested by Philo's language when he retells the Aristean story of the elders on Pharos (*Mos.* 2.31–40). "For Philo, the question 'Why was the Torah received in Sinai?' has become, 'Why was the Greek Pentateuch received on the Pharos?'"[65]

In order to fully appreciate the extent to which Philo re-presents the scenes of creation and of Pharos to his readers, compensating for the absence of Sinai, we need to understand the special sense in which, although he distinguishes his interpretation from the text, he is himself, as interpreter, a compensation for the absent Moses.

In the Deuteronomic tradition, Philo emphasizes the uniqueness of Moses, to whom no other mortal can compare. Similarly, the Law of Nature is beyond mortal grasp, inexpressible and necessarily unwritten. However, as we have seen, it is possible for the life of a sage to *copy* the archetypal Law of Nature, and for a written collection of laws to express such a life, hence itself to constitute a copy of the Law of Nature. Correspondingly, it is possible for others to copy the life and vision of Moses (*Mos.* 1.158–159):

---

[65] Nina L. Collins, *The Library in Alexandria & the Bible in Greek* (VTSup 82; Leiden: Brill, 2000), 149.

... τὰ ἀθέατα φύσει θνητῇ κατανοῶν· καθάπερ τε γραφὴν εὖ δεδημιουργημένην ἑαυτὸν καὶ τὸν ἑαυτοῦ βίον εἰς μέσον προαγαγὼν πάγκαλον καὶ
θεοειδὲς ἔργον ἔστησε παράδειγμα τοῖς ἐθέλουσι μιμεῖσθαι. εὐδαίμονες δ᾽
ὅσοι τὸν τύπον ταῖς ἑαυτῶν ψυχαῖς ἐναπεμάξαντο ἢ ἐσπούδασαν ἐναπομά-
ξασθαι· φερέτω γὰρ ἡ διάνοια μάλιστα μὲν τὸ εἶδος τέλειον ἀρετῆς εἰ δὲ
μή, τὸν γοῦν ὑπὲρ τοῦ κτήσασθαι τὸ εἶδος ἀνενδοίαστον πόθον·

... Thus he [Moses] beheld what is hidden from the sight of mortal
nature, and, in himself and his life displayed for all to see, he has set
before us, like some well-wrought picture, a piece of work beautiful
and godlike, a model for those who are willing to copy it. Happy are
they who imprint, or strive to imprint, that image in their souls. For
it were best that the mind should carry the form of virtue in perfection,
but, failing this, let it at least have the unflinching desire to possess
that form.

The absence of Sinai is no accident. For Sinai signifies to Philo, not
the moment at which the Law was given by God to Moses and
thence to Israel, but rather the moment at which Moses surpassed
the ability of humans in his comprehension of creation. But Sinai
does not vanish into nothingness. Instead, it becomes omnipresent,
since Moses' divine vision pervades both the Pentateuch and its correct interpretation, underwriting their authority. Only through the
unique Sinai event does it become possible for the written law of a
particular nation to serve as the perfect copy of the unwritten Law
of Nature. Nor does Moses vanish into nothingness, beyond mortal
ken.[66] Instead, he too becomes omnipresent, pervading not only the
Pentateuch, but also its correct interpretation. For it is also possible
to copy Moses, although one cannot *be* Moses, any more than a
written law can *be* the Law of Nature.

Here it is crucial to note the way in which Philo inherits the
fourth feature of Mosaic Discourse: attribution to Moses. According
to Philo, the Decalogue was spoken by God in His own person with
His prophet for interpreter (*Mos.* 1.188). This seems to mean that,
while God Himself revealed the ten principal laws, it was Moses,
acting as prophetically inspired interpreter, who derived from them
the special laws. Thus Moses is the author of the Pentateuch, but
only insofar as he is the authorized interpreter of the word of God.

---

[66] For a discussion of ancient Jewish interpretive traditions on the death and
burial of Moses see J. L. Kugel, "Chapter 25: The Life of Torah," in *The Bible As
It Was*, 536–44.

Thus Philo's own interpretive activity can be regarded as copying the interpretive activity of Moses himself. Similarly, Philo describes his interpretations as—at least occasionally—inspired, using terms similar to those he employs to characterize the inspiration of Moses.[67] But Philo never ascribes to himself the highest level of inspiration, attained by Moses: total displacement of reason by the divine spirit.[68] Thus Philo the inspired interpreter is a stand-in for Moses the inspired interpreter. Philo's presence compensates for Moses' absence. By the logic of original and copy, Philo's interpretations may be ascribed to Moses even when Philo self-consciously refers to his own interpretive activity. Thus the authority of Philo's interpretations is derivative from the authority of Moses and, ultimately, from the authority of the Law of Nature itself. Philo's readers cannot be present at Sinai any more than they can become Moses.[69] But, thanks to Philo, they can be present at Pharos and they can be granted a vision of creation itself,[70] as well as an understanding of the practical import of the Law of Nature.

Conclusion

I have argued that Philo participates in the Discourse of Moses. But there are two significant contrasts between this Hellenistic version and its Palestinian counterparts. First, whereas texts such as *Jubilees*

---

[67] John R. Levison, "Inspiration and the Divine Spirit in the Writings of Philo Judaeus," *JSJ* 26 (1995): 271–323, esp. 294–98; Richard D. Hecht, "Scripture and Commentary in Philo," *SBL Seminar Papers, 1981* (SBLSP 20; Chico, Calif.: Scholars Press, 1981), 129–64; B. Mack, "Moses on the Mountain Top," 16–28; David E. Aune, *Prophecy in Early Christianity and the Ancient Mediterranean World* (Grand Rapids: Eerdmans, 1983), 147–52; S. G. Sowers, *The Hermeneutics of Philo and Hebrews*, 28–43.

[68] J. R. Levison, "Inspiration and the Divine Spirit in the Writings of Philo Judaeus," 284, 301.

[69] D. M. Hay, "Philo's View of Himself as an Exegete: Inspired, But not Authoritative," 40–52; J. R. Levison, "Inspiration and the Divine Spirit in the Writings of Philo Judaeus," 271–323; David Winston, "Two Types of Mosaic Prophecy According to Philo," in *SBL Seminar Papers, 1988* (SBLSP 27; Atlanta: Scholars Press, 1988): 442–55. See also Abraham Terian's discussion of *Anim.* 7 (where Philo writes: μὲν γάρ εἰμι ἑρμηεὺς ἀλλ' οὐ διδάσκαλος ["I am an interpreter and not a teacher"]) in *Philonis Alexandrini de Animalibus: The Armenian Text with an Introduction, Translation, and Commentary* (Chico, Calif.: Scholars Press, 1981), 116–17.

[70] For a discussion of the extensive use of vision and visual perception with respect to God in Philo's writings see Ellen Birnbaum, *The Place of Judaism in Philo's Thought: Israel, Jews, and Proselytes* (BJS 290; SPM 2; Atlanta: Scholars Press, 1996), esp. 69–127.

and the Temple Scroll subordinate the figure of Moses to the law of Moses, Philo subordinates the Law of Moses to the figure of Moses, so that the written law may express the life of a sage. Second, whereas *Jubilees* and the Temple Scroll, following the lead of Deuteronomy, seek to weave existing traditions and their own interpretations into a single seamless whole attributed to Moses, Philo distinguishes explicitly between Mosaic Scripture and his own interpretations.

In both cases, Philo makes central use of the logic of copy and original in order to fuse Hellenistic philosophy with the traditions of Second Temple Judaism. As an expression of the life of the sage, the law of Moses is a copy of the Law of Nature. As an inspired interpreter, initiated by Moses (*Cher.* 49), Philo is a copy of Moses, and Philonic interpretations are copies of Mosaic originals. Thus, although, like Deuteronomy, Philo insists on the uniqueness and ultimacy of both Moses the prophet and the Law of Moses, Philo—no less than the Deuteronomists and the authors of *Jubilees* and the Temple Scroll—continues to participate in the dynamic process of Second Temple Torah.

CHAPTER FOUR

CONSTRUCTING CONTINUITIES
AND THE DANGERS OF ANACHRONISM

Later Developments of Mosaic Discourse

How much continuity, and how much discontinuity, do we find in the development of scriptural and interpretive traditions? More specifically, how much continuity, and how much discontinuity, is there between Second Temple and rabbinic traditions? Responses to this recurring question diverge widely. But much depends on the dimension along which one is measuring. For example, James Kugel finds considerable continuity between Second Temple and rabbinic literature by examining interpretive motifs,[1] while Jacob Neusner[2] finds radical discontinuity between the rabbinic project and its Second Temple predecessors. Relativized to content and form respectively, these claims need not conflict. In this study, I have been concerned

---

[1] James L. Kugel, *In Potiphar's House: The Interpretive Life of Biblical Texts* (Cambridge, Mass.: Harvard University Press, 1994), 267: "Early exegetical documents of various sorts seem to argue, by their very form as well as by the overwhelming store of exegetical motifs shared among them—and this despite their highly diverse origins and orientations—that there existed well before the common era a substantial body of standard explanations of various problems and peculiarities in the biblical text. These explanations were apparently not gathered and passed in written form, since no such document has survived or is even alluded to. Instead, they were passed on orally, perhaps taught to schoolchildren as part of their study of Scripture in literacy education, and/or communicated along with the public liturgical reading/translation/exposition of Scripture. . . . These interpretations were not of course merely passed on unaltered to subsequent generations: they were elaborated, and at times some were abandoned or even polemically attacked with new interpretations. Nevertheless, a corpus of methodological assumptions, as well as a good many specific interpretations, came to be shared even by the warring groups whose names and works we know from the end of this period. And it is this common inheritance—communicated orally, as suggested, perhaps through the position of Scripture—that is responsible for the common assumptions, and much common material, that we have seen to characterize the written sources that have survived from those early times." See also, idem, *The Bible As It Was*, 27–36; Hanokh Albeck, *Introduction to the Mishnah* (Jerusalem: Mosad Bialik and Tel Aviv: Dvir, 1967), 24 [Hebrew].

[2] See Jacob Neusner, *Early Rabbinic Judaism: Historical Studies in Religion, Literature and Art* (SJLA 13; Leiden: Brill, 1975), esp. 34–49; idem, *From Politics to Piety: The Emergence of Pharisaic Judaism* (Englewood Cliffs, N.J.: Prentice Hall, 1973).

with an additional, previously unexplored dimension: the mode in which authority is claimed for an interpretive version of biblical traditions. Elements of both form and content pertain to this dimension of continuity and discontinuity.

In my conceptualization of one such mode—Mosaic Discourse— I have taken pains to avoid two kinds of anachronism. First, I have sought to avoid the imposition of contemporary conceptions of the authority of texts and their authors upon ancient texts and authorial attributions constructed in accordance with very different norms. Second, I have shown how, within a family of approaches to the question of authorization, there could be both continuity and variation. Indeed, I have argued that Mosaic Discourse was sufficiently compelling and robust to survive in Hellenistic Alexandria, under conditions, and in the presence of conceptions of textuality and authorship, quite different from those in Palestine. It would be anachronistic to impose, upon one stage in the development of Mosaic Discourse, a conception proper to another stage.

Therefore, the thesis that Mosaic Discourse continues within rabbinic literature must be explored with due caution, taking care to avoid both kinds of anachronism.[3] There is a strong *prima facie* case to be made for this thesis. To be sure, the Rabbis do not rewrite the Bible in Deuteronomic fashion.[4] But neither does Philo. And we find in rabbinic literature considerable efforts to derive by *midrash* from Scripture associated with Moses what might otherwise be called non-Mosaic laws; the characterization of certain underived laws as

---

[3] A parallel thesis about early Christian texts also merits investigation. Some of the features we have discussed thus far are certainly present in many early Christian traditions. While we can point to important differences and distinctive developments, it is also the case that there is profound continuity. See, e.g., D. P. Moessner, "Paul and the Pattern of the Prophet like Moses in Acts," 203–12; idem, "Jesus and the 'Wilderness Generation'," 319–40; D. M. Hay, "Moses Through New Testament Spectacles," 240–52; D. C. Allison Jr., *The New Moses*.

[4] On the question of whether rabbinic texts participate in the "Rewritten Bible," see Paul Mandel, "Midrashic Exegesis and its Precedents in the Dead Sea Scrolls," *DSD* 8 (2001): 149–68. Mandel states: ". . . in certain parts of the Reworked Pentateuch and the Rewritten Bible texts (*Jubilees*, Temple Scroll, Genesis Apocryphon), the texts themselves become more foreign to a reader of rabbinic texts: the interpretive 'conceit,' which in these texts masks the interpretation under the guise of what purports to be an authentic (Torah) revelation, is largely absent from the early midrashic texts [but does reappear in early medieval midrashic texts, such as *Midrash Wayyisaʻu* or the *Chronicles of Moses*]" (155; 155 n. 16). On this last point, see Joseph Dan, *The Hebrew Story in the Middle Ages* (Jerusalem: Keter, 1994 [Hebrew]), 20–23, 133–41.

Halakah le-Moshe mi-Sinai;[5] and the general idea that rabbinic author-ity rests on a second Torah, תורה שבעל פה (Oral Torah) given to Moses at Sinai along with תורה שבכתב (Written Torah).[6]

---

[5] Numerous references to *Halakha le-Moshe mi-Sinai* appear in rabbinic literature, the earliest occurring in the Mishnah and the Tosephta. See, e.g., *m. Pe'ah* 2:6; *m. 'Ed.* 8:7; *m. Yad.* 4:3; *t. Yad.* 2:16; *b. Menaḥ.* 32a; *b. Meg.* 24b; *b. Ḥag.* 3a.; *b. Šabb.* 89b.

David Weiss Halivni insists that this term should really be understood as an Amoraic development. See his discussion in *Revelation Restored: Divine Writ and Critical Responses* (Boulder, Colo.: Westview, 1997): "Except for one possible reference in Peah, the Mishnah never alludes to a historical *Halakha le-Moshe mi-Sinai* as a deci-sive factor in halakha. The Tannaim did not deny the existence of *Halakha le-Moshe mi-Sinai* or, hypothetically, its power to decide halakha, but they did not avail them-selves of it for practical decisions" (56–57). Underlying Halivni's comments are the echoes of over a century of fierce debate among Rabbis and scholars of rabbinic literature, a debate that has medieval roots.

As several medievals of the Tosaphist school already noted, some laws said to be *Halakha le-Moshe mi-Sinai* are known to be rabbinic and not biblical. For exam-ple, on *m. Yad.* 4:3 (see also *b. Ḥag.* 3a), the Tosaphist, Rabbi Samson ben Abraham of Sens (late twelfth-early thirteenth century) writes "לאו דווקא למשה מסיני" because the Mishnah explicitly ascribes a post-Mosaic origin to the law in question. He then contrasts the version in *t. Yad.* 2:16, which, he argues, does suggest that the tradi-tion is *Halakha le-Moshe mi-Sinai*. In a later discussion, the Rosh (R. Asher ben Yehiel, 1250–1327) compares a similar case in *b. Šabb.* 11a, where the prohibition against reading by the light of a candle is called "אמת"; as the Rosh points out, accord-ing to *y. Šabb.* Ch. 1, halakha 3, every usage of "אמת" should be understood as marking a *Halakha le-Moshe mi-Sinai*. Yet, according to the Rosh, the prohibition is clearly rabbinic (*Hilkhot Miqvaot* 5). The Rosh cites the Ri (R. Isaac ben Samuel of Dampierre, ca. 1185) in support of his position that some laws are called *Halakha le-Moshe mi-Sinai* but are merely *like Halakha le-Moshe mi-Sinai* and acquire the author-ity of Sinaitic legislation.

See also the following discussions: Isaac H. Weiss, *Dor Dor Vedorshav Zur Geshikhte fun der jüdische Tradition, Vol. 1* (1871–1891; repr., Berlin: Platt and Minkus, 1924), 73 n. 2; Yehoshua Heshel Schorr, "Halakha le-Moshe mi-Sinai," *He-Halutz* 2 (1857): 29–50; Shmuel Safrai, "Halakhah le-Moshe mi-Sinai: History or Theology?" in *Mehqerei Talmud* (ed. Y. Sussman and D. Rosenthal; Jerusalem: Hebrew University, 1990 [Hebrew]), 11–38; D. W. Halivni, "Chapter 2: Overcoming Maculation," and "Afterward: Continuous Revelation," in *Revelation Restored: Divine Writ and Critical Responses*, 47–74, 87–89 and corresponding notes on 95–100, especially 96 n. 5; Jay M. Harris, *How Do We Know This? Midrash and the Fragmentation of Modern Judaism* (Albany: State University of New York Press, 1995), 101 and 298 n. 115 and n. 116; Christine E. Hayes, "Halakhah le-Moshe mi-Sinai in Rabbinic Sources: A Methodological Case Study," in *The Synoptic Problem in Rabbinic Literature* (ed. S. J. D. Cohen; BJS 326; Atlanta: Scholars Press, 2000), 61–118.

[6] This tradition is represented in early rabbinic traditions. See, e.g., *m. Qidd.*, chapter 4, Mishnah 14; *t. Qidd.*, chapter 5; *Sifre Deb., Wezot Habberakha*, par. 351; *Sifra, Parshat Beḥuqotai*, Chapter 8:13; *'Abot R. Nat.* (A) 15; *b. Ber.* 5a; *b. Šabb.* 31a. See J. L. Kugel, "Chapter 20: At Mount Sinai (Exodus 19–24)," in *The Bible As It Was*, 402–4 for discussion of the following two motifs, "Moses Was Given More than the Torah" and "Oral Teachings from Moses." See also, Hanokh Albeck,

While full investigation of this thesis lies outside the scope of this project, I want to point out three false moves that have been made, moves that can be avoided with the help of the concept of Mosaic Discourse. In each case, a feature of later, rabbinic literature has been supposedly discovered in a Second Temple text. Thus, *midrash halakhah* has been found in Ezra-Nehemiah, while תורה שבעל פה has been found in both *Jubilees* and Philo. In all three cases, there is a genuine continuity, which may indicate the rabbinic continuation of Mosaic Discourse. But, in all three cases, the continuity has been formulated in an anachronistic way that fails to acknowledge variation and transformation. The concept of Mosaic Discourse, I will argue, enables us to get the balance right.

Ezra and the Torah of Moses

There is a puzzling phenomenon in Ezra-Nehemiah. Certain laws that do not occur in the Pentateuch are nevertheless attributed to the Torah of Moses. Yet the text of the Pentateuch must have been fixed, for public reading occurred.[7] How is this to be understood?

First, let us consider the courses of the priesthood. No pre-exilic or exilic tradition mentions the particular groupings of priests and Levites mentioned in Ezra-Nehemiah.[8] Nevertheless, in Ezra 6:18, these "courses" of priests and the "divisions" of Levites are said to have been arranged in accordance with "the book of Moses."[9]

Introduction to the Mishnah, 3–39, esp. 3–4 and 3 n. 7; Peter Schäfer, "Das 'Dogma' von der Mündlichen Torah im Rabbinischen Judentum," in *Studien zur Geschichte und Theologie des rabbinischen Judentums* (Leiden: Brill, 1978), 153–97; Ephraim E. Urbach, "The Written Law and the Oral Law," in *The Sages* (Cambridge, Mass.: Harvard University Press, 1979), 286–314.

[7] Rainer Albertz states: "Traditionally the canonization of the Pentateuch is associated with the mission of Ezra, which according to Ezra 7.1–8 took place in the seventh year of Artaxerxes, i.e., 458 or 398. According to the Aramaic text of Ezra 7.11–26, which has the style of a confirmatory document sent by the Persian king, Ezra, who is called 'priest' and 'scribe' of the law of the God of heaven (v. 12), is explicitly authorized by the Persian court . . ." (*A History of Israelite Religion in the Old Testament Period, Volume II: From the Exile to the Maccabees* [trans. J. Bowden; OTL; 2 vols.; Louisville: Westminster/John Knox, 1994], 2:466).

[8] S. Japhet, "Law and 'The Law' in Ezra-Nehemiah," 114; H. G. M. Williamson, "The Origins of the Twenty-Four Priestly Courses," in *Studies in the Historical Books of the Old Testament* (ed. J. A. Emerton; VTSup 30; Leiden: Brill, 1979), 251–68.

[9] The term "courses" as referring to the courses of priests or Levites occurs only in post-exilic texts (1 and 2 Chronicles, Ezra, and Nehemiah). There is one additional

והקימו כהניא בפלגתהון ולויא במחלקתהון על עבידת אלהא די בירושלם
ככתב ספר משה

> They established priests in their courses and levites in their divisions
> for the service of the God of Jerusalem in accordance with the writing
> of the book of Moses.

In 2 Chr 35:4–5, the *very same* priestly organization is also attributed to a pre-exilic authority. But this time the authority is said to
be, not Moses, but *David and Solomon*. Sara Japhet notes that Ezra-
Nehemiah had a choice: the priestly courses could have been attributed to Moses *or* to David, either of whom were pre-exilic authorities.[10]
Thus, the choice of Moses was *deliberate* and motivated by theological considerations. It seems to me that Japhet's point raises a further question. If the author who ascribed the priestly courses to the
book of Moses did so with precision and in deliberate rejection of
the idea that they originated with the Davidic monarchy, then we
are faced with a problem. What could be meant by the ascription
of a law to a book in which the law does not appear? How, for
that matter, could one hope to get away with such an ascription, if
the book in question was public property?

I will return to these questions shortly. First, I want to consider
another case: the problem of the returnees who married foreigners
during the exile.

When Ezra was told of extensive intermarriage among the returning exiles, his response was not unlike that of previous Israelite leaders when they were faced with impending doom: he rent his clothing
and prayed to God (Ezra 9:3–7):

(3) וכשמעי את הדבר הזה קרעתי את בגדי ומעילי ואמרטה משער ראשי וזקני
ואשבה משומם (4) ואלי יאספו כל חרד בדברי אלהי ישראל על מעל הגולה
ואני ישב משומם עד למנחת הערב (5) ובמנחת הערב קמתי מתעניתי ובקרעי

---

usage of "courses" in Ezek 44:29 where reference is made to the land apportioned
to the Levites but this seems to be an alternative usage, also found in Josh 12:7
and 18:10, where it refers to the portions of land which were granted to the Israelite
tribes.

The term "divisions" appears only twice in post-exilic traditions: Ezra 6:18 and
2 Chr 35:5 and refers to divisions of the priests (Ezra) or to the clans (2 Chr). Also,
2 Chr 35:5 refers to the divisions of the Levites. See also the equivalent term in
the Aramaic portions of the MT, e.g., Neh 11:36; 1 Chr 23:6; 24:1; 26:1; 2 Chr
8:14.

[10] S. Japhet, "Law and 'The Law' in Ezra-Nehemiah," 114 ff.

בנדי ומעילי ואכרעה על ברכי ואפרשה כפי אל 'הוה אלהי (6) ואמרה אלהי בשתי
ונכלמתי להרים אלהי פני אליך כי עונתינו רבו למעלה ראש ואשמתנו נדלה
עד לשמים (7) מימי אבתינו אנחנו באשמה נדלה עד היום הזה ובעוונתינו נתנו אנ
תנו תלכ'נ כהנינו ביד מלכי הארצות בחרב בשבי ובבזה ובבשת פנים כהיום הזה

When I heard this matter I tore my tunic and my robe and I tore
out some hair from my head and my beard and I sat, horrified . . . I
spread out my hands to the LORD, my God and I said: 'My God, I
am too ashamed and humiliated to lift up my face to you, my God,
for our sins have multiplied upon our head and our guilt has extended
to the heavens. Since the days of our ancestors, we are in a state of
great guilt, until this very day. Because of our sins, we, our kings, and
our priests were given over into the hands of the kings of the lands,
to the sword, to captivity, to plunder and to shame, just like this day.'

Soon after, Ezra issued the following proclamation in Ezra 9:12:

ועתה בנותיכם אל תתנו לבניהם ובנתיהם אל תשאו לבניכם ולא תדרשו שלמם
וטובתם עד עולם למען תחזקו ואכלתם את טוב הארץ והורשתם לבניכם עד עולם

Now, do not give your daughters to their sons, and do not marry their
daughters to your sons. Do not seek their welfare and well-being ever.

What follows in the next chapter of Ezra is indeed noteworthy: one
of Ezra's officials, Shecaniah ben Yehiel, referred to Ezra's proclamation as divine law. In Ezra 10:3, Shecaniah says:

(3) ועתה נכרת ברית לאלהינו להוציא כל נשים הנולד מהם בעצת אדני והחרדים
במצות אלהינו וכתורה יעשה

Let us make a covenant to our God to send out all of the women
and anyone born from them in keeping with the plan of the LORD
and those who tremble at the command of our God, let him act in
accordance with the Torah.

Many scholars have assumed that, when Shecaniah said that intermarriage should be counteracted "in accordance with the Torah,"
he was saying that intermarriage was prohibited by the Torah of
Moses. There is a strong *pentateuchal basis* for such a prohibition.[11]
The pentateuchal source that is repeatedly cited is Deut 7:3 "do not
make marriages with them; do not give your daughter to his son;
and do not take his daughter for your son." However, it must be
noted that this prohibition is specifically about the local nations and

---

[11] For further discussion of the ban on foreign marriage see chapter 1, n. 28.

does not reflect a general prohibition against intermarriage. Further-more, despite very insightful and creative attempts to explain the relationship between earlier pentateuchal traditions and Ezra's pro-hibition, Deuteronomy contains no *explicit* commandment to divorce foreign women and to expel their children. Indeed, there is no gen-eral prohibition against intermarriage anywhere in the Pentateuch. How are we to explain Shecaniah's claim that this law is Torah? Is it new law? Or, is it part of the old Mosaic Torah?

Most scholars agree that we should understand this passage from Ezra as an early example of interpretation of earlier biblical tradi-tions[12]—namely, that Ezra interprets texts like Deuteronomy 7, and thereby claims that the resulting law reflects the *correct* reading of what was intended by Moses in the Torah.[13] Indeed the same story could be told about Ezra's priestly courses—namely, that this orga-nization of the priests and levites is said to be what Moses intended, or what David and Solomon envisioned.[14]

---

[12] E.g., Yehezkel Kaufmann, *History of Israelite Religion* (8 vols.; Tel Aviv: Bialik Institute, 1964 [Hebrew]), 8:291–93; J. L. Kugel, *The Bible As It Was*, 237–38; J. D. Levenson, "Last Four Verses in Kings," 358 n. 19; J. Blenkinsopp, *Ezra-Nehemiah*, 175 ff. On page 189, Blenkinsopp writes: "The requirement that this be done 'according to the law' is puzzling at first sight, since Pentateuchal law nowhere requires an Israelite to divorce his foreign wife. We must conclude that what is implied here is a particular interpretation of law, and specifically a rigorist inter-pretation of the Deuteronomic law forbidding marriage with the native popula-tion. ... This, then, would be one of several indications in the book of the crucial importance of biblical interpretation as a factor in the struggle to determine the identity and character of the community." On this point see also M. Fishbane, *Biblical Interpretation*, 107–29.

[13] See also Gen 15:19–20; Exod 3:8; 3:17; 33:2; 34:11; Lev 24:10–23; Num 27:1–11; Judg 3:5. For texts which are contemporaneous with Ezra 10 and reflect a similar position, namely that *intermarriage* is tantamount to treachery, see Ezra 10:2; 10:5; 10:10; Neh 1:8; 13:25–27 (9:8 is also relevant although it does not pre-serve the same verb used in Ezra 10); 1 Chr 2:7; 5:27; 9:1; 2 Chr 12:2; 26:1; 26:6; 26:18; 28:19; 28:22; 29:6; 29:19; 30:7; 33:19; 36:14.

[14] Among other serious difficulties, the returnees were clearly divided on the ques-tions of Davidic leadership and the constitution of the priesthood. On the former, see Sara Japhet, "Sheshbazzar and Zerubbabel—Against the Background of the Historical and Religious Tendencies of Ezra-Nehemiah," *ZAW* 94 (1982): 66–98. In this article, Japhet contrasts Zechariah's and Haggai's celebration of a Davidic descendant to Ezra-Nehemiah's silence concerning the Davidic connections of these Second Temple leaders. On the problem of the priesthood, see, e.g., Ezra 2:61–62. Some scholars have suggested that this difficulty was due to the tensions between the Samaritan community in Shechem and the newly constituted community in Jerusalem. See, e.g., H. G. M. Williamson, "The Origins of the Twenty-Four Priestly Courses," 251–68.

I too agree that Ezra is engaged in the interpretation of earlier biblical traditions. However, it seems to me that this point has been repeatedly misformulated. It is important to understand the specific nature of inner-biblical interpretation and, in particular, inner-biblical Mosaic attribution. For what is at stake here is one of the main strategies through which Second Temple Judaism sought to authorize itself. Moreover, we need an understanding of Ezra's practice of inner-biblical interpretation that will allow us to make sense of pseudonymous attribution to Moses in Second Temple texts.

If we impose a post-canonical conception of Scripture and interpretation onto the Second Temple period, we will not be able to make sense of this practice. We must understand Second Temple conceptions of Scripture within their own context.

Here is an example of anachronistic imposition. Yehezkel Kaufmann suggested that what we find in Ezra (in chapters 9 and 10) is one of the earliest examples of inner-biblical interpretation practiced in a manner similar to what will later be designated as *midrash halakhah*. However, although he may be correct in identifying pentateuchal connections with Ezra's prohibition, it cannot be adequate to say, as Kaufmann does, that what we have here is a "genuine *midrash halakhah*" (מדרש הלכה ממש).[15] Perhaps one *could* reconstruct a midrashic derivation of the prohibition against intermarriage, or of the priestly courses and the levitical divisions. Nevertheless, it is essential that no such *derivation* is provided in the Ezra passages themselves. Nor is there any suggestion whatsoever that Ezra or Shecaniah might need to *justify* their attributions to the Law of Moses. The context in which these attributions were made must have differed significantly from the context in which *midrash halakhah* was practiced. The midrashists could not avoid the question of justification. They had to appeal to tradition and/or reasoning in order to authorize their dicta. In the age of *midrash halakhah*, the text of the Law of Moses had become a settled and stable object. I mean not merely that the corpus and the specific texts were relatively fixed—for this was already true in the time of Ezra—but rather that, for the *ba'alei midrash*, there was a clear distinction between *reading* or *citing* a passage and *interpreting* that passage. There is simply no evidence that the distinction between reading or citing *and* interpreting was clearly established by the time of Ezra.

---

[15] Y. Kaufmann, *History of Israelite Religion*, 8:293 [Hebrew].

Ezra could not offer authoritative interpretation without claiming that his reading was Mosaic in origin. But such literal ascription to Moses was no longer possible in Tannaitic or in later Amoraic traditions, which had either to offer a derivation from the biblical text or else to appeal to Oral Torah in order to authorize their interpretations.[16]

The concept of Scripture in Ezra-Nehemiah, is, I suggest, the following. Even if there was a collection of writings known as the Torah of Moses, and even if the term "Torah of Moses" was often used to refer to this collection, it does not follow that the primary function of the term was to *name* this collection of writings. Instead, it may well be that the primary function of this term was to confer authority. Since a particular collection substantially like the Pentateuch had gradually become the most authoritative collection of sacred writings, it makes sense that this collection was the most pre-eminent example of the Torah of Moses. Yet, it was also possible to describe some law or practice as Torah of Moses, even in the absence of any explicit pentateuchal basis.[17]

This account of the concept of Scripture helps us to understand how the texts known as Rewritten Bible and pseudepigrapha could proliferate in the Second Temple period. If we take the term Torah of Moses to designate authoritative sacred writings and their inherited or innovated authoritative interpretations, then we can view Rewritten Bible as an understandable attempt to authorize certain laws and practices by literally inscribing them back into Mosaic Torah. On the other hand, if we anachronistically impose the later conception that the Torah of Moses is the name of an authoritative

---

[16] For some useful discussions of the origin, development, and application of this term in rabbinic literature see Gerald J. Blidstein, "A Note on the Term *Torah She-B'al peh*," *Tarbiz* 42 (1973): 496–98; Robert Brody, "Chapter 6: The Struggle against Heresy," in *The Geonim of Babylonia and the Shaping of Medieval Jewish Culture* (New Haven, Conn.: Yale University Press, 1998), 83–99, esp. 83–85; Peter Schäfer, "Das 'Dogma' von der Mündlichen Torah im Rabbinischen Judentum," 153–97; Martin S. Jaffee, *Torah in the Mouth: Writing and Oral Tradition in Palestinian Judaism, 200 B.C.E.–400 C.E.* (Oxford: Oxford University Press, 2001), 15–61.

[17] See John P. Meier, "Chapter 31: Jesus and the Law: Reciprocal Illumination," in *The Four Final Enigmas: Law, Parables, Titles, and Death* (vol. 4 of *A Marginal Jew. Rethinking the Historical Jesus*; ABRL; 4 vols.; New York: Doubleday, forthcoming): "When we look at the whole of the Jewish Scriptures, the sense of the noun *tôrâ* in Hebrew covers a range of meanings that include 'instruction,' 'teaching,' 'direction,' 'directive,' or 'law,' transmitted in either oral or written form. Needless to say, not every occurrence of the word conveys the whole range of meanings; but often, beyond the denotation of the noun, there are various connotations or resonances."

corpus of texts, then attempts to rewrite the Bible can seem like unscrupulous exercises in literary forgery.

What seems to us to be an interpolation did not seem so to Ezra and his contemporaries.[18] Such procedures may have been the continuation of the work of Ezra and his *mebinim*. Just as there was no distinction between citing and interpreting, so too there was no clear distinction between interpreting and interpolating. It follows that, although there is a continuity between Ezra's interpretive Torah and rabbinic *midrash*, it would be anachronistic to assimilate the former to the latter. Ezra and the Rabbis operate against very different background presuppositions about textual authority and authorship.

Jubilees and תורה שבעל פה *(Oral Torah)*

I will now turn to the example of *Jubilees* and its heavenly and written tradition of interpretation that accompanies that "first law."

At the end of his useful study of *Jubilees'* invocations of the heavenly tablets,[19] García Martínez writes:

> But the most important conclusion which has, at least to my knowledge, not been hitherto pointed out, is that in more than half of the cases in *Jubilees* where the expression HT [Heavenly Tablets] is used, it indicates that the HT function in the same way as the Oral Torah (tôrah shebe'al peh) in Rabbinic Judaism. The HT constitute a hermeneutical recourse which permits the presentation of the "correct" interpretation of the Law, adapting it to the changing situations of life. . . . Thanks to the HT, which are at once the pre-existing Torah, the Book of Destiny, and the Oral Torah, the author is not only able to rewrite history, but also interpret the present and establish a course of conduct which might secure the future.[20]

---

[18] There are, however, well-established Muslim traditions that accuse Ezra of such falsification and pseudonymous attribution. However, the Muslim tradition was by no means monolithic. Some writers defended and even praised Ezra, while others challenged the authenticity of Judaism by claiming that Ezra's Torah was inauthentic. For discussion of the challenges and the history of biblical interpretation of Ezra among Muslim writers, see Hava Lazarus-Yafeh, *Intertwined Worlds: Medieval Islam and Bible Criticism* (Princeton: Princeton University Press, 1992), 19–74; Camilla Adang, *Muslim Writers on Judaism and the Hebrew Bible: From Ibn Rabban to Ibn Hazm* (Leiden: Brill, 1996), 192–255. For an example of a recent study which insists on the authenticity and reliability of Ezra's Torah and transmission, see D. W. Halivni, *Revelation Restored: Divine Writ and Critical Responses*.

[19] F. García Martínez, "The Heavenly Tablets in the Book of Jubilees," 243–60.

[20] Ibid., 259.

Since then, others have found an anticipation of the rabbinic concept of the oral Torah in *Jubilees*' mention of "the first Torah," which
implies that it understands itself as "the second Torah" given to
Moses at Sinai.[21]

In assessing this claim, we must first note the important distinction, drawn by Martin Jaffee, between the claim that there was an
oral activity of transmission and interpretation in Second Temple
times, which is hardly to be doubted, and the claim that this activity was conceptualized in Second Temple times as the rabbinic doctrine of תורה שבעל פה, which is almost certainly false. Jaffee writes:

> In this sense, the oral-performative literary life of Second Temple scribal
> culture is the foundation of what would later emerge in ideological
> garb among the rabbinic Sages as Torah in the Mouth, an oral tra-
> dition represented as a primordial and necessary complement to a
> canonical corpus of sacred writings fixed forever at the moment of
> their original delivery to the prophet from whose pen the text had
> come. But it must be stressed that, *during the Second Temple period itself*,
> there is little evidence for reflection upon text-interpretive or oral-
> performative tradition as a reality independent of the books they brought
> to life. It was, rather, the book itself that dominated the attention of
> those who produced and circulated it.[22]

In the particular case of *Jubilees*, there are two significant disanalo-
gies with later, rabbinic ways of claiming authority. First, the rabbinic idea of an *oral* Torah is surely one way of keeping text and
interpretation distinct, while insisting at the same time on the equal
authority of both. But, of course, *Jubilees* deliberately effaces that distinction by rewriting the Torah. Indeed, from its opening words
onwards,[23] the Book of *Jubilees* calls attention to its own writtenness,
demonstrating an extraordinary interest in writing itself, as well as

---

[21] See C. Werman, "'The תורה and the תעודה engraved on the Tablets," 75–103;
Aharon Shemesh and Cana Werman, "Halakhah at Qumran: Genre and Authority,"
DSD 10 (2003): forthcoming; M. Kister, "על שני מטבעות לשון בספר היובלים," 294–300.
See also the earlier discussion of J. M. Baumgarten, "The Unwritten Law in the
Pre-Rabbinic Period," 13–39.

[22] M. S. Jaffee, *Torah in the Mouth*, 20.

[23] See the prologue of *Jubilees*: "These are the words regarding the divisions of
the times of the law and of the testimony, of the events of the years, of the weeks
of their jubilees throughout all the years of eternity as he related (them) to Moses
on Mt. Sinai when he went up to receive the stone tablets—the law and the commandments—on the Lord's orders as he had told him that he should come up to
the summit of the mountain."

in writing's ability to confer authority. This is most evident in *Jubilees*' insertion of the acts and products of writing at several apparently gratuitous points in its version of familiar biblical stories. I will give just two of the many available examples.

When, for example, Noah divided the earth among his children, he did so by means of a book:

(8:11) When he [Noah] summoned his children, they came to him—they and their children. He divided the earth into the lots which his three sons would occupy. They reached out their hands and took the book from the bosom of their father Noah.

No book is mentioned in Genesis in conjunction with Noah. But how else—as *Jubilees* did not even have to ask—could Noah have established an authoritative and lasting division of the land, forestalling future disputes? Nor is this the only writing that is associated with Noah. In two additional passages, *Jubilees* refers to the "book [or writings] of Noah."[24] Noah must have recorded and then transmitted the divine word in writing, for embodiment in writing is central to *Jubilees*' notion of authoritative tradition.

No less familiar than the Noahide division is the story of Joseph the righteous, resisting the temptation to commit adultery with Mrs. Potiphar. In *Jubilees*' version, writing played *two* essential roles in Joseph's act of resistance:

---

[24] For additional references to the "book(s)" or "writings" of Noah in *Jubilees* see 10:12–14; 21:10. See also 1QapGen 5:29; 1 Enoch 82:1–6; *Aram. Levi Doc.* 57. For the reconstruction of 1QapGen 5:29 see Matthew Morgenstern, Elisha Qimron, and Daniel Sivan (with an appendix by Gregory Bearman and Sheila Spiro), "The Hitherto Unpublished Columns of the Genesis Apocryphon," *AbrN* 33 (1995): 30–41, esp. 41. For a brief comparison between the Genesis Apocryphon and the book of *Jubilees*, see C. A. Evans, "The Genesis Apocryphon and the Rewritten Bible," 153–65, esp. 156–58 and 162–64. See also, J. L. Kugel, *The Bible As It Was*, 406–7. In his discussion, Kugel cites *Aram. Levi Doc.* 57 and 1 Enoch 82:1–6 as illustrations of this interpretive motif.

A considerable amount of secondary literature focuses on the question whether or not written traditions called the "book(s) of Noah" existed in the Second Temple period. See, e.g., Richard C. Steiner, "The Heading of the *Book of the Words of Noah* on a Fragment of the Genesis Apocryphon: New Light on a 'Lost' Work," *DSD* 2 (1995): 66–71; Florentino García Martínez, *Qumran and Apocalyptic: Studies on the Aramaic Texts from Qumran* (STDJ 9; Leiden: Brill, 1992), 24–44; Nathaniel Schmidt, "The Apocalypse of Noah and the Parables of Enoch," in *Oriental Studies Published in Commemoration of the Fortieth Anniversary of Paul Haupt* (ed. C. Adler and A. Ember; Baltimore: Johns Hopkins University Press, 1926), 111–23. However, not all scholars are in agreement as to the existence of such a "book of Noah." See, e.g., Jack P. Lewis, *A Study of the Interpretation of Noah and the Flood in Jewish and Christian Literature* (Leiden: Brill, 1978), 10–15.

(39:5) Now Joseph was well formed and very handsome. The wife of his master looked up, saw Joseph, loved him, and pleaded with him to lie with her. (6) But he did not surrender himself. He remembered the Lord and what his father Jacob would read to him from the words of Abraham—that no one is to commit adultery with a woman who has a husband; that there is a death penalty which has been ordained for him in heaven before the most high Lord. The sins will be entered regarding him in the eternal books forever before the Lord. (7) Joseph remembered what he had said and refused to lie with her.

Here Joseph recalls the voice of his father, reading to him from an ancestral book. Moreover what Joseph recalls from the book is not simply that adultery is prohibited, but rather that the prohibition is so severe that an act of adultery will be inscribed upon "eternal books forever before the Lord."[25]

To be sure, other ancient biblical interpretations also claim that Joseph refused to sin because of the teaching his father had taught him, but *Jubilees* modifies this claim by stating that there was a book involved.[26] Apparently, the author(s) of *Jubilees* thought it crucial to assert that a *book* had set out the prohibition so valiantly obeyed by Joseph, and likewise that an act of eternal *inscription* had determined on high the penalty that would follow the transgression of that law.

The second major disanalogy between *Jubilees* and rabbinic claims to authority concerns the role of Sinai. For the Rabbis, Sinai is the crucial moment of revelation and Moses is the primary recipient and tradent of revelation. They may, on occasion, assert that a certain law or practice is patriarchal in origin. But, in general, the authority of law and practice depends on revelation at Sinai, and it is at Sinai that Moses is said to have received both the written and oral Torot. In contrast, *Jubilees* repeatedly draws attention to the notion that Moses is not the first to receive the written calendrical and historical revelations to which so much importance is attached. These doctrines are said to be based on a written, heavenly tradition that long pre-dates Sinai.[27] Drawing upon Second Temple traditions known to us from other sources, this written tradition is associated in *Jub.* 4:16–19 with Enoch, who was simultaneously the first literate human,

[25] J. L. Kugel, "Part I: Joseph in the Bible," in *In Potiphar's House*, 23.
[26] See J. L. Kugel, *The Bible As It Was*, 258.
[27] Later versions of these claims are preserved in rabbinic traditions e.g., *Pirqe R. El.* ch. 8 (Warsaw, 1852); reprinted with commentary of David Luria (Jerusalem, 1970).

the first master of calendrical knowledge, and the first "to write a testimony" as the eternal scribe of human history.

(4:16) In the eleventh jubilee [491–539] Jared took a wife for himself, and her name was Barakah, the daughter of Rasu'eyal, the daughter of his father's *brother*, in the fourth week of this jubilee [512–18]. She gave birth to a son for him during the fifth week, in the fourth year, of the jubilee [522], and he named him Enoch. (17) He was the first of mankind who were born on the earth who learned (the art of) writing, instruction, and wisdom and who wrote down in a book the signs of the sky in accord with the fixed pattern of their months so that mankind would know the seasons of the years according to the fixed patterns of each of their months. (18) He was the first to write a testimony. He testified to mankind in the generations of the earth: The weeks of the jubilees he related, and made known the sabbaths of the years, as we had told him. (19) While he slept he saw in a vision what has happened and what will occur—how things will happen for mankind during their history until the day of judgment. He saw everything and understood. He wrote a testimony for himself and placed it upon the earth against all mankind and for their history.

Indeed, it is with Enoch, according to both *Jubilees* and 1 Enoch, that pre-Sinaitic sacred writing originates. Below is *Jubilees'* explanation of the passage from Gen 5:21–24 stating that Enoch "walked with God":[28]

(4:20) During the twelfth jubilee, in its seventh week [582–88] he took a wife for himself. Her name was Edni, the daughter of Daniel, the daughter of his father's *brother*. In the sixth year of this week [587] she gave birth to a son for him, and he named him Methuselah. (21) He was, moreover, with God's angels for six jubilees of years. They showed him everything on earth and in the heavens—the dominion of the sun—and he wrote down everything. (22) He testified to the Watchers who had sinned with the daughters of men because these had begun to mix with earthly women so that they became defiled. Enoch testified against all of them. (23) He was taken from human society, and we led him into the Garden of Eden for (his) greatness and honor. Now he is there writing down the judgment and condemnation of the world and all the wickedness of mankind. (24) Because of him the flood water did not come on any of the land of Eden because he was placed there as a sign and to testify against all people in order to tell all the deeds of history until the day of judgment.

---

[28] On the history of interpretation of Gen 5:21–24, see J. L. Kugel, *The Bible As It Was*, 100–7.

Thus, Enoch is eternally recording a written record of the actions of all human beings in the heavens.[29] Long before Moses ascended Mount Sinai, the calendrical and historical tradition inscribed upon the heavenly tablets was transmitted, in the form of a written tradition, to Enoch and then Noah and the patriarchs. To underscore the divine authority of this written transmitted tradition, repeated revelations to its tradents are recorded. But it nevertheless seems vital to *Jubilees* to emphasize the continuity of transmission, and, in the light of *Jubilees'* assumption about the intimate link between authority and writing, it is hardly surprising that the transmission of the tradition must be accompanied by the transmission of literacy. Thus, although Abraham came from a family of idol worshippers, in *Jub.* 11:14–17, it is reported that his writing instructor was his father, Terah. Abraham had to withdraw from the community of idolaters before he could receive divine revelation. Yet it was to his father's ancient books that God directed him:

> (12:25) Then the Lord God said to me: 'Open his [Abram's] mouth and his ears to hear and speak with his tongue in the revealed language'. For from the day of the collapse it had disappeared from the mouth(s) of all mankind. (26) I opened his mouth, ears, and lips and began to speak Hebrew with him—in the language of creation. (27) He took his fathers' books[30] (they were written in Hebrew) and copied them. From that time he began to study them, while I was telling him everything that he was unable (to understand). He studied them throughout the six rainy months.

So essential for the authority of teaching is continuous written tradition,[31] that *Jubilees* must find continuity even where it must also

---

[29] See also *Jub.* 10:17. The claim that the calendar, the history of the creation of the world and the cosmos are already written upon heavenly tablets is attested in a number of texts at Qumran. See, e.g., the discussion of 4Q180 by Armin Lange: "The predestined and pre-existent order of the world was inscribed on the heavenly tablets and revealed to Moses on Mount Sinai in the form of the Torah. Thus, the sapiential idea of a pre-existent order of the world is fused with the motif of the heavenly tablets and the Torah. Here it is of importance to recognize that the epochal pattern of history itself is part of this predestined order of world and history" ("Wisdom and Predestination in the Dead Sea Scrolls," *DSD* 2 [1995]: 340–54, citation 353).

[30] For a helpful discussion of this passage and of the question of whether a book or books of Noah existed, see J. C. VanderKam, *The Book of Jubilees*, 2:116. See also R. C. Steiner, "The Heading of the *Book of the Words of Noah* on a Fragment of the Genesis Apocryphon," 67–68 n. 13.

[31] E.g., later on in *Jub.* 19:13–15, Jacob also learns to write.

emphasize discontinuity: between the first patriarch and the idolatrous society whose errors he fled in order to found a distinct and separate people.[32] In *Jubilees*, Abraham's rejection of idolatry and discovery of the truth are given a bookish twist.

Rediscovered by Abraham, the tradition revealed to Enoch on heavenly tablets and transmitted to future generations by Enoch the testimonial scribe, is then transmitted via Jacob and Levi to Amram and, finally, to Moses, and the transmission is punctuated by further revelations of heavenly texts. Thus, when *Jubilees* retells the story of Jacob's revelation at Bethel, the events which will befall his children in the future are revealed in the form of heavenly books, which he must write down once he awakens.[33] God reassures Jacob about his ability to recall what he read in his vision:

> (32:24) "Do not be afraid because everything will happen just as you have seen and read. Now you write down everything just as you have seen and read." (25) Then Jacob said: "Lord, how shall I remember everything just as I have read and seen?" He said to him: "I will remind you of everything." (26) When he had gone from him, he awakened and remembered everything that he had read and seen. He wrote down all the things that he had read and seen.

The narrative in Genesis leaves the content and significance of Jacob's vision unclear. But *Jubilees* tells us both the historical content of Jacob's vision, which turns out to be prophetic, and the authoritative basis of that prophetic history, which carries weight because it is inscribed on tablets, from which Jacob reads with the help of an angel. *Jubilees* reports that Jacob was daunted by the responsibility of accurately transcribing what he had read, and that he was blessed with divine assurance that his transcription would indeed be accurate. Jacob, in turn, gives his books to Levi:

---

[32] See Josh 24:2.

[33] According to 11QT 29:7–9 Jacob received a divine covenant at Bethel. See Yigael Yadin, *The Temple Scroll*, 1:182; 2:128–29. See also: J. Schwartz, "Jubilees, Bethel and the Temple of Jacob," 63–85; J. L. Wentling, "Unraveling the Relationship," 61–73; D. D. Swanson, "'A Covenant Just Like Jacob's,'" 273–86; M. O. Wise, "The Covenant of Temple Scroll XXIX, 3–10," 49–60; idem, "The Eschatological Vision of the Temple Scroll," 155–72. For additional texts reflecting the importance of Jacob's dream in Second Temple literature, see, e.g., *T. Levi* 9:3–5; Philo, *De Somniis*; *The Ladder of Jacob*. For further discussion of the interpretive traditions which grew out of Gen 28:11–17, see J. L. Kugel, "Levi's Elevation to the Priesthood in Second Temple Writings," 1–64; idem, "The Ladder of Jacob," 209–28; idem, "The Ladder Was a Message," in *The Bible As It Was*, 211–13; J. C. VanderKam, "*Jubilees*' Exegetical Creation of Levi the Priest," 359–73.

> (45:16) He [Jacob] gave all his books and the books of his fathers to
> his son Levi so that he could preserve them and renew them for his
> sons until today.

This is of no small significance, since Moses is of course a Levite.[34]
It should be no surprise by now that, although Exodus makes no
mention of any connection between Moses and his Levite father,
Jubilees reports that Amram taught Moses the art of writing:

> (47:9) Afterwards, when you had grown up, you were brought to the
> pharaoh's *daughter* and became her child. Your father *Amram* taught
> you (the art of writing).

We are not explicitly told that Moses received the written tradition
of books from Amram. But we may nevertheless say that, when
Moses received that tradition from the angel of the presence on
Mount Sinai, he was inheriting a tradition long known to his family, an inheritance for which he had been prepared when his father
taught him to write.

While such specific examples illustrate *Jubilees'* interest in writing,
they also lead us to what certainly was, for *Jubilees*, a related question, namely, that of the book's own claim to authority. For *Jubilees*,
authoritative teaching consistently takes the form of writing including, prominently, writing that is found on heavenly tablets whose
contents are revealed to humans and then transmitted in written
books.[35] Indeed, such teachings are not only doubly written, but also
archaic, dating literally to the origin of the world.

This view of authoritative doctrine has significant implications for
the status of Mosaic Torah. For, when Moses transcribed a revelation
of heavenly tablets at Sinai, he was repeating a scene that had already
occurred numerous times, and even the historical and calendrical
contents of his revelation had long been practiced,[36] revealed, and

---

[34] For some discussion of the importance of the process of transmission from
Noah to Levi (via Shem, Abraham, and Jacob), see John M. Allegro, *The Dead Sea
Scrolls and the Christian Myth* (Amherst, N.Y.: Prometheus, 1992), 65–66.

[35] J. C. VanderKam convincingly argues that although *Jubilees* refers to the heavenly written traditions (e.g., tablets, books, writings), in several ways they all refer
to the same written heavenly collection. See his discussion in *Enoch and the Growth
of an Apocalyptic Tradition* (CBQMS 16; Washington, D.C.: Catholic Biblical Association
of America, 1984), 151.

[36] M. Fishbane writes, "It is significant to observe that a number of exegetical
traditions are authorized in the Book of *Jubilees* by their observance by the pious
patriarchs themselves" (*Biblical Interpretation*, 528). This way of authorizing an exegetical

transmitted.[37] The point of *Jubilees'* massive elaboration and contextualization of the Sinai scene is, of course, to undergird the authority of its own interpretation of the Law, especially of calendrical law, which must have been a hotly contested issue. While the authority of Moses' revelation at Sinai is invoked on behalf of the solar calendar, that authority is at the same time downgraded. Moses was not unique; he was one of many bookish heroes charged with the transcription of heavenly tablets. These traditions originated in the heavens and are a direct product of divine utterance, perhaps even divine writing. This too should be seen as an authority-claiming strategy: in a time of conflicting interpretations and practices, authority rests with those who possess not only the traditions of Moses, but also the archaic books of Enoch.

In contrast to the familiar Christian claim to *supersede* the Sinaitic covenant with a *new* covenant, which also emerges from Second Temple disputes about law and its authority, *Jubilees* invokes an *archaic*, pre-Sinaitic covenant, whose pre-eminence depends on its claim to *precede* Sinai.[38] Any interpretation of the Law that was not based on knowledge of this older covenant was *ipso facto* inauthentic, even if it appeared to be based on pentateuchal texts, for those texts could be authentically read only through the lens of the primordial tradition. On the basis of such ideas, Second Temple sectarians challenged the practice of the Jerusalem establishment, which they regarded as inauthentic.[39] In the case of *Jubilees*, it should hardly

---

tradition continues in later rabbinic traditions. Cf. the rabbinic attempt to authorize the law of ערוב תבשילין in *Ber. Rab.*, *Parsha Vayiggash*, 95:3 (ed. Theodor-Albeck; Jerusalem: Wahrmann, 1965), 1189, lines 4–5; *b. Yoma* 28b.

[37] This point is made by a number of scholars, e.g., J. C. VanderKam in "The Putative Author of the Book of Jubilees," 213. In addition, A. Lange notes a connection between 4Q180 and *Jub.* 1:27 in "Wisdom and Predestination in the Dead Sea Scrolls," 353 n. 31.

[38] For additional discussion of pre-Sinaitic law see, G. A. Anderson, "The Status of the Torah Before Sinai," 1–30; J. M. Baumgarten, "The Unwritten Law in the Pre-Rabbinic Period," 13–38; J. L. Kugel, "The Jubilees Apocalypse," 322–38.

[39] A similar claim, one might argue, continues in early Christian traditions such as the *Epistle to the Hebrews* where the authority of Jesus is said to have preceded that of Aaron the priest and Moses the lawgiver, long before Sinai. See, e.g., Harold W. Attridge, *The Epistle to the Hebrews: A Commentary on the Epistle to the Hebrews* (Hermeneia; Philadelphia: Fortress, 1989), 54 n. 58 and n. 59; M. R. D'Angelo, "Chapter Four: Moses Likened to the Son of God According to Glory: The Theological Function of Moses in Hebrews," in *Moses in the Letter to the Hebrews*, 151–200.

surprise us, in light of the above evidence of *Jubilees'* repeated association of authority with writing, that the authentic pre-Sinaitic tradition is presented as written on heavenly tablets, from which angels
dictate to select human scribes.[40] Even if it is ultimately concluded
that both *Jubilees'* appeal to heavenly tablets and rabbinic appeal to
Torah she-b'al peh are participants in Mosaic Discourse, we are dealing here with very different conceptions of the authority of text and
author.

Unwritten Natural Law and Written Mosaic Law

Considerable confusion has resulted from the fact that Philo refers
to the Law of Nature as *unwritten* law.[41] Some, who are inclined to

---

[40] A number of prominent scholars have connected *Jubilees'* repeated appeal to
pre-Mosaic authority with the following passage from 1 Macc 1:11: "In those days
certain renegades came out from Israel and misled many, saying 'Let us go and
make a covenant with the Gentiles around us, for since we separated from them
many disasters have come upon us.'" *Jubilees'* repeated insistence upon pre-Sinaitic
written law can be understood as a challenge to those "renegades" who had a very
different conception of pre-Mosaic life. If this is the correct context for *Jubilees'*
claims, then *Jubilees* should be dated roughly around the time of Antiochus IV
(175–164). There are additional arguments for such a dating. See J. C. VanderKam,
"The Origins and Purposes of the Book of Jubilees," 3–24. On page 21, VanderKam
writes: "*Jubilees'* emphatic insistence on the election of the Jewish people from the
very beginning and on the claim that the pre-Mosaic ancestors lived according to
the pentateuchal law directly addresses such assertions. The writer says in effect
that there never was such a pristine, 'golden' time. The law was always there on
the heavenly tablets and, beginning with Adam and Eve, the chosen, those joined
to God in the covenant, lived by those laws as they were revealed to them." For
similar claims about the historical context in which *Jubilees* appeals to pre-Mosaic,
heavenly traditions see, e.g., John C. Endres, *Biblical Interpretation of the Book of Jubilees*
(CBQMS 18; Washington, D.C.: Catholic Biblical Association of America, 1987),
226–38; Eberhard Schwarz, *Identität durch Abgrenzung: Abgrenzungsprozesse in Israel im 2.
vorchristlichen Jahrhundert und ihre traditionsgeschichtlichen Voraussetzungen. Zugleich ein Beitrag
zur Erforschung des Jubiläenbuches* (Europäische Hochschulschriften 23/162; Frankfurt:
Lang, 1982), 99–126.
[41] Philo is not alone in identifying unwritten law with the Law of Nature. The
identification is common among Hellenistic writers, who thereby sought an ancient
pedigree for their new concept. For example, Stoics sought a Socratic precedent in
Xenophon, *Mem.* 4.4.19–21. See G. Striker, "Plato's Socrates and the Stoics,"
241–51. The unwritten law referred to in early Greek texts was divine, eternal and
superior to written law, and in these respects it was like the Law of Nature referred
to in later texts. However, there is a significant historical development of the term
"unwritten law" in Greek literature. When Sophocles, Socrates, or Aristotle spoke
of unwritten law, they were referring to certain norms obeyed in all known societies that were considered worthy of respect, norms that could therefore be assumed

view Philo as more of a Hellenist than a Jew, have taken him to be thereby conceding that the written Law of Moses has a secondary status.[42] Others, who are inclined to view him as more Jew than Hellenist, have taken him to be thereby invoking a proto-rabbinic oral law.[43] I believe that *neither* position is correct. However, there is a kernel of truth in the anachronistic idea that Philo had a proto-type of the oral law, a kernel of truth that must be carefully distinguished from the idea's misleading formulation.

Here, for example, is a characterization of Abraham that might be wrongly taken to show that Philo takes the unwritten Law of Nature to be superior to the written Law of Moses (*Abr.* 274–276):

πρεσβύτερος μὲν οὖν καὶ πρῶτος ἔστι τε καὶ λεγέσθω ὁ ἀστεῖος, νεώτερος δὲ καὶ ἔσχατος πᾶς ἄφρων, τὰ νεωτεροποιὰ καὶ ἐν ἐσχατιαῖς ταττόμενα μετιών. ταῦτα μὲν οὖν ἐπὶ τοσοῦτον εἰρήσθω. τῷ δὲ πλήθει καὶ μεγέθει τῶν ἐπαίνων ἐπιτιθεὶς ὥσπερ τινὰ καφαλὴν τοῦ σοφοῦ φησιν, ὅτι τὸν θεῖον νόμον καὶ τὰ θεῖα προστάγματα πάντα ἐποίησεν ὁ ἀνὴρ οὗτος (), οὐ γράμμασιν ἀναδιδαχθείς, ἀλλ᾽ ἀγράφῳ τῇ φύσει σπουδάσας ὑγιαινούσαις καὶ ἀνόσοις ὁρμαῖς ἐπακολουθῆσαι· περὶ δὲ ὧν ὁ θεὸς ὁμολογεῖ, τί προσῆκεν ἀνθρώπους ἢ βεβαιότατα πιστεύειν; τοιοῦτος ὁ βίος τοῦ πρώτου καὶ ἀρχη-

to be either of divine origin or, at any rate, of some origin that the gods themselves would respect. They seem to have had no notion that such norms might be derived from nature, whether human or cosmic. These earlier Greeks understood unwritten law to be *social* in origin, even if it was universal. So when Antigone (450–460) appeals to the "gods' unwritten and secure practices" which "live not just now and yesterday, but always forever," the appeal is to a social norm which is eternally binding. Later Hellenistic thinkers fused the ancient concept of unwritten law with the new Stoic idea of Natural Law; unwritten law thereby came to be understood as *natural* in origin, contrary to its original usage. For an incisive study of the Law of Nature in the Letter of James see Matt A. Jackson-McCabe, *Logos and Law in the Letter of James: The Law of Nature, the Law of Moses, and the Law of Freedom* (NovTSup 100; Leiden: Brill, 2001), esp. 29–134.
   [42] André Myre develops a view of a higher law where Mosaic Law is ultimately superseded by the higher law in the following three articles: "La loi l'ordre cosmique et politique selon Philon d'Alexandrie," *ScEs* 24 (1972): 217–47; idem, "La loi et la Pentateuque selon Philon d'Alexandrie," *ScEs* 25 (1973): 208–25; idem, "La Loi de la Nature et la loi Mosaic selon Philon d'Alexandrie," *ScEs* 28 (1976): 163–81, esp. 176ff. See also E. R. Goodenough, *By Light, Light*, 73–96; Samuel Sandmel, *Philo's Place in Judaism: A Study of Conceptions of Abraham in Jewish Literature* (New York: KTAV, 1971), 109.
   [43] Earle Hilgert, "Philo Judaeus et Alexandrinus," in *The School of Moses: Studies in Philo and Hellenistic Religion* (ed. J. P. Kenney; BJS 304; Atlanta: Scholars Press, 1995), 1–15; Naomi G. Cohen, *Philo Judaeus: His Universe of Discourse* (BEATAJ 24; Frankfurt am Main: Lang, 1995); idem, "The Jewish Dimension of Philo's Judaism," 165–86; Samuel Belkin, *Philo and the Oral Law* (Cambridge, Mass.: Harvard University Press, 1940).

γέτου τοῦ ἔθνους ἐστίν, ὡς μὲν ἔνιοι φήσουσι, νόμιμος, ὡς δ' ὁ παρ' ἐμοῦ
λόγος ἔδειξε, νόμος αὐτὸς ὢν καὶ θεσμὸς ἄγραφος.

So, then the man of worth is elder and first, and so must he be called;
but younger and last is every fool who pursues the ways which belong
to rebellious youth and stand lowest in the list. So much for all this,
but to these praises of the Sage, so many and so great, Moses adds
this crowning saying "that this man did the divine law and the divine
commands." He did them, not taught by written words, but unwritten nature gave him the zeal to follow where wholesome and untainted
impulse led him. And when they have God's promises before them
what should men do but trust in them most firmly? Such was the life
of the first, the founder of the nation, one who obeyed the law, some
will say, but rather, as our discourse has shown, himself a law and an
unwritten statute.

In short, Abraham followed the law because he succeeded in grasping the unwritten law of nature by means of his own reason.[44] This

---

[44] The claim that Abraham kept the commandments or, more generally, that
"the patriarchs fulfilled the commandments," appears in a number of rabbinic traditions. For example, b. Yoma 28b, reports that Abraham *fulfilled* the commandments,
suggesting that he was *commanded* to observe them, whereas m. Qidd. 4:14 says that
Abraham *performed* the commandments, without any suggestion that he was acting
under orders. Commentators struggle with the question: what is the relationship
between this Amoraic tradition and the much older Mishnaic tradition? The Maharsha'
(Samuel Eliezer ben Edels, 1555–1631) in his b. Yoma 28b (ad loc), suggests that
m. Qidd. 4:14 is claiming that Abraham only performed the positive commandments.
The passage from b. Yoma, however, suggests that Abraham was commanded to do
all of the *mitzvot* and thus he has an obligation to *fulfill* them. This, the Maharsha'
argues, is implied in the verb *to fulfill*. Cf. t. Qidd., chapter 5 (Zuckermandel, 344).
The tradition that the patriarchs established the fixed prayers is a particular manifestation of this claim, e.g., *Tanḥuma Yelamdenu, Parsha Chayyei Sarah*, 5 (Vienna, 1863).
This tradition that the patriarchs instituted prayers also appears in b. Ber. 26b.
See Rashi (Solomon ben Isaac, 1040–1105) ad loc. Rashi's comment on b. Ber. 26b
suggests that the debate consists of whether the patriarchs instituted the prayers
(prior to Sinai) or whether the Great Assembly instituted the prayers (during the
Second Temple period). This is a very interesting comment by Rashi because
nowhere in the passage (b. Ber. 26b) does it suggest that this institution of prayer
which corresponds to the sacrifices was instituted prior to the destruction in 70 c.e.
But, b. Ber. 33a describes prayer as one of a number of things that the Great
Assembly instituted without the any reference to the correspondence between daily
sacrifice and daily prayer. Perhaps Rashi's comment on b. Ber. 26b was influenced
by the tradition preserved in b. Ber. 33a. Similarly, the beraitot cited in b. Ber. 26b;
y. Ber. 2:1, as well as the discussion of instituted prayers in t. Ber. 3:1, say nothing
about *when* the prayers were instituted (pre-destruction or post-destruction). The
Rabbis, however, reported that prayers were already said in conjunction with the
daily temple sacrifices by the *mishmarot*. On this see m. Ta'an. 4:2; *massechet Sof* 17:5.
With the *exception* of the b. Ber. 26b and the *She'iltot de Rav Achai Gaon, Parsha Lech
Lecha, She'ilta* 8 (Jerusalem 1986), 44, all other witnesses to this Midrash (*Ber. Rab.,*

is a remarkable achievement, which sets Abraham apart from those who are fortunate enough to live after the time of Moses, who need only to obey the written law (*Abr.* 16):[45]

πολλὰ μὲν οὖν οἱ νομοθέται, πολλὰ δὲ οἱ πανταχοῦ νόμοι πραγματεύονται περὶ τοῦ τὰς ψυχὰς τῶν ἐλευθέρων ἐλπίδων χρηστῶν ἀναπλῆσαι· ὁ δ᾽ ἄνευ παραινέσεως δίχα τοῦ κελευσθῆναι γενόμενος εὔελπις ἀγράφῳ μὲν νόμῳ δὲ πάλιν αὐτομαθεῖ τὴν ἀρετὴν ταύτην πεπαίδευται, ὃν ἡ φύσις ἔθηκε.

Great indeed are the efforts expended both by lawgivers and by laws in every nation in filling the souls of free men with comfortable hopes; but he who gains this virtue of hopefulness without being led to it by exhortation or command has been educated into it by a law which nature has laid down, a law unwritten yet intuitively learnt.

However, the fact that Abraham's pre-Sinaitic *achievement* is greater than the achievement of Jews who obey the written Law of Moses does not imply that the unwritten law is greater than the written law.[46] Rather, the unwritten Law of Nature is *embodied* by written

---

Tanḥuma Yelamdenu and the Palestinian Talmud) attribute the claim that the patriarchs instituted the prayers to Rabbi Yehoshua ben Levi. This position (that the patriarchs instituted the prayers) in *b. Berakhot* and *She'iltot*, however, is attributed to Rabbi Yossi ben Ḥanina.

For further discussion about the version in the Babylonian Talmud see Raphael N. Rabinowitz, *Diqduqei Sofrim* (12 vols.; Jerusalem: Magnes, 1968), 1:133–35; 133 n. ב; 135 notes ש, ר, פ in the *haggahot*; *Pirqe R. El.*, chapter 8 and *Ber. Rab.* 68:9 (Albeck, 799). See also, Maimonides *Sefer haMitzvot, shoresh sheni*: "All that was not heard at Sinai in full clarity is considered *Divrei Sofrim*." Maimonides argues that *Divrei Sofrim* refers to the thirteen hermeneutical rules. It is less clear from the earlier rabbinic sources that there is *necessarily* a clear distinction between *Divrei Sofrim* and *Oral Torah*. See, e.g., *b. ʿErub.* 21b; *m. Ber.* 1:5; *m. Yebam.* 2:4; *b. Yebam.* 21a; *t. Taʿan.* 2:6.

On this motif, see, E. E. Urbach, *The Sages*, 335–36; Isaak Heinemann, *Darkhei Ha'Aggada* (Jerusalem: Magnes, 1949), 35–39; Israel M. Ta-Shema in his article "Abraham: In the Aggadah," *Encyclopedia Judaica* 2:115; H. Albeck's expanded notes (*hashlamot vetosaphot*) to his commentary on *m. Qidd.* 4:14, in his *Shisha Sidrei Mishnah* (Jerusalem: Mosad Bialik and Tel Aviv: Dvir, 1952) where he implies that *Jubilees* and Philo are two proto-rabbinic traditions which have *the same* view as the Rabbis. Albeck is not alone in this respect and until very recently, many scholars assumed (and some still do) that elements of shared interpretation suggested straightforward continuity between the Second Temple and Rabbinic periods.

[45] On this passage, see John W. Martens, "Unwritten Law in Philo: A Response to Naomi G. Cohen," *JJS* 43 (1992): 38–45: "The unwritten law is not only the physical representative of the law of nature, but it is the law of nature itself. Of course, a physical representation of the law of nature is the law of nature, but here the connection is made explicit" (44 n. 31).

[46] In *Spec.* 4.150, Philo writes: "Praise cannot be duly given to one who obeys

Mosaic Law,[47] which is therefore "stamped, as it were, with the seals of nature itself" (*Mos.* 2.14). It is just this idea—that a written text can have the highest authority, here conceived as the authority of nature—that is all but unthinkable for the Hellenistic mind, yet it is just this idea that is essential for Philo's Jewish commitment to Mosaic Torah. Those who miss this aspect of Philo's thinking are missing what is revolutionary about his use of Hellenistic terms to authorize a sacred, written text.

What of those who take Philo's unwritten law to be a prototype of the rabbinic תורה שבעל פה?[48] There is an important kernel of truth here, for Philo explicitly acknowledges his indebtedness to what he takes to be ancient, extra-pentateuchal interpretive traditions. Even when he does not register this fact explicitly, comparison of his work with other Second Temple texts or with later rabbinic texts shows that his interpretations include inherited elements of what would later be called rabbinic תורה שבעל פה.[49]

However, it is nonetheless misleading to say that Philo is refer-ring to an oral Torah when he speaks of unwritten law. First, as I

---

the written laws, since he acts under the admonition of restraint and the fear of punishment. But he who faithfully observes the unwritten deserves commendation, since the virtue which he displays is freely willed."

[47] Many scholars have argued for this position. See, for example, Isaak Heinemann, "Die Lehre vom Ungeschriebenen Gesetz im jüdischen Schriftum," *HUCA* 4 (1930–31): 149–71, esp. 152 ff.; H. A. Wolfson, *Philo*; P. Borgen, *Philo of Alexandria: An Exegete For His Time*; V. Nikiprowetsky, "Loi De Moïse, Loi De Nature, Sagesse," 116–54; J. W. Martens, "Philo and the 'Higher' Law," 309–22; idem, "Unwritten Law in Philo," 38–45; R. A. Horsley, "The Law of Nature in Philo and Cicero," 35–59.

[48] See, e.g., S. Belkin, *Philo and the Oral Law*. Although N. G. Cohen claims that she is not arguing for Belkin's position, she nevertheless suggests in much of her writing that the connection between *unwritten law* and the rabbinic *oral law* can be argued in a number of cases. See N. G. Cohen, *Philo Judaeus*; idem, "'Agraphos Nomos' in Philo's Writings—a New Examination," *Da'at* 15 (1985): 5–20 [Hebrew]; idem, "The Jewish Dimension of Philo's Judaism," 165–86. I maintain that such a reading is misleading and blurs an important feature of Philo's appropriation of the ancient Greek *unwritten law* and his larger project of arguing for the universal impor-tance of Mosaic Law. This is accomplished in part by demonstrating that Judaism, like ancient Greek traditions, has an unwritten law and unwritten custom which is ancient and authoritative. Ellen Birnbaum argues that Cohen misunderstands Philo's universalist project ("Review of *Philo Judaeus: His Universe of Discourse*, by Naomi G. Cohen," *StPhA* 8 [1996]: 189–96). For a very helpful evaluation of the existing scholarship on the relationship between Philo and Judaism see E. Hilgert, "Philo Judaeus et Alexandrinus," 1–15.

[49] This has been amply demonstrated most recently by P. Borgen, *Philo of Alexandria An Exegete For His Time*; and J. L. Kugel, *The Bible As It Was*. In addition, see the earlier work of S. Belkin, *Philo and the Oral Law*, and N. G. Cohen, *Philo Judaeus*; idem, "The Jewish Dimension of Philo's Judaism."

have already indicated, the term "*agraphos nomos*" is a standard Greek term and is used by Philo, as by his Stoic contemporaries, to refer to the Law of Nature. Second, even if Philo inherited and shared many of the interpretive traditions that would later be called rabbinic תורה שבעל פה,[50] that name carries with it a very specific conception of the authority of these traditions, a conception that is quite different from Philo's conception of unwritten law.[51]

The Rabbis who used the term understood the authority of their interpretive traditions to be based on the fact that these traditions had been transmitted through a chain of identifiable tradents, a chain beginning with God's transmission to Moses of both the written Torah and its equally authoritative extra-pentateuchal interpretations and accompaniments. On this conception, the authority of a tradition depends on its origination in God's revelation to Moses on Sinai and on the accuracy of its subsequent transmission.[52] The idea reflects a particular mode of oral pedagogy that may be traced back to the Tannaitic period and that continued and developed in the Amoraic and later Geonic periods.[53] As I have said, Philo certainly shared versions of many of the traditions that were passed down to the Rabbis in this way.[54] He also regarded the institution of the public reading of Mosaic Torah, accompanied by authorized exposition as an extremely important feature of Judaism, a feature which was almost certainly derived from the practice initiated in Neh 8:1–8.[55]

---

[50] On the use and development of this term in rabbinic literature see G. J. Blidstein, "A Note on the Term *Torah She-B'al peh*," 496–98; P. Schäfer, "'Das 'Dogma' von der Mündlichen Torah im Rabbinischen Judentum"; E. E. Urbach, "The Written Law and the Oral Law," 286–314; R. Brody, "Chapter 6: The Struggle against Heresy," in *The Geonim of Babylonia and the Shaping of Medieval Jewish Culture*, 83–99, esp. 83–85.

[51] J. L. Kugel, "At Mt. Sinai," in *The Bible As It Was*: "This conception is quite distinct from the concept of 'unwritten law' in Philo, which is hardly to be equated with the 'oral Torah' of later rabbinic literature" (401 n. 19).

[52] See, e.g., *m. Abot* 1:1.

[53] See the recent studies by Michael S. Berger, *Rabbinic Authority* (New York: Oxford University Press, 1998) and by R. Brody, *The Geonim of Babylonia and the Shaping of Medieval Jewish Culture*.

[54] For example, "I will . . . tell the story of Moses as I have learned it, both from sacred books, the wonderful monuments of his wisdom which he has left behind him, and from some of the elders of the nation; for I always interwove what I was told with what I read, and thus believed myself to have a closer knowledge than others of his life's history" (*Mos.* 1.4). For additional examples and discussion of the "traditions of the elders" see J. L. Kugel, *The Bible As It Was*, 400–1.

[55] "What then did he [Moses] do? *He required them to assemble in the same place on these seventh days, and sitting together in a respectful and orderly manner hear the laws read so*

Yet Philo's conception of the authority of interpretive traditions was
entirely different both from earlier Second Temple conceptions, such
as that found in the book of *Jubilees*, and from later rabbinic conception. For Philo, the pentateuchal and extra-pentateuchal traditions were authoritative because they were congruent with Natural
Law. Even if a tradition were *known* because it was handed down
orally through the generations, Philo would not have regarded the
tradition's *authority* as based on *the particularity of its mode of transmission*. Instead, he would have regarded its authority as based on *the
universality of its content*. This brings out an extremely important point:
interpreters may share a body of interpretive traditions, yet differ
significantly in the ways they conceive of the basis of the authority
of those traditions.

Like the Rabbis, Philo certainly believed that the unwritten law
included not only written pentateuchal texts but also extra-pentateuchal customs and interpretive traditions. But, unlike the Rabbis,
he did not privilege oral transmission; he believed, as we saw in the book
of *Jubilees*, that some of the extra-pentateuchal interpretive traditions
were *written down*. Furthermore, Philo sometimes suggests that the
work of the interpretive traditions of the elders or the fathers was
precisely to show the universal significance of Mosaic Law, to show
how that particular law is in fact a copy of the Law of Nature.
Here, for example, is his description of the Therapeutae (*Contempl.*
28–29 [Colson, LCL]):

> τὸ δὲ ἐξ ἑωθινοῦ μέχρις ἑσπέρας διάστημα σύμπαν αὐτοῖς ἐστιν ἄσκησις·
> ἐντυγχάνοντες γὰρ τοῖς ἱεροῖς γράμμασι φιλοσοφοῦσι τὴν πάτριον φιλοσοφίαν
> ἀλληγοροῦντες, ἐπειδὴ σύμβολα τὰ τῆς ῥητῆς ἑρμηνείας νομίζουσιν ἀπο-
> κεκρυμμένης φύσεως ἐν ὑπονοίαις δηλουμένης. ἔστι δὲ αὐτοῖς καὶ συγ-
> γράμματα παλαιῶν ἀνδρῶν, οἳ τῆς αἱρέσεως ἀρχηγέται γενόμενοι πολλὰ

---

that none should be ignorant of them. And indeed they do always assemble and sit
together, most of them in silence except when it is the practice to add something
to signify approval of what is read. *But some priest who is present or one of the elders
reads the holy laws to them and expounds them point by point till about the late afternoon, when
they depart having gained both expert knowledge of the holy laws and considerable advance in
piety.* Do you think that this marks them as idlers or that any work is equally vital
to them? And so they do not resort to persons learned in the law with questions
as to what they should do or not do, nor yet by keeping independent transgress in
ignorance of the law, but any one of them whom you attack with inquiries about
their ancestral institutions can answer you readily and easily. The husband seems
competent to transmit knowledge of the laws to his wife, the father to his children,
the master to his slaves" (*Hypoth.* 7.12). Emphasis is mine.

μνημεῖα τῆς ἐν τοῖς ἀλληγορουμένοις ἰδέας ἀπέλιπον, οἷς καθάπερ τισὶν ἀρχετύποις χρώμενοι μιμοῦνται τῆς προαιρέσεως τὸν τρόπον· ὥστε οὐ θεωροῦσι μόνον, ἀλλὰ καὶ ποιοῦσιν ᾄσματα καὶ ὕμνους εἰς τὸν θεὸν διὰ παντοίων μέλῶν καὶ μελῶν, ἃ ῥυθμοῖς σεμνοτέροις ἀναγκαίως χαράττουσι.

The interval between early morning and evening is spent entirely in spiritual exercise. They read the Holy Scriptures and seek wisdom from their ancestral philosophy by taking it as an allegory, since they think that the words of the literal text are symbols of something whose hidden nature is revealed by studying the underlying meaning. They have also writings of men of old, the founders of their ways of thinking, who left many memorials of the form used in allegorical interpretation and these they take as a kind of archetype and imitate the method in which this principle is carried out. And so they do not confine themselves to contemplation but also compose hymns and psalms to God in all sorts of meters and melodies which they write down with the rhythms necessarily made more solemn.

One important implication of the above passage is that the interpretive traditions have not exhausted the work of interpretation. There is more work to be done, in imitation of the traditions, and of course it is not only the Therapeutae who continue this work, but also Philo himself. Thus Philo associates his own practice of allegorical interpretation, which brings out the spiritual or universal meaning of particular laws, with the Therapeutae and hence with their ancient interpretive traditions (*Contempl.* 78):[56]

αἱ δὲ ἐξηγήσεις τῶν ἱερῶν γραμμάτων γίνονται δι᾽ ὑπονοιῶν ἐν ἀλληγορίαις· ἅπασα γὰρ ἡ νομοθεσία δοκεῖ τοῖς ἀνδράσι τούτοις ἐοικέναι ζῴῳ καὶ σῶμα μὲν ἔχειν τὰς ῥητὰς διατάξεις, ψυχὴν δὲ τὸν ἐναποκείμενον ταῖς λέξεσιν ἀόρατον νοῦν, ἐν ᾧ ἤρξατο ἡ λογικὴ ψυχὴ διαφερόντως τὰ οἰκεῖα θεωρεῖν, ὥσπερ κιὰ κατόπτρου τῶν ὀνομάτων ἐξαίσια κάλλη νοημάτων ἐμφαινόμενα κατιδοῦσα διὰ τὰ μὲν σύμβολα διαπτύξασα καὶ διακαλύψασα, γυμνὰ δὲ εἰς φῶς προαγαγοῦσα τὰ ἐνθύμια τοῖς δυναμένοις ἐκ μικρᾶς ὑπομνήσεως τὰ ἀφανῆ διὰ τῶν φανερῶν θεωρεῖν.

---

[56] Philo should be considered in light of a long pre-Philonic history of allegorical interpretation. For an extensive, but somewhat problematic reconstruction of such a history see Richard Goulet, *La Philosophie de Moïse: Essai de Reconstitution d'un Commentaire Philosophique Prephilonien du Pentateuque* (Paris: J. Vrin, 1987). See also David T. Runia's very thorough and critical review of Goulet's book in *JTS* 40 (1989): 590–602. For an insightful study of Philo and 1 Corinthians, arguing for an underlying pre-Philonic exegetical tradition, see Gregory E. Sterling, "Wisdom among the Perfect: Creation Traditions in Alexandrian Judaism and Corinthian Christianity," *NovT* 37 (1995): 355–84.

> The exposition of the sacred Scriptures treats the inner meaning conveyed in allegory. For to these people the whole law book seems to resemble a living creature with the literal ordinances for its body and for its soul the invisible mind laid up in its wording. It is in this mind especially that the rational soul begins to contemplate the things akin to itself and looking through the words as through a mirror beholds the marvelous beauties of the concepts, unfolds and removes the symbolic coverings and brings forth the thoughts and sets them bare to the light of day for those who need but a little reminding to enable them to discern the inward and hidden through the outward and visible.

Although Philo's method of allegorical interpretation is clearly akin to the methods of contemporaneous Greek and Roman interpreters of Homer, Philo claims that the method is part of Jewish heritage.[57] But it is not the inherited character of the method that renders it authoritative; rather, it is the method's goal. For the goal of allegorical interpretation is to demonstrate the authority of the Law of Moses by showing how that law embodies the Law of Nature. Allegorical interpretation is necessary especially in the case of Mosaic laws that are binding only on the Jews. For it is one thing to say that universally binding laws are authoritative because they are congruent with nature, but in what sense are these particular laws authoritative? Philo maintains that even these particular laws have a universal significance that may be brought out by allegorical interpretation. The universal significance is the primary meaning and import of the Law,[58] but this does not mean that the Law is to govern all peoples or that Jews who understand the Law's meaning are thereby exempt from obeying it. For example, circumcision is explained as a law that improves the virtue of men and controls their passions (*Spec.* 1.2–11). Holidays such as Passover are explained as having both national and cosmological significance:[59]

---

[57] It is important to see that, although the allegorist is in one sense reading Scripture through Hellenistic eyes, in another sense he is subordinating Hellenistic culture to Scripture. For further discussion see, e.g., David Dawson, "Philo: The Reinscription of Reality," in *Allegorical Readers and Cultural Revision in Ancient Alexandria* (Berkeley and Los Angeles: University of California Press, 1992), 73–126, esp. 82 ff.

[58] P. Borgen, *Philo of Alexandria: An Exegete For His Time*, 144.

[59] Another interesting illustration of Philo's insistence upon the universal significance of the Jewish holidays can be seen in *Spec.* 2.188–192 on the particular, i.e., national, and universal significance of the sounding of the Trumpet at the beginning of the first month, i.e., the Jewish new year.

(*Spec.* 2.150):[60]

Συνάπτει δὲ τοῖς διαβατηρίοις ἑορτὴν διάφορον ἔχουσαν καὶ οὐ συνήθη τροφῆς χρῆσιν, ἄζυμα, ἀφ' οὗ καὶ ὠνόμασται. διττὸς δὲ ὁ περὶ αὐτῆς λόγος, ὁ μὲν ἴδιος τοῦ ἔθνους ἕνεκα τῆς λεχθείσης ἀποικίας, ὁ δὲ κοινὸς κατὰ φύσεως ἀκολουθίαν καὶ τὴν τοῦ κόσμου παντὸς ἁρμονίαν.

With the Crossing-feast he combines one in which the food consumed is of a different and unfamiliar kind, namely, unleavened bread, which also gives its name to the feast. This may be regarded from two points of view, one peculiar to the nation, referring to the migration just mentioned, the other universal, following the lead of nature, and in agreement with the general cosmic order.

(*Spec.* 2.156):

ἡ δὲ ἑορτὴ πάλιν ἐφ' ἡμέρας ἑπτὰ ἄγεται δι' ἣν ἔλαχεν ἐν κόσμῳ ὁ ἀριθμὸς προνομίαν τε καὶ τιμήν, ἵνα μηδὲν τῶν εἰς εὐθυμίαν καὶ πάνδημον εὐφροσύνην καὶ εὐχαριστίαν τὴν πρὸς τὸν θεὸν ἀπολείπηται τῆς ἱερᾶς ἑβδομάδος, ἣν ἀρχὴν καὶ πηγὴν ἀνθρώποις ἀγαθῶν ἁπάντων εἶναι διενοήθη.

Again, the feast is held for seven days to mark the precedence and honor which the number holds in the universe, indicating that nothing which tends to cheerfulness and public mirth and thankfulness to God should fail to be accompanied with memories of the sacred seven which He intended to be the source and fountain to men of all good things.

Similarly, Philo claims that the bringing of the sheaf has universal significance (*Spec.* 2.162):[61]

Ἑορτὴ δέ ἐστιν ἐν ἑορτῇ ἡ μετὰ τὴν πρώτην εὐθὺς ἡμέραν, ἥτις ἀπὸ τοῦ συμβεβηκότος ὀνομάζεται δράγμα· τοῦτο γὰρ ἀπαρχὴ προσάγεται τῷ βωμῷ καὶ τῆς χώρας, ἣν ἔλαχε τὸ ἔθνος οἰκεῖν, καὶ τῆς συμπάσης γῆς, ὡς εἶναι τὴν ἀπαρχὴν καὶ τοῦ ἔθνους ἰδίαν καὶ ὑπὲρ ἅπαντος ἀνθρώπων γένους κοινήν.

---

[60] Philo then continues (*Spec.* 1.151 ff.) to explain the cosmic reason for the placing of Passover as the first month, although it was, in other biblical texts, the seventh month. Furthermore, he explains the seasonal significance in conjunction with the movements of the sun and the moon, i.e., the cosmological significance of the Passover festival.

[61] The festival of the 'sheaf' culminates in the Feast of Weeks, *Shavuoth*. See *Spec.* 2.162–163 and *Spec.* 2.176: "The festival of the Sheaf ... indicated in the law, is also in fact anticipatory of another greater feast. For it is from it that the fiftieth day is reckoned, by counting seven sevens, which are then crowned with the sacred number by the monad, which is an incorporeal image of God, Whom it resembles because it also stands alone."

> But within the feast (of Passover) there is another feast following directly
> after the first day. This is called the "Sheaf," a name given to it from
> the ceremony which consists in bringing to the altar a sheaf as a first-
> fruit, both of the land which has been given to the nation to dwell in
> and of the whole earth, so that it serves that purpose both to the
> nation in particular and for the whole human race in general.

In general, the authority of an interpretive tradition *does not rest*, for
Philo, on God's transmission of those traditions to the interpreter via
Moses and a chain of tradents. It rests rather on the tradition's ability to bring out the universal significance of Mosaic Torah, thus to
demonstrate the congruence of Mosaic Torah with the Law of Nature
and to show the unparalleled authority of Mosaic Torah itself.

Consequently, Philo does not always claim that his allegorical interpretations are inherited from the elders or the fathers. He sometimes
takes the liberty of interpreting Mosaic Law on his own by using
his "love of knowledge to peer into each of them [sacred messages]
and unfold and reveal what is not known to the multitude" (*Spec.*
3.6) without claiming to possesses any ancient Jewish tradition. At
other times he is critical of the procedures of other interpreters, both
of those who are overly literal (*Migr.* 44–45), neglecting universal
significance, and of those who are overly allegorical (*Migr.* 89–90),
ignoring the practical normativity of the law for a particular people.[62] In these passages, we see Philo's concern to authorize the Law
of Moses in the universal terms appropriate to his Hellenistic context, *without compromising the particularity of the Law* and its place in particular Jewish society. As we have seen, for Philo, the unwritten law
is the Law of Nature, whose universally acknowledged authority
underlies the authority of Mosaic Law because Mosaic Law is the
most perfect particular, written copy of Natural Law.[63] That is to
say, Natural Law is embodied by the pentateuchal and extra-pentateuchal laws and traditions of the Jews, both written and oral.
Those traditions therefore participate in a universally acknowledged
ground of authority, even though they are particular in many of
their legal requirements. Thus Philo invokes a Hellenistic concep-

---

[62] For discussion of Philo's criticism of other exegetes see, D. M. Hay, "References
to Other Exegetes in Philo's *Quaestiones*," 81–97; P. Borgen, "Philo of Alexandria,"
ANRW 21.1:126–28.
[63] See D. Winston's helpful discussion of the relationship between Torah, i.e.,
Mosaic Law, and Natural Law in "Two Types of Mosaic Philosophy," 442–55.

tion of the normativity of unwritten nature in order to authorize an inherited body of Jewish writings along with their inherited or developed interpretations.

Like *Jubilees*, Philo understands himself as teaching a tradition that dates back, not merely to Sinai, but to creation. Like the Rabbis, Philo understands the interpretation of Scripture to be distinct from Scripture itself. However, in spite of his continuities with both Second Temple interpretive traditions on the one hand, and rabbinic ideas about the distinctness of Scripture and interpretation on the other, Philo's conception of the authority of Scripture and of its interpretation distinguishes him from both. We can make the relevant distinctions, and thus avoid anachronism, while simultaneously acknowledging genuine continuities, if we regard Philo and *Jubilees*—and, perhaps, some rabbinic traditions—as members of the family of texts that I have characterized as Mosaic Discourse. The pursuit of family resemblances and inheritances should not blind us to the reality of generational and cultural variation. One should expect this variation to be immense, far greater than the range I have considered in this book. For Mosaic Discourse remains a living force in the imagination and in the soul of Judaism and Christianity throughout the centuries.[64]

---

[64] For studies of Mosaic Discourse (although these authors do not use the term) in later Judaism and Christianity see Elliot R. Wolfson, *Through a Speculum that Shines: Vision and Imagination in Medieval Jewish Mysticism* (Princeton: Princeton University Press, 1994), esp. 326–92, and D. C. Allison Jr., *The New Moses*.

—

BIBLIOGRAPHY

Adang, Camilla. *Muslim Writers on Judaism and the Hebrew Bible: From Ibn Rabban to Ibn Hazm.* Leiden: Brill, 1996.

Albeck, Hanokh. *Introduction to the Mishnah.* Jerusalem: Mosad Bialik and Tel Aviv: Dvir, 1967 (Hebrew).

———., ed. *Shisha Sidrei Mishnah.* Jerusalem: Mosad Bialik, 1957–59 (Hebrew).

Albertz, Rainer. *A History of Israelite Religion in the Old Testament Period, Volume II: From the Exile to the Maccabees.* Translated by John Bowden. Old Testament Library. Louisville: Westminster/John Knox, 1994.

Albright, William F. "A Catalogue of Early Hebrew Lyric Poems (Psalm LXVIII)." *Hebrew Union College Annual* 23 (1950): 1–39.

Alexander, Philip S. "Retelling the Old Testament." Pages 99–121 in *It is Written: Scripture Citing Scripture. Essays in Honour of Barnabas Lindars, SSF.* Edited by D. A. Carson and H. G. M. Williamson. Cambridge: Cambridge University Press, 1988.

Allegro, John M. *The Dead Sea Scrolls and the Christian Myth.* Amherst, N.Y.: Prometheus, 1992.

Allison, Dale C., Jr. *The New Moses: A Matthean Typology.* Minneapolis: Fortress, 1993.

Alon, Gedaliah. "The Levitical Uncleanness of Gentiles." Pages 146–89 in *Jews, Judaism and the Classical World.* Translated by Israel Abrahams. Jerusalem: Magnes, 1977.

Anderson, Gary A. "The Status of the Torah Before Sinai: The Retelling of the Bible in the Damascus Document and the Book of Jubilees." *Dead Sea Discoveries* 1 (1994): 1–29.

Assmann, Jan. *Moses the Egyptian: The Memory of Egypt in Western Monotheism.* Cambridge, Mass.: Harvard University Press, 1997.

———. *The Search for God in Ancient Egypt.* Translated by David Lorton. Ithaca: Cornell University Press, 2001.

Attridge, Harold W. *The Epistle to the Hebrews: A Commentary on the Epistle to the Hebrews.* Hermeneia. Philadephia: Fortress, 1989.

Aune, David E. *Prophecy in Early Christianity and the Ancient Mediterranean World.* Grand Rapids: Eerdmans, 1983.

Baltzer, Klaus. *The Covenant Formulary in Old Testament, Jewish, and Early Christian Writings.* Translated by David E. Green. Philadelphia: Fortress, 1971.

Barthélemy, Dominique, and Jósef T. Milik. "1Q22 (Dires de Moïse)." Pages 91–97 in *Qumrân Cave I.* Discoveries in the Judaean Desert 1. Oxford: Clarendon, 1955.

Baumgarten, Joseph M. "The Calendar of the Book of Jubilees and the Bible." *Tarbiz* 32 (1962): 317–28. Repr. pages 101–14 in *Studies in Qumran Law.* Studies in Judaism in Late Antiquity 24. Leiden: Brill, 1977.

———. "The Calendars of the Book of Jubilees and the Temple Scroll." *Vetus Testamentum* 37 (1987): 71–78.

———. "The Unwritten Law in the Pre-Rabbinic Period." *Journal for the Study of Judaism* 3 (1972): 7–29. Repr. pages 13–39 in *Studies in Qumran Law.* Studies in Judaism in Late Antiquity 24. Leiden: Brill, 1977.

Beegle, Dewy M. "Moses." Pages 909–18 in vol. 4 of *The Anchor Bible Dictionary.* Edited by David Noel Freedman et al. 6 vols. New York: Doubleday, 1992.

Belkin, Samuel. *Philo and the Oral Law.* Cambridge, Mass.: Harvard University Press, 1940.

Berger, Michael S. *Rabbinic Authority.* New York: Oxford University Press, 1998.

Bernstein, Moshe J. "4Q159 Fragment 5 and the 'Desert Theology' of the Qumran Sect." *Dead Sea Discoveries* 9 (2002): 75–103.

———. "4Q252: From Re-Written Bible to Biblical Commentary." *Journal of Jewish Studies* 45 (1994): 2–27.

———. "Angels at the Aqedah: A Study in the Development of a Midrashic Motif." *Dead Sea Discoveries* 7 (2000): 263–91.

———. "Introductory Formulas for Citation and Re-citation of Biblical Verses in the Qumran Pesharim." *Dead Sea Discoveries* 1 (1994): 30–70.

———. "Pentateuchal Interpretation at Qumran." Pages 128–59 in vol. 1 of *The Dead Sea Scrolls after Fifty Years: A Comprehensive Assessment*. Edited by Peter W. Flint and James C. VanderKam. 2 vols. Leiden: Brill, 1998–99.

———. "Re-Arrangement, Anticipation and Harmonization as Exegetical Features in the Genesis Apocryphon." *Dead Sea Discoveries* 3 (1996): 37–57.

Berrin, Shani. "Qumran Pesharim." In *Biblical Interpretation at Qumran*. Edited by Matthias Henze. Grand Rapids: Eerdmans, forthcoming.

Birnbaum, Ellen. *The Place of Judaism in Philo's Thought: Israel, Jews, and Proselytes*. Brown Judaica Series 290. Studia Philonica Monographs 2. Atlanta: Scholars Press, 1996.

———. Review of Naomi G. Cohen, *Philo Judaeus: His Universe of Discourse*. *Studia Philonica* 8 (1996): 189–96.

Bland, Kalman P. "Moses and the Law According to Maimonides." Pages 49–66 in *Mystics, Philosophers, and Politicans: Essays in Jewish Intellectual History in Honor of Alexander Altmann*. Edited by Jehuda Reinharz and Daniel Swetschinski, with collaboration of Kalman P. Bland. Durham, N.C.: Duke University Press, 1982.

Blank, Sheldon H. "The Dissident Laity in Early Judaism." *Hebrew Union College Annual* 19 (1945–46): 1–42.

Blenkinsopp, Joseph. *Ezra-Nehemiah: A Commentary*. Old Testament Library. Philadelphia: Westminster, 1988.

———. *Isaiah 1–39: A New Translation with Introduction and Commentary*. Anchor Bible 19. New York: Doubleday, 2000.

———. "The Mission of Udjahorresnet and Those of Ezra and Nehemiah." *Journal of Biblical Literature* 106 (1987): 409–21.

———. *The Pentateuch: An Introduction to the First Five Books of the Bible*. Anchor Bible Reference Library. New York: Doubleday, 1992.

———. "The Prophetic Biography of Isaiah." Pages 13–26 in *Mincha: Festgabe für Rolf Rendtorff zum 75. Geburtstag*. Edited by Erhard Blum. Neukirchen Vluyn: Neukirchener Verlag, 2000.

———. "Was the Pentateuch the Civic and Religious Constitution of the Jewish Ethnos in the Persian Period?" Pages 41–62 in *Persia and Torah: The Theory of Imperial Authorization of the Pentateuch*. Society of Biblical Literature Symposium Series 17. Atlanta: Society of Biblical Literature, 2001.

Blidstein, Gerald J. "A Note on the Term *Torah She-B'al peh*." *Tarbiz* 42 (1973): 496–98 (Hebrew).

Blum, Erhard. *Studien zur Komposition des Pentateuch*. Beihefte zur Zeitschrift für die alttestamentliche Wissenschaft 189. Berlin: de Gruyter, 1990.

Boccaccini, Gabriele. *Beyond the Essene Hypothesis: The Parting of Ways between Qumran and Enochic Judaism*. Grand Rapids: Eerdmans, 1998.

Bockmuehl, Markus. "Natural Law in Second Temple Judaism." *Vetus Testamentum* 45 (1995): 17–44.

———. *Revelation and Mystery in Ancient Judaism and Pauline Christianity*. Grand Rapids: Eerdmans, 1997.

Bokser, Baruch M. "Approaching Sacred Space." *Harvard Theological Review* 78 (1985): 279–99.

Boorer, Suzanne. *The Promise of the Land as Oath: A Key to the Formation of the Pentateuch.* Beihefte zur Zeitschrift für die alttestamentliche Wissenschaft 205. Berlin: de Gruyter, 1992.

Borgen, Peder. "Philo of Alexandria: A Critical and Synthetical Survey of Research Since World War II." *ANRW* 21.1:98–154. Part 2, *Principat,* 21.1. Edited by H. Temporini and W. Haase. Berlin: de Gruyter, 1984.

———. *Philo of Alexandria: An Exegete for his Time.* Novum Testamentum Supplements 86. Leiden: Brill, 1997.

Bowie, Ewen Lyall. "Apollonius of Tyana: Tradition and Reality." *ANRW* 16.2:1652–99. Part 2, *Principat,* 16.2. Edited by H. Temporini and W. Haase. Berlin: de Gruyter, 1978.

Brady, Monica Walsh. "Prophetic Traditions at Qumran: A Study of 4Q383–391." 2 vols. Ph.D. diss., The University of Notre Dame, 2000.

Brettler, Marc Z. *The Creation of History in Ancient Israel.* London: Routledge, 1995.

Brin, Gershon. "Regarding the Connection between the *Temple Scroll* and the Book of *Jubilees.*" *Journal of Biblical Literature* 112 (1993): 108–09.

———. *Studies in Biblical Law: From the Hebrew Bible to the Dead Sea Scrolls.* Journal for the Study of the Old Testament Supplement Series 176. Sheffield: JSOT Press, 1994.

Brody, Robert. "Chapter 6: The Struggle against Heresy." Pages 83–99 in *The Geonim of Babylonia and the Shaping of Medieval Jewish Culture.* New Haven, Conn.: Yale University Press, 1998.

Brooke, George J. "Between Authority and Canon: The Significance of Reworking the Bible for Understanding the Canonical Process." Paper presented at the Seventh Orion International Symposium: Reworking the Bible at Qumran in the Context of Second Temple Judaism. Hebrew University of Jerusalem, January 17, 2002; Orion Conference Proceedings Series, forthcoming. Online: *http://orion.mscc.huji.ac.il/orion/symposiums/7th/.*

———. "The Genre of 4Q252: From Poetry to Pesher." *Dead Sea Discoveries* 1 (1994): 160–79.

———. "Rewritten Bible." Pages 777–81 in vol. 2 of *Encyclopedia of the Dead Sea Scrolls.* Edited by Lawrence H. Schiffman and James C. VanderKam. 2 vols. Oxford: Oxford University Press, 2000.

Broshi, Magen. "The Gigantic Dimensions of the Visionary Temple in the Temple Scroll." *Biblical Archaeology Review* 13, no. 6 (November/December 1987): 36–37.

Brox, Norbert. "Falsche Verfasserangaben: zur Erklärung der früchristlichen Pseudepigraphie." *Stuttgarter Bibelstudien* 79 (1975): 11–67.

Büchler, Adolph. "Family Purity and Family Impurity in Jerusalem Before the Year 70 C.E." Pages 64–98 in *Studies in Jewish History: the Adolph Büchler Memorial Volume.* Edited by Israel Brodie and Joseph Rabbinowitz. London: Oxford University Press, 1956.

———. "The Levitical Impurity of the Gentile in Palestine Before the Year 70." *Jewish Quarterly Review* 17 (1926): 1–81.

———. "Studies in the Book of Jubilees." *Revue des études juives* 82 (1926): 253–74.

Burgmann, Hans. "11QT: The Sadducean *Torah.*" Pages 257–63 in *Temple Scroll Studies: Papers presented at the International Symposium on the Temple Scroll. Manchester, December 1987.* Edited by George J. Brooke. Journal for the Study of the Pseudepigrapha Supplement Series 7. Sheffield: Sheffield Academic, 1989.

Burkert, Walter. *Greek Religion: Archaic and Classical.* Translated by John Raffan. Cambridge, Mass.: Harvard University Press, 1985.

Calabi, Francesca. *The Language and the Law of God: Interpretation and Politics in Philo of Alexandria.* Edited by Jacob Neusner. University of South Florida Studies in the History of Judaism 188. Atlanta: Scholars Press, 1998.

Callaway, Philip. "Source Criticism of the Temple Scroll: The Purity Laws." *Revue de Qumran* 12 (1986): 213–22.

Cavell, Stanley. "The Fact of Television." Pages 235–68 in *Themes Out of School: Effects and Causes.* San Francisco: North Point Press, 1984. Repr., Chicago: University of Chicago Press, 1988.

———. *Pursuits of Happiness: The Hollywood Comedy of Remarriage.* Cambridge, Mass.: Harvard University Press, 1981.

Chapman, Stephen B. "'The Law and the Words' as a Canonical Formula within the Old Testament." Pages 26–74 in *The Interpretation of Scripture in Early Judaism and Christianity: Studies in Language and Tradition.* Edited by Craig A. Evans. Journal for the Study of the Pseudepigrapha Supplement Series 33. Studies in Scripture in Early Judaism and Christianity 7. Sheffield: Sheffield Academic, 2000.

Charlesworth, James H. "The Date of Jubilees and of the Temple Scroll." Pages 193–204 in *SBL Seminar Papers, 1985.* Society of Biblical Literature Seminar Papers 24. Atlanta: Scholars Press, 1985.

———. "In the Crucible: The Pseudepigrapha as Biblical Interpretation." Pages 120–43 in *The Pseudepigrapha and Early Biblical Interpretation.* Edited by James H. Charlesworth and Craig A. Evans. Journal for the Study of the Pseudepigrapha Supplement Series 14. Studies in Scripture and Early Judaism and Christianity 2. Sheffield: Sheffield Academic, 1993.

———. "The Significance of the New Edition of the Old Testament Pseudepigrapha." Pages 11–28 in *La Littérature Intertestamentaire: Colloque de Strasbourg (17–19 Octobre 1983).* Paris: Presses Universitaires de France, 1985.

———., ed. *The Old Testament Pseudepigrapha.* 2 vols. Garden City, N.Y.: Doubleday, 1985.

Childs, Brevard S. *The Book of Exodus: A Critical, Theological Commentary.* Old Testament Library. Louisville: Westminster, 1976.

Claburn, W. Eugene. "The Fiscal Basis of Josiah's Reforms." *Journal of Biblical Literature* 92 (1953): 11–22.

Coats, George W. *Moses: Heroic Man, Man of God.* Journal for the Study of the Old Testament Supplement Series 57. Sheffield: Almond, 1988.

Cogan, Mordechai, and Hayim Tadmor. *II Kings: A New Translation.* Anchor Bible 11. New York: Doubleday, 1988.

Cohen, Naomi G. "'Agraphos Nomos' in Philo's Writings—a New Examination." *Da'at* 15 (1985): 5–20 (Hebrew).

———. "The Jewish Dimension of Philo's Judaism—An Elucidation of de Spec. Leg. IV 132–150." *Journal of Jewish Studies* 38 (1987): 165–86.

———. *Philo Judaeus: His Universe of Discourse.* Beiträge zur Erforschung des Alten Testaments und des Antiken Judentums 24. Frankfurt: Lang, 1995.

Cohen, Shaye J. D. "Conversion to Judaism in Historical Perspective: From Biblical Israel to Postbiblical Judaism." *Conservative Judaism* 36.4 (1983): 31–45.

———. "Crossing the Boundary and Becoming a Jew." *Harvard Theological Review* 82 (1989): 13–33.

———. "From the Bible to the Talmud: The Prohibition of Intermarriage." *Hebrew Annual Review* 7 (1983): 23–39.

———. "The Origins of the Matrilineal Principle in Rabbinic Law." *Association for Jewish Studies Review* 10 (1985): 19–53.

Cohon, Samuel S. "Authority in Judaism." *Hebrew Union College Annual* 11 (1936): 593–646.

Collins, John J. "Chapter 8: The Diaspora Setting." Pages 135–57 in *Jewish Wisdom in the Hellenistic Age.* Old Testament Library. Louisville: Westminster/John Knox, 1997.

———. "Cult and Culture: The Limits of Hellenization in Judea." Pages 38–61 in *Hellenism in the Land of Israel.* Edited by John J. Collins and Gregory E.

Sterling. Christianity and Judaism in Antiquity Series 13. Notre Dame: University of Notre Dame Press, 2001.

————. "The Impact of Dogmatism on Rational Discourse: Comments on the Paper of Michael Dummett." Pages 23–30 in *Hermes and Athena: Biblical Exegesis and Philosophical Theology*. Edited by Eleonore Stump and Thomas P. Flint. Notre Dame: University of Notre Dame Press, 1993.

————., and Gregory E. Sterling, eds. *Hellenism in the Land of Israel*. Christianity and Judaism in Antiquity Series 13. Notre Dame: University of Notre Dame Press, 2001.

Collins, Nina L. *The Library in Alexandria & the Bible in Greek*. Vetus Testamentum Supplements 82. Leiden: Brill, 2000.

Cooper, John M. "Eudaimonism, the Appeal to Nature, and 'Moral Duty' in Stoicism." Pages 261–84 in *Aristotle, Kant, and the Stoics: Rethinking Happiness and Duty*. Edited by Stephen Engstrom and Jennifer Whiting. New York: Cambridge University Press, 1996.

Cross, Frank Moore. *The Ancient Library of Qumran*. 3d ed. Sheffield: Sheffield Academic and Minneapolis: Fortress, 1995.

————. "The Themes of the Book of Kings and the Structure of the Deuteronomistic History." Pages 274–89 in *Canaanite Myth and Hebrew Epic: Essays in the History of the Religion of Israel*. Cambridge, Mass.: Harvard University Press, 1973.

————., and David Noel Freedman. "Josiah's Revolt Against Assyria." *Journal of Near Eastern Studies* 12 (1953): 56–58.

————., and Shemaryahu Talmon, eds. *Qumran and the History of the Biblical Text*. Cambridge, Mass.: Harvard University Press, 1975.

D'Angelo, Mary Rose. *Moses in the Letter to the Hebrews*. Society of Biblical Literature Dissertation Series 42. Missoula, Mont.: Scholars Press, 1979.

Dan, Joseph. *The Hebrew Story in the Middle Ages*. Jerusalem: Keter, 1994 (Hebrew).

Davenport, Gene L. *The Eschatology of the Book of Jubilees*. Studia post-biblica 20. Leiden: Brill, 1971.

Davidson, Maxwell J. *Angels at Qumran: A Comparative Study of 1Enoch 1–36, 72–108 and Sectarian Writings from Qumran*. Journal for the Study of the Pseudepigrapha Supplement Series 11. Sheffield: JSOT Press, 1992.

Davies, John A. "The *Temple Scroll* from Qumran and the Ultimate Temple." *Reformed Theological Review* 57 (1998): 1–21.

Davies, Philip R. *In Search of 'Ancient Israel'*. Journal for the Study of the Old Testament Supplement Series 148. Sheffield: JSOT Press, 1992.

Dawson, David. "Philo: The Reinscription of Reality." Pages 73–126 in *Allegorical Readers and Cultural Revision in Ancient Alexandria*. Berkeley and Los Angeles: University of California Press, 1992.

DeFilippo, Joseph G., and Phillip T. Mitsis. "Socrates and Stoic Natural Law." Pages 252–71 in *The Socratic Movement*. Edited by Paul A. Vander Waerdt. Ithaca: Cornell University Press, 1994.

Dietrich, Walter. *Prophetie und Geschichte*. Forschungen zur Religion und Literatur des Alten und Neuen Testaments 108. Göttingen: Vandenhoeck & Ruprecht, 1972.

Dillon, John M. *The Middle Platonists: 80 B.C. to A.D. 220*. Ithaca: Cornell University Press, 1996.

————. "A Response to Runia and Sterling." *Studia Philonica Annual* 5 (1993): 151–55.

Dimant, Devorah. "Apocrypha and Pseudepigrapha at Qumran." *Dead Sea Discoveries* 1 (1994): 151–59.

————. *Qumran Cave 4. Parabiblical Texts, Part 4: Pseudo-Prophetic Texts*. Discoveries in the Judaean Desert 21. Oxford: Clarendon, 2001.

Doran, Robert. "The Non-Dating of Jubilees: Jub 34–38; 23:14–32 in Narrative Context." *Journal for the Study of Judaism* 20 (1989): 1–11.

Edelman, R. "To 'annot Exodus xxxii 18." *Vetus Testamentum* 16 (1966): 355.

Edwards, Mark J., and Simon Swain, eds. *Portraits: Biographical Representation in the Greek and Latin Literature of the Roman Empire.* Oxford: Clarendon, 1997.

Eissfeldt, Otto. *The Old Testament: An Introduction.* Translated by Peter Ackroyd. New York: Harper & Row, 1966.

Elman, Yaakov. *Authority and Tradition: Toseftan Baraitot in Talmudic Babylonia.* New York: Michael Scharf Publication Trust of the Yeshiva University Press and Hoboken, N.J.: KTAV, 1994.

Endres, John C. *Biblical Interpretation in the Book of Jubilees.* Catholic Biblical Quarterly Monograph Series 18. Washington, D.C.: Catholic Biblical Association of America, 1987.

Eppel, Robert. "Les tables de la Loi et les tables célestes." *Revue d'histoire et de philosophie religieuse* 17 (1937): 401–12.

Epstein, Louis. "Intermarriage." Pages 145–219 in *Marriage Laws in the Bible and Talmud.* Cambridge, Mass.: Harvard University Press, 1942.

Eshel, Esther. "Hermeneutical Approaches to Genesis in the Dead Sea Scrolls." Pages 1–12 in *The Book of Genesis in Jewish and Oriental Christian Interpretation: A Collection of Essays.* Edited by Judith Frishman and Lucas Van Rompay. Leuven: Peeters, 1997.

Eskenazi, Tamara C., and Eleanore P. Judd. "Marriage to a Stranger in Ezra 9–10." Pages 266–85 in *Second Temple Studies: 2. Temple Community in the Persian Period.* Edited by Tamara C. Eskenazi and Kent H. Richards. Journal for the Study of the Old Testament Supplement Series 175. Sheffield: JSOT Press, 1994.

Eslinger, Lyle. "Josiah and the Torah Book: Comparison of 2 Kgs 22:1–23:28 and 2 Chr 34:1–35:19." *Hebrew Annual Review* 10 (1986): 37–62.

Evans, Craig A. "The Genesis Apocryphon and the Rewritten Bible." *Revue de Qumran* 13 (1988): 153–65.

Eynikel, Erik. *The Reform of King Josiah and the Composition of the Deuteronomistic History.* Oudtestamentische Studiën 33. Leiden: Brill, 1996.

Falk, Daniel K. "Moses, Texts of." Pages 577–81 in vol. 1 of *Encyclopedia of the Dead Sea Scrolls.* Edited by Lawrence H. Schiffman and James C. VanderKam. 2 vols. Oxford: Oxford University Press, 2000.

Fideler, David, and Kenneth S. Guthrie, eds. *The Pythagorean Sourcebook and Library.* Grand Rapids: Phanes, 1988.

Fishbane, Michael. *Biblical Interpretation in Ancient Israel.* Oxford: Clarendon, 1985. Repr., Oxford: Clarendon Paperbacks, 1988.

———. "Chapter 10: Use, Authority and Interpretation of Mikra at Qumran." Pages 339–77 in *Mikra: Text, Translation, Reading and Interpretation of the Hebrew Bible in Ancient Judaism and Early Christianity.* Edited by Martin J. Mulder. Compendia rerum iudaicarum ad Novum Testamentum 2.1. Assen: Van Gorcum and Minneapolis: Fortress, 1990.

———. *The Garments of Torah: Essays in Biblical Hermeneutics.* Bloomington, Ind.: Indiana University Press, 1989. Repr., 1992.

Fletcher-Louis, Crispin. "4Q374: A Discourse on the Sinai Tradition: The Deification of Moses and Early Christology." *Dead Sea Discoveries* 3 (1996): 236–52.

———. *All the Glory of Adam: Liturgical Anthropology in the Dead Sea Scrolls.* Studies on the Texts of the Desert of Judah 42. Leiden: Brill, 2002.

Forster, Edward M. *Anonymity: An Enquiry.* London: Hogarth, 1925.

Foucault, Michel. "What is an Author?" Pages 205–22 in *Michel Foucault: Aesthetics, Method, and Epistemology. Vol. 2.* Edited by James D. Faubion. Translated by Josué V. Harari and modified by Robert Hurley. New York: The New Press, 1998.

Fowden, Garth. *The Egyptian Hermes: A Historical Approach to the Late Pagan Mind.* Cambridge: Cambridge University Press, 1986.

Frankel, David. *The Murmuring Stories of the Priestly School: A Retrieval of Ancient Sacerdotal Lore.* Vetus Testamentum Supplements 89. Leiden: Brill, 2002.

Franks, Paul W. "Kant and Hegel on the Esotericism of Philosophy." Ph.D. diss., Harvard University, 1993.

Fraser, Peter Marshall. "Chapter 5: The Cults of Alexandria." Pages 189–301 in vol. 1 of *Ptolemaic Alexandria.* 3 vols. Oxford: Clarendon, 1972.

Frei, Peter. "Die persische Reichsautorisation: Ein Überblick." *Zeitschrift für altorientalische und biblische Rechtgeschichte* 1 (1995): 1–35. Repr., and translated as: "Persian Imperial Authorization: A Summary." Pages 5–40 in *Persia and Torah: The Theory of Imperial Authorization of the Pentateuch.* Translated by James W. Watts. Society of Biblical Literature Symposium Series 17. Atlanta: Society of Biblical Literature, 2001.

———. "Zentralgewalt und Lokalautonomie im Achämenidenreich." Pages 5–132 in Peter Frei and Klaus Koch, *Reichsidee und Reichsorganisation im Perserreich.* 2d enl. ed. Orbis biblicus et orientalis 55. Freiburg: Universitätsverlag and Göttingen: Vandenhoeck & Ruprecht, 1996.

Freudenthal, J. *Alexander Polyhistor und die von ihm erhaltenen Reste jüdischer und samaritanischer Geschichtsweke.* Breslau, 1875.

García Martínez, Florentino. "The Heavenly Tablets in the Book of Jubilees." Pages 243–60 in *Studies in the Book of Jubilees.* Edited by Matthias Albani, Jörg Frey, and Armin Lange. Tübingen: Mohr Siebeck, 1997. Repr., and translated by M. T. Davis from "Las Tablas Celestes en el Libro de los Jubileos." Pages 333–49 in *Palabra y Vida: Homenaje a José Alonso Díaz en su 70 cumpleaños.* Edited by Antonio Vargas Machuca and Gregorio Ruiz. Publicationes de la Universidad Pontifica Comillias Madrid, Series 1, Estudios 58. Madrid: Ediciones Universidad de Comillias, 1984.

———. *Qumran and Apocalyptic: Studies on the Aramaic Texts from Qumran.* Studies on the Texts of the Desert of Judah 9. Leiden: Brill, 1992.

———. "Temple Scroll." Pages 927–33 in vol. 2 of *Encyclopedia of the Dead Sea Scrolls.* Edited by Lawrence H. Schiffman and James C. VanderKam. 2 vols. Oxford: Oxford University Press, 2000.

———., and Eibert J. C. Tigchelaar, eds. *The Dead Sea Scrolls Study Edition.* 2 vols. Leiden: Brill and Grand Rapids: Eerdmans, 1997–98.

Geljon, Abraham C. "Moses as Example: The Philonic Background of Gregory of Nyssa's *De Vita Moysis.*" Ph.D. diss., University of Leiden, 2000.

Goodenough, Erwin Ramsdell. *By Light, Light: The Mystic Gospel of Hellenistic Judaism.* New Haven, Conn.: Yale University Press, 1935.

———. "Philo's Exposition of the Law and His De Vita Mosis." *Harvard Theological Review* 26 (1933): 109–25.

Goody, Jack. *Literacy, Family, Culture and the State: The Interface Between the Written and the Oral.* Cambridge: Cambridge University Press, 1987.

Goulet, Richard. *La Philosophie de Moïse: Essai de Reconstitution d'un Commentaire Philosophique Préphilonien du Pentateuque.* Paris: J. Vrin, 1987.

Grafton, Anthony. *Forgers and Critics: Creativity and Duplicity in Western Scholarship.* Princeton: Princeton University Press, 1990.

———. Introduction to *Prolegomena to Homer (1795).* Translated with introduction and notes by Anthony Grafton, Glenn W. Most, and James E. G. Zetzel. Princeton: Princeton University Press, 1985.

———. "Jacob Bernays, Joseph Scaliger, and Others." Pages 279–98 in *Bring Out Your Dead: The Past as Revelation.* Cambridge, Mass.: Harvard University Press, 2001.

———. "Protestant Versus Prophet: Isaac Casaubon on Hermes Trismegistus." *Journal of the Warburg and Courauld Institutes* 46 (1983): 78–93.

Griffen, Miriam T., and E. Margaret Atkins, eds. *Cicero: On Duties.* Cambridge Texts in the History of Political Thought. Cambridge: Cambridge University Press, 1991.

Gruen, Eric S. "Jewish Perspectives on Greek Culture." Pages 62–93 in *Hellenism in the Land of Israel*. Edited by John J. Collins and Gregory E. Sterling. Christianity and Judaism in Antiquity Series 13. Notre Dame: University of Notre Dame Press, 2001.

Hadas, Moses, and Morton Smith. *Heroes and Gods: Spiritual Biographies in Antiquity*. Edited by Ruth Nanda Anshen. Religious Perspectives 13. New York: Harper & Row, 1965.

Halivni, David Weiss. *Revelation Restored: Divine Writ and Critical Responses*. Boulder, Colo.: Westview, 1997.

Haran, Menahem. "Book-Scrolls in Israel in Pre-Exilic Times." *Journal of Jewish Studies* 33 (1982): 161–73.

Harris, Jay Michael. *How Do We Know This? Midrash and the Fragmentation of Modern Judaism*. Albany: State University of New York Press, 1995.

Hay, David M. "Defining Allegory in Philo's Exegetical World." Pages 55–68 in *SBL Seminar Papers, 1994*. Society of Biblical Literature Seminar Papers 33. Atlanta: Scholars Press, 1994.

———. "Moses Through New Testament Spectacles." *Interpretation* 44 (1990): 240–52.

———. "Philo of Alexandria." Pages 357–79 in *The Complexities of Second Temple Judaism: Justification and Variegated Nomism, Vol. 1*. Edited by D. A. Carson, Peter T. O'Brien, and Mark A. Seifrid. Wissenschaftliche Untersuchungen zum Neuen Testament, Reihe 2:140. Tübingen: J. C. B. Mohr, 2001.

———. "Philo's References to Other Allegorists." *Studia Philonica* 6 (1979–80): 41–76.

———. "Philo's View of Himself as an Exegete: Inspired, But Not Authoritative." *Studia Philonica Annual* 3 (1991): 40–52.

———. "References to Other Exegetes in Philo's *Quaestiones*." Pages 81–97 in *Both Literal and Allegorical: Studies in Philo of Alexandria's Questions and Answers on Genesis and Exodus*. Edited by David M. Hay. Brown Judaic Studies 232. Atlanta: Scholars Press, 1991.

Hayes, Christine E. *Gentile Impurities and Jewish Identities: Intermarriage and Conversion from the Bible to the Talmud*. New York: Oxford University Press, forthcoming.

———. "Halakhah le-Moshe mi-Sinai in Rabbinic Sources: A Methodological Case Study." Pages 61–118 in *The Synoptic Problem in Rabbinic Literature*. Edited by Shaye J. D. Cohen. Brown Judaica Series 326. Atlanta: Scholars Press, 2000.

———. "Intermarriage and Impurity in Ancient Jewish Sources." *Harvard Theological Review* 92 (1999): 3–36.

Hecht, Richard D. "Scripture and Commentary in Philo." Pages 129–64 in *SBL Seminar Papers, 1981*. Society of Biblical Literature Seminar Papers 20. Chico, Calif.: Scholars Press, 1981.

Heinemann, Isaak. *Darkhei Ha'Aggada*. Jerusalem: Magnes, 1949 (Hebrew).

———. "Die Lehre vom Ungeschriebenen Gesetz im jüdischen Schrifttum." *Hebrew Union College Annual* 4 (1930–31): 149–71.

Hengel, Martin. "Anonymität, Pseudepigraphie und 'Literarische Fälschung' in der jüdisch-hellenistischen Literatur." Pages 231–308 with discussion 309–29 in *Pseudepigrapha I*. Edited by Kurt von Fritz. Vandoeuvres-Geneve: Fondation Hardt, 1972.

Hilgert, Earle. "Philo Judaeus et Alexandrinus." Pages 1–15 in *The School of Moses: Studies in Philo and Hellenistic Religion*. Edited by John P. Kenney. Brown Judaica Series 304. Atlanta: Scholars Press, 1995.

Himmelfarb, Martha. "Levi, Phineas, and the Problem of Intermarriage at the Time of the Maccabean Revolt." *Jewish Studies Quarterly* 6 (1999): 1–24.

———. "Sexual Relations and Purity in the Temple Scroll and the Book of Jubilees." *Dead Sea Discoveries* 6 (1999): 11–36.

Holladay, Carl R. *Fragments from Hellenistic Jewish Authors. Vol. IV: Orphica*. Society of Biblical Literature Texts and Translations 40. Society of Biblical Literature Pseudepigrapha Series 14. Atlanta: Scholars Press, 1996.

————. *Theios Aner in Hellenistic Judaism: A Critique of the Use of This Category in the New Testament Christology.* Society of Biblical Literature Dissertation Series 40. Missoula, Mont.: Scholars Press, 1977.

Hölscher, Gustav. "Das Buch der Könige, seine Quellen und seine Redaktion." Pages 158–213 in ΕΥΧΑΡΙΣΤΗΡΙΟΝ: *Studien zur Religion und Literatur des Alten und Neuen Testaments.* Forschungen zur Religion und Literatur des Alten und Neuen Testaments 36/1. Edited by H. Schmidt. Göttingen: Vandenhoeck & Ruprecht, 1923.

————. "Kompisition und Ursprung des Deuteronomiums." *Zeitschrift für die alttestamentliche Wissenschaft* 40 (1922): 161–255.

Horsley, Richard A. "The Law of Nature in Philo and Cicero." *Harvard Theological Review* 71 (1978): 35–59.

Horst, Friedrich. "Die Kultsreform des Königs Josia (II Rg. 22–23)." *Zeitschrift der deutschen morgenländischen Gesellschaft* 77 (1923): 220–35.

Jackson-McCabe, Matt A. *Logos and Law in the Letter of James: The Law of Nature, the Law of Moses, and the Law of Freedom.* Novum Testamentum Supplements 100. Leiden: Brill, 2001.

Jacobson, Howard. *A Commentary on Pseudo-Philo's* Liber Antiquitatum Biblicarum, *with Later Text and English Translation.* 2 vols. Arbeiten zur Geschichte des Antiken Judentums und des Urchristentums 31. Leiden: Brill, 1996.

Jaffee, Martin S. *Torah in the Mouth: Writing and Oral Tradition in Palestinian Judaism, 200 B.C.E.–400 C.E.* Oxford: Oxford University Press, 2001.

Japhet, Sara. *I & II Chronicles: A Commentary.* Old Testament Library. Louisville: Westminster/John Knox, 1993.

————. *The Ideology of the Book of Chronicles and its Place in Biblical Thought.* Translated by Anna Barber. Beiträge zur Erforschung des Alten Testaments und des antiken Judentums 9. 2d rev. ed. Frankfurt: Lang, 1997.

————. "Law and 'The Law' in Ezra-Nehemiah." Pages 99–115 in *Proceedings of the Ninth World Congress of Jewish Studies.* Edited by David Assaf. Jerusalem: Magnes, 1985.

————. "Sheshbazzar and Zerubbabel—Against the Background of the Historical and Religious Tendencies of Ezra-Nehemiah." *Zeitschrift für die Alttestamentliche Wissenschaft* 94 (1982): 66–98.

Jaubert, A. "Le calendrier des Jubilés et de la secte de Qumrân. Ses origins bibliques." *Vetus Testamentum* 3 (1953): 250–64.

————. "Le calendrier des Jubilés et les jours liturgiques de la semaine." *Vetus Testamentum* 7 (1957): 35–61.

Johnson, M. D., trans. "The Life of Adam and Eve." Pages 249–95 in vol. 2 of *The Old Testament Pseudepigrapha.* Edited by James H. Charlesworth. 2 vols. New York: Doubleday, 1985.

Joseph, Joy. *'Re-Lecturing' of Deuteronomy (Chapter [sic] 12–26) in the Post-Exilic Period.* Berlin: Logos Verlag, 1997.

Kamesar, Adam. Review of Peder Borgen, *Philo of Alexandria: An Exegete for His Time. Journal of Theological Studies* 50 (1999): 753–58.

Kaufmann, Yehezkel. *History of Israelite Religion.* 8 vols. Tel Aviv: Bialik Institute, 1964 (Hebrew).

Keefer, Kyle. "A Postscript to the Book: Authenticating the Pseudepigrapha." Pages 232–41 in *Reading Bibles, Writing Bodies: Identity and The Book.* Edited by Timothy K. Beal and David M. Gunn. London: Routledge, 1997.

Kennett, Robert H. *Deuteronomy and the Decalogue.* Cambridge: Cambridge University Press, 1920.

Kenney, John P., ed. *The School of Moses: Studies in Philo and Hellenistic Religion.* Brown Judaic Studies 304. Studia Philonica Monographs 1. Atlanta: Scholars Press, 1995.

Kister, Menahem. "על שני מטבעות לשון בספר היובלים" *Tarbiz* 70 (2001): 289–300.

Klawans, Jonathan. *Impurity and Sin in Ancient Judaism*. New York: Oxford University Press, 2000.

———. "Notions of Gentile Impurity in Ancient Judaism." *Association for Jewish Studies Review* 20 (1995): 285–312.

Knohl, Israel. *The Sanctuary of Silence: The Priestly Torah and the Holiness School*. Minneapolis: Fortress, 1995.

Knoppers, Gary N. "An Achaemenid Imperial Authorization of Torah in Yehud?" Pages 115–34 in *Persia and Torah: The Theory of Imperial Authorization of the Pentateuch*. Society of Biblical Literature Symposium Series 17. Atlanta: Society of Biblical Literature, 2001.

———. "Intermarriage, Social Complexity, and Ethnic Diversity in the Geneaology of Judah." *Journal of Biblical Literature* 120 (2001): 15–30.

———. "Rethinking the Relationship between Deuteronomy and the Deuteronomistic History: The Case of Kings." *Catholic Biblical Quarterly* 63 (2001): 393–415.

———. "A Reunited Kingdom in Chronicles?" *Proceedings, Eastern Great Lakes and Midwest Biblical Societies* 9 (1989): 74–88.

———. *Two Nations Under God: The Deuteronomistic History of Solomon and the Dual Monarchies. Volume 2: The Reign of Jeroboam, the Fall of Israel, and the Reign of Josiah.* Harvard Semitic Monographs 53. Atlanta: Scholars Press, 1994.

Koester, Helmut. "'ΝΟΜΟΣ ΦΥΣΕΩΣ': The Concept of Natural Law in Greek Thought." Pages 521–41 in *Religions in Antiquity: Essays in Memory of Erwin Ramsdell Goodenough*. Edited by Jacob Neusner. Studies in the History of Religions (Supplement to *Numen*) 14. Leiden: Brill, 1968.

Koskenniemi, Erkki. "Apollonius of Tyana: A Typical ΘΕΙΟΣ ΑΝΗΡ?" *Journal of Biblical Literature* 117 (1998): 455–67.

Kugel, James L. *The Bible As It Was*. Cambridge, Mass.: Harvard University Press, 1997.

———. "The Bible in the University." Pages 143–65 in *The Hebrew Bible and Its Interpreters*. Edited by William H. Propp, Baruch Halpern, and David N. Freedman. Winona Lake, Ind.: Eisenbrauns, 1990.

———. "Early Interpretation: The Common Background of Late Forms of Biblical Exegesis." Pages 11–106 in James L. Kugel and Rowan A. Greer, *Early Biblical Interpretation*. Library of Early Christianity 3. Philadelphia: Westminster, 1986.

———. "The Holiness of Israel and the Land in Second Temple Times." Pages 21–32 in *Texts, Temples, and Traditions: A Tribute to Menahem Haran*. Edited by Michael V. Fox et al. Winona Lake, Ind.: Eisenbrauns, 1996.

———. *In Potiphar's House: the Interpretive Life of Biblical Texts*. San Francisco: Harper, 1990. 2d ed., repr., Cambridge, Mass.: Harvard University Press, 1994.

———. "The Jubilees Apocalypse." *Dead Sea Discoveries* 1 (1994): 322–37.

———. "The Ladder of Jacob." *Harvard Theological Review* 88 (1995): 209–28.

———. "Levi's Elevation to the Priesthood in Second Temple Writings." *Harvard Theological Review* 86 (1993): 1–64.

———. "The Story of Dinah in the Testament of Levi." *Harvard Theological Review* 85 (1992): 1–34.

Lambert, Wilfred G. "Ancestors, Authors, and Canonicity." *Journal of Cuneiform Studies* 11 (1957): 1–14.

Lange, Armin. "Wisdom and Predestination in the Dead Sea Scrolls." *Dead Sea Discoveries* 2 (1995): 340–54.

Lazarus-Yafeh, Hava. *Intertwined Worlds: Medieval Islam and Bible Criticism*. Princeton: Princeton University Press, 1992.

Lehmann, Manfred R. "The Temple Scroll as a Source of Sectarian Halakhah." *Revue de Qumran* 9 (1978): 579–88.

Lehming, Sigo. "Versuch zu Ex. xxxii." *Vetus Testamentum* 19 (1960): 16–50.

Leiman, Sid Z. *The Canonization of Hebrew Scripture: The Talmudic and Midrashic Evidence.* Transactions of the Connecticut Academy of Arts and Sciences 47. Hamden, Conn.: Archon Books, 1976.

Levenson, Jon D. *The Hebrew Bible, the Old Testament, and Historical Criticism: Jews and Christians in Biblical Studies.* Louisville: Westminster/John Knox, 1993.

———. "The Last Four Verses in Kings." *Journal of Biblical Literature* 103 (1984): 353–61.

———. *Sinai and Zion: An Entry into the Jewish Bible.* San Francisco: Harper & Row, 1985.

———. "Sources of Torah: Psalm 119 and the Modes of Revelation in Second Temple Judaism." Pages 559–74 in *Ancient Israelite Religion: Essays in Honor of Frank Moore Cross.* Edited by Patrick D. Miller Jr., Paul D. Hanson, and S. Dean McBride. Philadelphia: Fortress, 1987.

———. "Who Inserted the Book of the Torah?" *Harvard Theological Review* 68 (1975): 203–33.

Levin, Christoph. "Joschija im deuteronomistischen Geschichtswerk." *Zeitschrift für die alttestamentliche Wissenschaft* 96 (1984): 351–71.

Levin, David Michael. "The Living Body of Tradition." *Religious Traditions* 5 (1983): 45–61.

Levine, Baruch A. "The Temple Scroll: Aspects of its Historical Provenance and Literary Character." *Bulletin of the American Schools of Oriental Research* 232 (1978): 5–23.

Levine, Étan. "The Transcription of the Torah Scroll." *Zeitschrift für die Alttestamentliche Wissenschaft* 94 (1982): 99–105.

Levinson, Bernard M. "The Case for Revision and Interpolation within the Biblical Legal Corpora." Pages 37–59 in *Theory and Method in Biblical and Cuneiform Law.* Edited by Bernard M. Levinson. Journal for the Study of the Old Testament Supplement Series 181. Sheffield: Sheffield Academic, 1994.

———. *Deuteronomy and the Hermeneutics of Legal Innovation.* New York: Oxford University Press, 1997.

Levison, John R. "Inspiration and the Divine Spirit in the Writings of Philo Judaeus." *Journal for the Study of Judaism* 26 (1995): 271–323.

———. "The Prophetic Spirit as an Angel According to Philo." *Harvard Theological Review* 88 (1995): 189–208.

Lewis, Jack P. *A Study of the Interpretation of Noah and the Flood in Jewish and Christian Literature.* Leiden: Brill, 1978.

Lim, Timothy H., Hector L. MacQueen, and Calum M. Carmichael, eds. *On Scrolls, Artefacts and Intellectual Property.* Journal for the Study of the Pseudepigrapha Supplement Series 38. Sheffield: Sheffield Academic, 2001.

Lohfink, Norbert. "The Cult Reform of Josiah of Judah: 2 Kings 22–23 as a Source for the History of Israelite Religion." Pages 459–76 in *Ancient Israelite Religion: Essays in Honor of Frank Moore Cross.* Edited by Patrick D. Miller Jr., Paul D. Hanson, and S. Dean McBride. Philadelphia: Fortress, 1987.

———. "Recent Discussions on 2 Kings 22–23: The State of the Question." Pages 36–61 in *A Song of Power and the Power of Song: Essays on the Book of Deuteronomy.* Edited by Duane L. Christensen. Sources for Biblical and Theological Study 3. Winona Lake, Ind.: Eisenbrauns, 1993. Repr. and translated by Linda M. Maloney from "Zur neuern Diskussion über 2 Kön 22–23." Pages 24–48 in *Das Deuteronomium: Entstehung, Gestalt und Botschaft.* Edited by Norbert Lohfink. Bibliotheca ephemeridum theologicarum lovaniensium 68. Leuven: Leuven University Press, 1985.

———. "Was There a Deuteronomistic Movement?" Pages 36–66 in *Those Elusive Deuteronomists: The Phenomenon of Pan-Deuteronomism.* Edited by Linda S. Schearing and Steven L. McKenzie. Journal for the Study of the Old Testament Supplement Series 268. Sheffield: Sheffield Academic, 1999.

Lord, Albert B. *The Singer of Tales.* Cambridge, Mass.: Harvard University Press, 1960.

Mach, Michael. *Entwicklungsstadien des jüdischen Engelglaubens in vorrabinischer Zeit.* Texte und Studien zum antiken Judentum 34. Tübingen: J. C. B. Mohr, 1992.

Mack, Burton. "Moses on the Mountaintop." Pages 16–28 in *The School of Moses: Studies in Philo and Hellenistic Religion.* Edited by John P. Kenney. Brown Judaica Studies 304. Studia Philonica Monographs 1. Atlanta: Scholars Press, 1995.

———. "Under the Shadow of Moses: Authorship and Authority in Hellenistic Judaism." Pages 299–318 in *SBL Seminar Papers, 1982.* Society of Biblical Literature Seminar Papers 21. Chico, Calif.: Scholars Press, 1982.

Maier, Johann. *The Temple Scroll: An Introduction, Translation and Commentary.* Translated by Richard T. White. Journal for the Study of the Old Testament Supplement Series 34. Sheffield: JSOT Press, 1985; translation of *Die Tempelrolle vom Toten Meer.* Munich: Ernst Reinhart Verlag, 1978.

Mandel, Paul. "Midrashic Exegesis and its Precedents in the Dead Sea Scrolls." *Dead Sea Discoveries* 8 (2001): 149–68.

Marshall, Robert C. "Moses, Oedipus, Structuralism and History." *Religious Traditions* 5 (1983): 245–66.

Martens, John W. "Philo and the 'Higher' Law." Pages 309–22 in *SBL Seminar Papers, 1991.* Society of Biblical Literature Seminar Papers 30. Atlanta: Scholars Press, 1991.

———. "Unwritten Law in Philo: A Response to Naomi G. Cohen." *Journal of Jewish Studies* 43 (1992): 38–45.

McCready, Wayne O. "A second Torah at Qumran?" *Studies in Religion* 14 (1985): 5–15.

McKirahan, Richard D., Jr. "Chapter 19: The NOMOS-PHYSIS Debate." Pages 390–413 in *Philosophy Before Socrates: An Introduction with Texts and Commentary.* Indianapolis: Hackett, 1994.

Meade, David G. *Pseudonymity and Canon: An Investigation into the Relationship of Authorship and Authority in Jewish and Earliest Christian Tradition.* Tübingen: J. C. B. Mohr, 1986. Repr., Grand Rapids: Eerdmans, 1987.

Meeks, Wayne A. "Moses as God and King." Pages 354–71 in *Religions in Antiquity: Essays in Memory of Erwin Ramsdell Goodenough.* Edited by Jacob Neusner. Studies in the History of Religions (Supplement to *Numen*) 14. Leiden: Brill, 1968.

———. *The Prophet-King: Moses Traditions and the Johannine Christology.* Novum Testamentum Supplements 14. Leiden: Brill, 1967.

Meier, John P. "Chapter 31: Jesus and the Law: Reciprocal Illumination." In *The Four Final Enigmas: Law, Parables, Titles, and Death.* Vol. 4 of *A Marginal Jew: Rethinking the Historical Jesus.* Anchor Bible Reference Library. 4 vols. New York: Doubleday, forthcoming.

Menn, Esther Marie. *Judah and Tamar (Genesis 38) in Ancient Jewish Exegesis: Studies in Literary Form and Hermeneutics.* Journal for the Study of Judaism Supplement Series 51. Leiden: Brill, 1997.

Metzger, Bruce M. "Literary Forgeries and Canonical Pseudepigrapha." *Journal of Biblical Literature* 91 (1972): 3–24.

Milgrom, Jacob. "The Concept of Impurity in *Jubilees* and the *Temple Scroll.*" *Revue de Qumran* 16 (1993): 277–84.

———. *Leviticus 1–16: A New Translation with Introduction and Commentary.* Anchor Bible 3. New York: Doubleday, 1991.

———. "Religious Conversion and the Revolt for the Formation of Israel." *Journal of Biblical Literature* 101 (1982): 169–76.

————. "Scriptural Foundation and Deviation in the Laws of Purity of the Temple Scroll." Pages 83–99 in *Archaeology and History in the Dead Sea Scrolls: The New York University Conference in Memory of Yigael Yadin.* Edited by James H. Charlesworth, Philip R. Davies, James R. Mueller and James C. VanderKam. Journal for the Study of the Pseudepigrapha Supplement Series 8. Journal for the Study of the Old Testament/American Schools of Oriental Research Monographs 2. Sheffield: JSOT Press, 1990.

Milik, Josef T. *The Books of Enoch: Aramaic Fragments of Qumrân Cave 4.* Oxford: Clarendon, 1976.

Miller, Patrick D., Jr. "Deuteronomy and Psalms." Pages 318–36 in *Israelite Religion and Biblical Theology: Collected Essays.* Journal for the Study of the Old Testament Supplement Series 267. Sheffield: Sheffield Academic, 2000. Repr. from *Journal of Biblical Literature* 118 (1999): 3–18.

————. "'Moses My Servant': The Deuteronomic Portrait of Moses." Pages 301–12 in *A Song of Power and the Power of Song: Essays on the Book of Deuteronomy.* Edited by Duane L. Christensen. Sources for Biblical and Theological Study 3. Winona Lake, Ind.: Eisenbrauns, 1993. Repr. from *Interpretation* 41 (1987): 245–55.

Mink, Hans-Aage. "The Use of Scripture in the Temple Scroll and the Status of the Scroll as Law." *Scandinavian Journal of the Old Testament* 1 (1987): 20–50.

Moessner, David P. "Jesus and the 'Wilderness Generation': The Death of the Prophet like Moses according to Luke." Pages 319–40 in *SBL Seminar Papers, 1982.* Society of Biblical Literature Seminar Papers 21. Chico, Calif.: Scholars Press, 1982.

————. "Luke 9:1–50: Luke's Preview of the Journey of the Prophet like Moses of Deuteronomy." *Journal of Biblical Literature* 102 (1983): 575–605.

————. "Paul and the Pattern of the Prophet like Moses in Acts." Pages 203–12 in *SBL Seminar Papers, 1983.* Society of Biblical Literature Seminar Papers 22. Chico, Calif.: Scholars Press, 1982.

Momigliano, Arnaldo. *The Classical Foundations of Modern Historiography.* Sather Classical Lectures 54. Berkeley and Los Angeles: University of California Press, 1990.

————. *The Development of Greek Biography: Four Lectures.* Cambridge, Mass.: Harvard University Press, 1971.

Morgenstern, Matthew, Elisha Qimron, and Daniel Sivan, with an appendix by Gregory Bearman and Sheila Spiro. "The Hitherto Unpublished Columns of the Genesis Apocryphon." *Abr-Nahrain* 33 (1995): 30–41.

Mowinckel, Sigmund. *The Psalms in Israel's Worship.* 1 vol. Oxford: Basil Blackwell, 1982. Repr. from rev. Eng. ed. in 2 vols.; translated by D. R. Ap-Thomas; Oxford: Basil Blackwell, 1962. Translation from 1st German ed. 1951.

Mulder, Martin Jan, ed. *Mikra: Text, Translation, Reading and Interpretation of the Hebrew Bible in Ancient Judaism and Early Christianity.* Compendia rerum iudaicarum ad Novum Testamentum 2.1. Assen: Van Gorcum and Minneapolis: Fortress, 1990.

Myre, André. "La loi de la Nature et la loi Mosaic selon Philon d'Alexandrie." *Science et esprit* 28 (1976): 163–81.

————. "La loi et la Pentateuque selon Philon d'Alexandrie." *Science et esprit* 25 (1973): 208–25.

————. "La loi l'ordre cosmique et politique selon Philon d'Alexandrie." *Science et esprit* 24 (1972): 217–47.

Najman, Hindy. "Angels at Sinai: Exegesis, Theology and Interpretative Authority." *Dead Sea Discoveries* 7 (2000): 313–33.

————. "Authoritative Writing and Interpretation: A Study in the History of Scripture." Ph.D. diss., Harvard University, 1998.

————. "Interpretation as Primordial Writing: Jubilees and Its Authority Conferring Strategies." *Journal for the Study of Judaism* 30 (1999): 379–410.

———. "The Law of Nature and the Authority of Mosaic Law." *Studia Philonica Annual* 11 (1999): 55–73.

———. Review of Gabriele Boccaccini, *Beyond the Essene Hypothesis*. *Association for Jewish Studies Review*, forthcoming.

———. "Torah of Moses: Pseudonymous Attribution in Second Temple Writings." Pages 202–16 in *The Interpretation of Scripture in Early Judaism and Christianity: Studies in Language and Tradition*. Edited by Craig A. Evans. Journal for the Study of the Pseudepigrapha Supplement Series 33. Studies in Scripture in Early Judaism and Christianity 7. Sheffield: Sheffield Academic, 2000.

———. "A Written Copy of the Law of Nature: An Unthinkable Paradox." In *The Law of Nature: Ancient Origins and Contemporary Transformations*. Edited by Hindy Najman, David K. O'Connor, and Gregory E. Sterling. Forthcoming.

Nelson, Richard D. *The Double Redaction of the Deuteronomistic History*. Journal for the Study of the Old Testament Supplement Series 18. Sheffield: JSOT Press, 1981.

Neusner, Jacob. *Early Rabbinic Judaism: Historical Studies in Religion, Literature and Art*. Studies in Judaism in Late Antiquity 13. Leiden: Brill, 1975.

———. *From Politics to Piety: The Emergence of Pharisaic Judaism*. Englewood Cliffs, N.J.: Prentice-Hall, 1973.

———. *Rabbinic Traditions about the Pharisees before 70*. 3 vols. Leiden: Brill, 1971.

Newsom, Carol A. "4Q374: A Discourse on the Exodus/Conquest Tradition." Pages 40–52 in *The Dead Sea Scrolls. Forty Years of Research*. Edited by Devorah Dimant. Studies on the Texts of the Desert of Judah 10. Leiden: Brill, 1992.

Nickelsburg, George W. E. "Chapter Two: Stories of Biblical and Early Post-Biblical Times." Pages 33–87 in *Jewish Writings of the Second Temple Period: Apocrypha, Pseudepigrapha, Qumran Sectarian Writings, Philo, Josephus*. Edited by Michael E. Stone. Compendia rerum iudaicarum ad Novum Testamentum 2.2. Assen: Van Gorcum and Philadephia: Fortress, 1984.

———. "Chapter Three: The Bible Rewritten and Expanded." Pages 89–156 in *Jewish Writings of the Second Temple Period: Apocrypha, Pseudepigrapha, Qumran Sectarian Writings, Philo, Josephus*. Edited by Michael E. Stone. Compendia rerum iudaicarum ad Novum Testamentum 2.2. Assen: Van Gorcum and Philadephia: Fortress, 1984.

Niehoff, Maren. *Philo on Jewish Identity and Culture*. Texte und Studien zum antiken Judentum 86. Tübingen: J. C. B. Mohr, 2001.

Nikiprowetsky, Valentin. *Le Commentaire De L'Ecriture Chez Philon D'Alexandrie*. Leiden: Brill, 1977.

Noth, Martin. *The Deuteronomistic History*. Journal for the Study of the Old Testament Supplement Series 15. Sheffield: Sheffield Academic, 1991. Translation of *Überlieferungsgeschichtliche Studien: Die sammelnden und bearbeitenden Geschichtswerke im Alten Testament*. 3d ed. Darmstadt: Wissenschaftliche Buchgesellschaft, 1967. 1st ed. 1943.

O'Brien, Mark A. *The Deuteronomistic History Hypothesis: A Reassessment*. Orbis biblicus et orientalis 92. Göttingen: Vandenhoeck & Ruprecht, 1989.

O'Connor, David K. "The Seductions of Socrates." *First Things* 114 (2001): 29–33.

Oestreicher, Theodor. *Das deuteronomistische Grundgesetz*. Beiträge zur Förderung christlicher Theologie 27/4. Gütersloh: Bertelsmann, 1923.

Olson, Dennis T. *Deuteronomy and the Death of Moses: A Theological Reading*. Overtures to Biblical Theology. Minneapolis: Fortress, 1994.

Olyan, Saul M. *A Thousand Thousands Served Him: Exegesis and the Naming of Angels in Ancient Judaism*. Texte und Studien zum antiken Judentum 36. Tübingen: J. C. B. Mohr, 1993.

Ong, Walter J. *Orality and Literacy: The Technologizing of the Word*. London: Methuen, 1982.

Orlov, Andrei A. "Overshadowed by Enoch's Greatness: 'Two Tablets' Traditions from the *Book of Giants* to *Palaea Historica.*" *Journal for the Study of Judaism* 32 (2001): 137–58.

Paul, Shalom M. "Heavenly Tablets and the Book of Life." *Journal of the Ancient Near Eastern Society of Columbia University* 5 (1973): 345–53.

Perlitt, Lothar. *Bundestheologie im Alten Testament.* Wissenschaftliche Monographien zum Alten und Neuen Testament 36. Neukirchen Vluyn: Neukirchener Verlag, 1969.

Perrot, Charles. *Pseudo-Philon: Les antiquités bibliques. Tome II: Introduction littéraire, commentaire et index.* Sources chrétiennes 230. Paris: Cerf., 1976.

Person, Raymond F. *Second Zechariah and the Deuteronomic School.* Journal for the Study of the Old Testament Supplement Series 167. Sheffield: JSOT Press, 1993.

Polzin, Robert. *Moses and the Deuteronomist: A Literary Study of the Deuteronomic History.* New York: Seabury, 1980.

Pomykala, Kenneth E. *The Davidic Dynasty Tradition in Early Judaism: Its History and Significance for Messianism.* Society of Biblical Literature Early Judaism and Its Literature 7. Atlanta: Scholars Press, 1995.

Porter, Jean. *Natural and Divine Law: Reclaiming the Tradition for Christian Ethics.* Grand Rapids: Eerdmans, 1999.

Qimron, Elisha. "Further New Readings in the Temple Scroll." *Israel Exploration Journal* 37 (1987): 31–35.

———. "לנוסחה של מגילת המקדש" *Lešonénu* 42 (1978): 136–45.

———. "New Readings in the Temple Scroll." *Israel Exploration Journal* 28 (1978): 161–72.

———. *The Temple Scroll: A Critical Edition with Extensive Reconstructions.* Judean Desert Studies. Beer Sheva: Ben-Gurion of the Negev and Jerusalem: Israel Exploration Society, 1996.

Rabinowitz, Raphael N. *Diqduqei Sofrim.* 12 vols. Jerusalem, Magnes, 1968.

Rad, Gerhard von. *Deuteronomy: A Commentary.* Old Testament Library. Philadelphia: Westminster, 1966.

———. *Das Geschichtsbild des chronistischen Werkes.* Stuttgart: Kohlhammer, 1930.

Ravid, Liora. "Issues in the Book of Jubilees." Ph.D. diss., Bar-Ilan University, 2001 (Hebrew).

Rendtorff, Rolf. "Esra und das 'Gesetz.'" *Zeitschrift für die Alttestamentliche Wissenschaft* 96 (1984): 165–84.

———. *The Problem of the Process of Transmission in the Pentateuch.* Journal for the Study of the Old Testament Supplement Series 89. Sheffield: JSOT Press, 1990.

Rochberg-Halton, Francesca. "Canonicity in Cuneiform Texts." *Journal of Cuneiform Studies* 36 (1984): 127–44.

Rogerson, John W. *Old Testament Criticism in the Nineteenth Century: England and Germany.* Philadelphia: Fortress, 1985.

Römer, Thomas. "Deuteronomy in Search of Origins." Pages 112–38 in *Reconsidering Israel and Judah: Recent Studies on the Deuteronomistic History.* Edited by Gary N. Knoppers and J. Gordon McConville. Sources for Biblical and Theological Study 8. Winona Lake, Ind.: Eisenbrauns, 2000. Repr. and translated by Peter T. Daniels from "Le Deutéronome à la quête des origins." Pages 65–98 in *Le Pentateuque: Débats et recherches.* Edited by Pierre Haudebert. Lectio divina 151. Paris: Cerf, 1992.

———., and Marc Z. Brettler. "Deuteronomy 34 and the Case for a Persian Hexateuch." *Journal of Biblical Literature* 119 (2000): 401–19.

Rose, Martin. "Bermerkungen zum historischen Fundament des Josia-Bildes in II Reg. 22f." *Zeitschrift für die alttestamentliche Wissenschaft* 89 (1977): 55–62.

Runia, David T. "God and Man in Philo of Alexandria." *Journal of Theological Studies* 39 (1988): 48–75. Repr. pages 48–74 in *Studia Patristica: Papers of the 1983 Oxford Patristics Conference.* Edited by Elizabeth A. Livingston. Studia patristica 18.2. Leuven: Peeters, 1989.

———. "The Language of Excellence in Plato's *Timaeus* and Later Platonism." Pages 11–37 in *Platonism in Late Antiquity*. Edited by Stephen Gersh and Charles Kannengiesser. Notre Dame: University of Notre Dame, 1992.

———. *Philo of Alexandria and the Timaeus of Plato*. 2 vols. Alblasserdam: Boekhandel, 1983.

———. *Philo of Alexandria*: On the Creation of the Cosmos according to Moses. *Introduction, Translation and Commentary*. Philo of Alexandria Commentary Series 1. Leiden: Brill, 2001.

———. Review of Richard Goulet, *La Philosophie de Moïse*. *Journal of Theological Studies* 40 (1989): 590–602.

———. "Was Philo a Middle Platonist? a Difficult Question Revisited." *Studia Philonica Annual* 5 (1993): 112–40.

Safrai, Shmuel. "Halakhah le-Moshe mi-Sinai: History or Theology?" Pages 11–38 in *Meḥqerei Talmud*. Edited by Yaakov Sussman and David Rosenthal. Jerusalem: Magnes, 1990 (Hebrew).

Sanders, Ed. P. *Paul and Palestinian Judaism: A Comparison of Patterns of Religion*. Philadelphia: Fortress, 1977.

Sanders, James A. "Introduction: Why the Pseudepigrapha?" Pages 13–19 in *The Pseudepigrapha and Early Biblical Interpretation*. Edited by James H. Charlesworth and Craig A. Evans. Journal for the Study of the Pseudepigrapha Supplement Series 14. Studies in Scripture and Early Judasim and Christianity 2. Sheffield: Sheffield Academic, 1993.

Sandmel, Samuel. "Philo's Place in Judaism: A Study of Conceptions of Abraham in Jewish Literature." *Hebrew Union College Annual* 25 (1954): 209–37.

Satran, David, trans. "Appendix: The Lives of the Prophets." Pages 121–28 in *Biblical Prophets in Byzantine Palestine: Reassessing the Lives of the Prophets*. Studia in Veteris Testamenti pseudepigraphica 11. Leiden: Brill, 1995.

Schäfer, Peter. "Das 'Dogma' von der Mündlichen Torah im Rabbinischen Judentum." Pages 153–97 in *Studien zur Geschichte und Theologie des rabbinischen Judentums*. Arbeiten zur Geschichte des antiken Judentums und des Urchristentums 15. Leiden: Brill, 1978.

Schiffman, Lawrence H. "The Construction of the Temple according to the *Temple Scroll*." *Revue de Qumran* 17 (1996): 555–71.

———. "The Deuteronomic Paraphrase of the Temple Scroll." *Revue de Qumran* 15 (1992): 543–67.

———. "The King, his Guard, and the Royal Council in the *Temple Scroll*." *American Academy for Jewish Research* 54 (1987): 237–59.

———. "The Sacrificial System of the *Temple Scroll* and the Book of Jubilees." Pages 217–33 in *SBL Seminar Papers, 1985*. Society of Biblical Literature Seminar Papers 24. Chico, Calif.: Scholars Press, 1985.

———. "The Temple Scroll and the Halakhic Pseudepigrapha of the Second Temple Period." Pages 121–31 in *Pseudepigraphic Perspectives: The Apocrypha and Pseudepigrapha in Light of the Dead Sea Scrolls. Proceedings of the International Symposium of the Orion Center for the Study of the Dead Sea Scrolls and Associated Literature, 12–14 January, 1997*. Edited by Esther G. Chazon and Michael E. Stone. Studies on the Texts of the Desert of Judah 31. Leiden: Brill, 1999.

———. "The *Temple Scroll* and the Nature of Its Law: The Status of the Question." Pages 37–55 in *The Community of the Renewed Covenant*. Edited by Eugene Ulrich and James C. VanderKam. Christianity and Judaism in Antiquity Series 10. Notre Dame: University of Notre Dame Press, 1994.

———. "The Theology of the Temple Scroll." *Jewish Quarterly Review* 85 (1994): 109–28.

Schlegel, Friedrich. "On Philosophy. To Dorothea." Page 316 in *Theory as Practice: A Critical Anthology of Early German Romantic Writings*. Edited and translated by Jochen Schulte-Sasse et al. Minneapolis: University of Minnesota Press, 1997.

Schmidt, Nathaniel. "The Apocalypse of Noah and the Parables of Enoch." Pages 111–23 in *Oriental Studies Published in Commemoration of the Fortieth Anniversary of Paul Haupt*. Edited by Cyrus Adler and Aaron Ember. Baltimore: Johns Hopkins University Press, 1926.

Schniedewind, William M. "The Chronicler as an Interpreter of Scripture." Pages 158–80 in *The Chronicler as Author: Studies in Text and Texture*. Edited by M. Patrick Graham and Steven L. McKenzie. Journal for the Study of the Old Testament Supplement Series 263. Sheffield: Sheffield Academic, 1999.

———. "Prophets and Prophecy in the Books of Chronicles." Pages 204–24 in *The Chronicler as Historian*. Edited by M. Patrick Graham, Kenneth G. Hoglund, and Steven L. McKenzie. Journal for the Study of the Old Testament Supplement Series 238. Sheffield: Sheffield Academic, 1997.

———. *The Word of God in Transition: From Prophet to Exegete in the Second Temple Period*. Journal for the Study of the Old Testament Supplement Series 197. Sheffield: Sheffield Academic, 1995.

Schorr, Yehoshua Heshel. "Halakha le-Moshe mi-Sinai." *He-Halutz* 2 (1857): 29–50.

Schwartz, Joshua. "Jubilees, Bethel and the Temple of Jacob." *Hebrew Union College Annual* 56 (1985): 63–85.

Schwarz, Eberhard. *Identität durch Abgrenzung: Abgrenzungsprozesse in Israel im 2. vorchristlichen Jahrhundert und ihre traditionsgeschichtlichen Voraussetzungen. Zugleich ein Beitrag zur Erforschung des Jubiläenbuches*. Europäische Hochschulschriften 23/162. Frankfurt: Lang, 1982.

Schweitzer, Steven J. "Reading Chronicles as Utopian Historiography: Continuity and Innovation in Service of the Cult." Paper presented at the National annual meeting of the SBL. Denver, Colo., November 18, 2001.

Sedley, David. "The nomothêtes in Plato's Cratylus." In *The Law of Nature: Ancient Origins and Contemporary Transformations*. Edited by Hindy Najman, David K. O'Connor, and Gregory E. Sterling. Forthcoming.

Seeligman, Isac L. "ניצני מדרש בספר דברי הימים" *Tarbiz* 49 (1979–80): 14–32.

Segal, Michael. "4QReworked Pentateuch or 4QPentateuch?" Pages 391–99 in *The Dead Sea Scrolls Fifty Years after Their Discovery: Proceedings of the Jerusalem Congress, July 20–25, 1997*. Edited by Lawrence H. Schiffman, Emanuel Tov, and James C. VanderKam. Jerusalem: Israel Exploration Society and the Shrine of the Book, 2000.

———. "Biblical Exegesis in 4Q158: Techniques and Genre." *Textus* 19 (1998): 45–62.

Shaver, Judson R. *Torah and the Chronicler's History Work: An Inquiry into the Chronicler's References to Laws, Festivals, and Cultic Institutions in Relationship to Pentateuchal Legislation*. Brown Judaica Series 196. Atlanta: Scholars Press, 1989.

Shemesh, Aharon. "The Origins of the Laws of Separatism: Qumran Literature and Rabbinic Halacha." *Revue de Qumran* 18 (1997): 223–41.

———., and Cana Werman. "Halakhah at Qumran: Genre and Authority." *Dead Sea Discoveries* 10 (2003): forthcoming.

Skehan, Patrick W., and Alexander A. Di Lella. *The Wisdom of Ben Sira: A New Translation with Notes*. Anchor Bible 39. New York: Doubleday, 1987.

Smend, Rudolf. "Das Gesetz und die Völker: Ein Beitrag zur deuteronomistischen Redaktionsgeschichte." Pages 494–509 in *Probleme biblischer Theologie: Festschrift Gerhard von Rad*. Edited by Hans W. Wolff. Munich: Kaiser, 1971.

Smith, Morton. "Prolegomena to a Discussion of Aretalogies, Divine Men, the Gospels and Jesus." *Journal of Biblical Literature* 90 (1971): 174–99.

———. "Pseudepigraphy in the Israelite Literary Tradition." Pages 189–215 with discussion 216–27 in *Pseudepigrapha I*. Edited by Kurt von Fritz. Vandoeuvres-Geneve: Fondation Hardt., 1972.

Smith-Christopher, Duane L. "Between Ezra and Isaiah: Exclusion, Transformation, and Inclusion of the 'Foreigner' in Post-Exilic Biblical Theology." Pages 117–42 in *Ethnicity and the Bible*. Edited by Mark G. Brett. Biblical Interpretation Series 19. Leiden: Brill, 1996.

———. "The Mixed Marriage Crisis in Ezra 9–10 and Nehemiah 13: A Study of the Sociology of Post-Exilic Judaean Community." Pages 243–65 in *Second Temple Studies: 2. Temple Community in the Persian Period*. Edited by Tamara C. Eskenazi and Kent H. Richards. Journal for the Study of the Old Testament Supplement Series 175. Sheffield: JSOT Press, 1994.

Sonnet, Jean-Pierre. *The Book Within the Book: Writing in Deuteronomy*. Biblical Interpretation Series 14. Leiden: Brill, 1997.

Sowers, Sidney G. *The Hermeneutics of Philo and Hebrews: A Comparison of the Interpretation in Philo Judaeus and the Epistle to the Hebrews*. Basel Studies of Theology 1. Richmond, Va.: John Knox, 1965.

Speyer, Wolfgang. "Fälschung, pseudepigraphische freie Erfindung und 'echte religiöse Pseudepigraphie'." Pages 331–66 with discussion 367–72 in *Pseudepigrapha I*. Edited by Kurt von Fritz. Vandoeuvres-Geneve: Fondation Hardt., 1972.

———. *Die Literarische Fälschung im Heidnischen und Christlichen Altertum: Ein Versuch Ihrer Deutung*. Munich: C. H. Beck'sche Verlagsbuchhandlung, 1971.

Spieckermann, Hermann. *Juda unter Assur in der Sargonidenzeit*. Forschungen zur Religion und Literatur des Alten und Neuen Testaments 129. Göttingen: Vandenhoeck & Ruprecht, 1982.

Steiner, Richard C. "The Heading of the *Book of the Words of Noah* on a Fragment of the Genesis Apocryphon: New Light on a 'Lost' Work." *Dead Sea Discoveries* 2 (1995): 66–71.

Sterling, Gregory E. "Judaism Between Jerusalem and Athens." Pages 263–301 in *Hellenism in the Land of Israel*. Edited by John J. Collins and Gregory E. Sterling. Christianity and Judaism in Antiquity Series 13. Notre Dame: University of Notre Dame Press, 2001.

———. "Philo and the Logic of Apologetics: An Analysis of the *Hypothetica*." Pages 412–30 in *SBL Seminar Papers, 1990*. Society of Biblical Literature Seminar Papers 29. Atlanta: Scholars Press, 1990.

———. "Platonizing Moses: Philo and Middle Platonism." *Studia Philonica Annual* 5 (1993): 96–111.

———. "Wisdom among the Perfect: Creation Traditions in Alexandrian Judaism and Corinthian Christianity." *Novum Testamentum* 37 (1995): 355–84.

Steudel, Annette. "There are No Further Columns in the *Temple Scroll*." *Revue de Qumran* 19 (1999): 131–36.

Stone, Michael E. "Categorization and Classification of the Apocrypha and Pseudepigrapha." *Abr-Nahrain* 24 (1986): 167–77.

———. "The Dead Sea Scrolls and the Pseudepigrapha." *Dead Sea Discoveries* 3 (1996): 270–95.

———. *Fourth Ezra: A Commentary on the Book of Fourth Ezra*. Hermeneia. Minneapolis: Fortress, 1990.

———., ed. *Jewish Writings of the Second Temple Period: Apocrypha, Pseudepigrapha, Qumran Sectarian Writings, Philo, Josephus*. Compendia rerum iudaicarum ad Novum Testamentum 2.2. Assen: Van Gorcum and Philadelphia: Fortress, 1984.

Strauss, Leo. *Natural Right and History*. Chicago: University of Chicago Press, 1953.

Striker, Gisela. "Origins of the Concept of Natural Law." Pages 209–20 in *Essays on Hellenistic Epistemology and Ethics*. New York: Cambridge University Press, 1996.

———. "Plato's Socrates and the Stoics." Pages 241–51 in *The Socratic Movement*. Edited by Paul A. Vander Waerdt. Ithaca: Cornell University Press, 1994.

Strugnell, John. "4Q375 (4QApocryphon of Moses[a] [*olim* 4QApocryphon of Moses B])," and "4Q376 (4QApocryphon of Moses[b]? [*olim* 4QLit of 3 Tongues of

Fire])." Pages 111–36 in *Qumran Cave 4. XIV, Parabiblical Texts, Part 2.* Discoveries in the Judaean Desert 19. Oxford: Clarendon, 1995.

————. "Moses-Pseudepigrapha At Qumran: 4Q375, 4Q376, and Similar Works." Pages 221–56 in *Archaeology and History in the Dead Sea Scrolls: The New York University Conference in Memory of Yigael Yadin.* Edited by James H. Charlesworth, Philip R. Davies, James R. Mueller and James C. VanderKam. Journal for the Study of the Pseudepigrapha Supplement Series 8. Journal for the Study of the Old Testament/American Schools of Oriental Research Monographs 2. Sheffield: JSOT Press, 1990.

Stuart, Duane Reed. *Epochs of Greek and Roman Biography.* Sather Classical Lectures 4. Berkeley: University of California Press, 1928.

Swain, Simon. "Biography and Biographic in the Literature of the Roman Empire." Pages 1–37 in *Portraits: Biographical Representation in the Greek and Latin Literature of the Roman Empire.* Edited by Mark J. Edwards and Simon Swain. Oxford: Clarendon, 1997.

Swanson, Dwight D. "'A Covenant Just Like Jacob's: the Covenant of 11QT29 and Jeremiah's New Covenant." Pages 273–86 in *New Qumran Texts and Studies: Proceedings of the First Meeting of the International Organization for Qumran Studies, Paris, 1992.* Edited by George J. Brooke with Florentino García Martínez. Studies on the Texts of the Desert of Judah 15. Leiden: Brill, 1994.

————. *The Temple Scroll and the Bible: The Methodology of 11QT.* Studies on the Texts of the Desert of Judah 14. Leiden: Brill, 1995.

Ta-Shema, Israel M. "Abraham: In the Aggadah." Page 115 in vol. 2 of *Encyclopedia Judaica.* 16 vols. New York: Macmillan, 1972.

Talbert, Charles H. "Biographies of Philosophers and Rulers as Instruments of Religious Propoganda in Mediterranean Antiquity." *ANRW* 16.2:1619–51. Part 2, *Principat,* 16.2. Edited by H. Temporini and W. Haase. Berlin: de Gruyter, 1978.

————. "The Myth of the Immortals in Mediterranean Antiquity." *Journal of Biblical Literature* 94 (1975): 419–36.

Terian, Abraham. *Philonis Alexandrini de Animalibus: The Armenian Text with an Introduction, Translation, and Commentary.* Chico, Calif.: Scholars Press, 1981.

Testuz, Michel. *Les Idées Religieuses du Livre des Jubilés.* Geneva: Librairie E. Droz and Paris: Librairie Minard, 1960.

Tiede, David L. *The Charismatic Figure As Miracle Worker.* Society of Biblical Literature Dissertation Series 1. Missoula, Mont.: University of Montana Press, 1972.

————. "The Figure of Moses in *The Testament of Moses.*" Pages 86–92 in *Studies on the Testament of Moses.* Edited by George W. E. Nickelsburg. Society of Biblical Literature Septuagint and Cognate Studies 4. Cambridge, Mass.: Society of Biblical Literature, 1973.

Tigay, Jeffrey H. *The Evolution of the Gilgamesh Epic.* Philadelphia: University of Pennsylvania Press, 1982.

Tobin, Thomas H. "Was Philo a Middle Platonist? Some Suggestions." *Studia Philonica Annual* 5 (1993): 147–50.

Toit, David S. du. *Theios Anthropos: Zur Verwendung von Θεῖος ἄνθρωπος und sinnverwandten Ausdrücken in der Literatur der Kaiserzeit.* Edited by Martin Hengel and Otfried Hofius. Wissenschaftliche Untersuchungen zum Neuen Testament, Reihe 2: 91. Tübingen: J. C. B. Mohr, 1997.

Tov, Emanuel. "Biblical Texts as Reworked in Some Qumran Manuscripts with Special Attention to 4QRP and 4QparaGen-Exod." Pages 111–34 in *The Community of the Renewed Covenant.* Edited by Eugene Ulrich and James C. VanderKam. Christianity and Judaism in Antiquity Series 10. Notre Dame: University of Notre Dame Press, 1994.

————. "Rewritten Bible Compositions and Biblical Manuscripts, with Special Attention to the Samaritan Pentateuch." *Dead Sea Discoveries* 5 (1998): 334–54.

————. "The Textual Status of 4Q364–367 (4QPP)." Pages 43–82 in vol. 1 of *The Madrid Qumran Congress: Proceedings of the International Congress on the Dead Sea Scrolls Madrid 18–21 March, 1991*. Edited by Julio Trebolle Barrera and Luis Vegas Montaner. 2 vols. Studies on the Texts of the Desert of Judah 11.1. Leiden: Brill, 1992.

————., and Sidnie White Crawford. "Reworked Pentateuch." Pages 187–351 in *Qumran Cave 4, VIII: Parabiblical Texts, Part 1*. Discoveries in the Judaean Desert 13. Oxford: Clarendon, 1994.

Trebolle Barrera, Julio. "The Authoritative Functions of Scriptural Works at Qumran." Pages 95–110 in *The Community of the Renewed Covenant*. Edited by Eugene Ulrich and James C. VanderKam. Christianity and Judaism in Antiquity Series 10. Notre Dame: University of Notre Dame Press, 1994.

————. "A 'Canon Within a Canon': Two Series of Old Testament Books Differently Transmitted, Interpreted and Authorized." *Revue de Qumran* 19 (2000): 383–99.

Ulrich, Eugene. "The Bible in the Making: The Scriptures at Qumran." Pages 77–94 in *The Community of the Renewed Covenant*. Edited by Eugene Ulrich and James C. VanderKam. Christianity and Judaism in Antiquity Series 10. Notre Dame: University of Notre Dame Press, 1994.

————. "The Dead Sea Scrolls and the Biblical Text." Pages 79–100 in vol. 1 of *The Dead Sea Scrolls after Fifty Years: A Comprehensive Assessment*. Edited by Peter W. Flint and James C. VanderKam. 2 vols. Leiden: Brill, 1998–99.

————. *The Dead Sea Scrolls and the Origins of the Bible*. Studies in the Dead Sea Scrolls and Related Literature. Grand Rapids: Eerdmans and Leiden: Brill, 1999.

————. "From Literature to Scripture: Reflections on the Growth of a Text's Authoritativeness." *Dead Sea Discoveries* 10 (2003): forthcoming.

Urbach, Ephraim E. "The Written Law and the Oral Law." Pages 286–314 in *The Sages: Their Concepts and Beliefs*. Translated by Israel Abrahams. Cambridge, Mass.: Harvard University Press, 1979.

VanderKam, James C. "The Angel of the Presence in the Book of Jubilees." *Dead Sea Discoveries* 7 (2000): 378–93.

————. "Authoritative Literature in the Dead Sea Scrolls." *Dead Sea Discoveries* 5 (1998): 382–402.

————. "Biblical Interpretation in *1 Enoch* and *Jubilees*." Pages 96–125 in *The Pseudepigrapha and Early Biblical Interpretation*. Edited by James H. Charlesworth and Craig A. Evans. Journal for the Study of the Pseudepigrapha Supplement Series 14. Studies in Scripture and Early Judaism and Christianity 2. Sheffield: Sheffield Academic, 1993.

————. *The Book of Jubilees*. Corpus scriptorum christianorum orientalium 510–511. Scriptores Aethiopici 87–88. 2 vols. Leuven: Peeters, 1989.

————. *Calendars in the Dead Sea Scrolls: Measuring Time*. The Literature of the Dead Sea Scrolls. London: Routledge, 1998.

————. "Chapter 2: 1 Enoch, Enochic Motifs, and Enoch in Early Christian Literature." Pages 33–101 in *The Jewish Apocalyptic Heritage in Early Christianity*. Edited by James C. VanderKam and William Adler. Compendia rerum iudaicarum ad Novum Testamentum 3.4. Assen: Van Gorcum and Minneapolis: Fortress, 1996.

————. "Das chronologische Konzept des Jubiläenbuches." *Zeitschrift für die alttestamentliche Wissenschaft* 107 (1995): 80–100. Repr. and translated as "Studies in the Chronology of the Book of Jubilees," pages 522–44 in *From Revelation to Canon: Studies in the Hebrew Bible and Second Temple Literature*. Journal for the Study of Judaism Supplement Series 62. Leiden: Brill, 2000.

————. *The Dead Sea Scrolls Today*. Grand Rapids: Eerdmans, 1994.

————. *Enoch and the Growth of an Apocalyptic Tradition*. Catholic Biblical Quarterly Monograph Series 16. Washington, D.C.: Catholic Biblical Association of America, 1984.

————. *An Introduction to Early Judaism*. Grand Rapids: Eerdmans, 2001.

————. "*Jubilees'* Exegetical Creation of Levi the Priest." *Revue de Qumran* 17 (1996): 359–73. Repr. pages 545–61 in *From Revelation to Canon: Studies in the Hebrew Bible and Second Temple Literature*. Journal for the Study of Judaism Supplement Series 62. Leiden: Brill, 2000.

————. "The Origins and Purposes of the *Book of Jubilees*." Pages 3–24 in *Studies in the Book of Jubilees*. Edited by Matthias Albani, Jörg Frey, and Armin Lange. Tübingen: J. C. B. Mohr, 1997.

————. "The Putative Author of the Book of Jubilees." *Journal of Semitic Studies* 26 (1981): 209–17. Repr. pages 439–47 in *From Revelation to Canon: Studies in the Hebrew Bible and Second Temple Literature*. Journal for the Study of Judaism Supplement Series 62. Leiden: Brill, 2000.

————. "Questions of Canon Viewed through the Dead Sea Scrolls." *Bulletin for Biblical Research* 11 (2001): 269–92.

————. Review of Gabriele Boccaccini, *Beyond the Essene Hypothesis*. *Rivista biblica italiana*, forthcoming.

————. "The Temple Scroll and the Book of Jubilees." Pages 211–36 in *Temple Scroll Studies: Papers Presented at the International Symposium on the Temple Scroll, Manchester, December 1987*. Edited by George J. Brooke. Journal for the Study of the Pseudepigrapha Supplement Series 7. Sheffield: JSOT Press, 1989.

————. *Textual and Historical Studies in the Book of Jubilees*. Harvard Semitic Monographs 14. Missoula, Mont.: Scholars Press, 1977.

————. "The Theology of the Temple Scroll: A Response to Lawrence H. Schiffman." *Jewish Quarterly Review* 85 (1994): 129–35.

————., and Josef T. Milik. "Jubilees." Pages 1–140 in *Qumran Cave 4. VIII: Parabiblical Texts Part I*. Discoveries in the Judaean Desert 13. Oxford: Clarendon, 1994.

Vander Waerdt, Paul A. "Zeno's Republic and the Origins of Natural Law." Pages 272–308 in *The Socratic Movement*. Edited by Paul A. Vander Waerdt. Ithaca: Cornell University Press, 1994.

Van Seters, John. "Creative Imitation in the Hebrew Bible." *Studies in Religion* 29 (2000): 395–409.

————. *In Search of History: Historiography in the Ancient World and the Origins of Biblical History*. New Haven, Conn.: Yale University Press, 1983. Repr., Winona Lake, Ind.: Eisenbrauns, 1997.

Vermes, Geza. *Scripture and Tradition in Judaism: Haggadic Studies*. 2d. rev. ed. Studia post-biblica 4. Leiden: Brill, 1973. 1st ed. 1961.

Vessey, Mark. "The Forging of Orthodoxy in Latin Christian Literature: A Case Study." *Journal of Early Christian Studies* 4 (1996): 495–513.

Wacholder, Ben Zion. *The Dawn of Qumran: The Sectarian Torah and the Teacher of Righteousness*. Cincinnati: Hebrew Union College, 1983.

————. "*Jubilees* as the Super Canon: Torah-Admonition versus Torah-Commandment." Pages 195–211 in *Legal Texts and Legal Issues: Proceedings of the Second Meeting of the International Organization for Qumran Studies, Cambridge 1995*. Edited by Moshe Bernstein, Florentino García Martínez, and John Kampen. Studies on the Texts of the Desert of Judah 23. Leiden: Brill, 1997.

————. "The Relationship between 11QTorah (The Temple Scroll) and the Book of Jubilees: One Single or Two Independent Compositions." Pages 205–16 in *SBL Seminar Papers, 1985*. Society of Biblical Literature Seminar Papers 24. Chico, Calif.: Scholars Press, 1985.

Waltke, Bruce K., and Michael O'Connor. *An Introduction to Biblical Hebrew Syntax*. Winona Lake, Ind.: Eisenbrauns, 1990.

Watts, James W. "The Legal Characterization of Moses in the Rhetoric of the Pentateuch." *Journal of Biblical Literature* 117 (1998): 415–26.

———. "Public Readings and Pentateuchal Law." *Vetus Testamentum* 45 (1995): 540–57.

Weinfeld, Moshe. *Deuteronomy and the Deuteronomic School.* Oxford: Clarendon, 1972.

———. "God versus Moses in the Temple Scroll: 'I do not speak on my own but on God's authority' (*Sifrei Deut.* Sec. 5; *John* 12, 48 f.)." *Revue de Qumran* 15 (1992): 175–80.

Weiss, Isaac H. *Dor Dor Vedorshav Zur Geshikhte fun der jüdische Tradition. Vol. 1.* 5 vols. Vienna: n.s., 1871–91. Repr., Berlin: Platt & Minkus, 1924.

Wells, Colin. *The Roman Empire.* Stanford, Calif.: Stanford University Press, 1984.

Wentling, Judith L. "Unraveling the Relationship between 11QT, the Eschatological Temple, and the Qumran Community." *Revue de Qumran* 14 (1989): 61–73.

Werman, Cana. "*Jubilees* 30: Building a Paradigm for the Ban on Intermarriage." *Harvard Theological Review* 90 (1997): 1–22.

———. "'The תורה and the תעודה' engraved on the Tablets." *Dead Sea Discoveries* 9 (2002): 75–103. Repr., and translated from "'התורה והתעודה' הכתובה על הלוחות" *Tarbiz* 68 (1999): 473–92.

Wette, Wilhelm Martin Leberecht de. *Dissertatio critico-exegetica, qua Deuteronomium a prioribus Pentateuchi libris diversum, alius cuiusdam recentioris auctoris opus esse monstratur.* Ienae: Literis Etzdorfii, 1805.

White Crawford, Sidnie. "Reworked Pentateuch." Pages 775–77 in vol. 2 of *Encyclopedia of the Dead Sea Scrolls.* Edited by Lawrence H. Schiffman and James C. VanderKam. 2 vols. Oxford: Oxford University Press, 2000.

———. "The 'Rewritten Bible' at Qumran: A Look at Three Texts." *Eretz-Israel* 26 (1999): 1–8.

———. *The Temple Scroll and Related Texts.* Companion to the Qumran Scrolls 2. Sheffield: Sheffield Academic, 2000.

———. "Three Fragments from Qumran Cave 4 and Their Relationship to the Temple Scroll." *Jewish Quarterly Review* 85 (1994): 259–73.

Whybray, Roger N. "annôt in Exodus xxxii 18." *Vetus Testamentum* 17 (1967): 122.

Wieder, Naphtali. "The 'Law-Interpreter' of the Sect of the Dead Sea Scrolls: The Second Moses." *Journal of Jewish Studies* 3 (1952): 158–75.

Wiesenberg, Ernest. "The Jubilee of Jubilees." *Revue de Qumran* 3 (1961–62): 3–40.

Willi, Thomas. *Die Chronik als Auslegung.* Forschungen zur Religion und Literatur des Alten und Neuen Testaments 106. Göttingen: Vandenhoeck & Ruprecht, 1972.

Williamson, H. G. M. *Israel in the Book of Chronicles.* Cambridge: Cambridge University Press, 1977.

———. "The Origins of the Twenty-Four Priestly Courses." Pages 251–68 in *Studies in the Historical Books of the Old Testament.* Edited by J. A. Emerton. Supplements to Vetus Testamentum 30. Leiden: Brill, 1979.

Wilson, Andrew M., and Lawrence M. Wills. "Literary Sources of the *Temple Scroll.*" *Harvard Theological Review* 75 (1982): 275–88.

Wilson, Robert R. "Who Was the Deuteronomist? (Who Was Not the Deuteronomist?): Reflections on Pan-Deuteronomism." Pages 67–82 in *Those Elusive Deuteronomists: The Phenomenon of Pan-Deuteronomism.* Edited by Linda S. Schearing and Steven L. McKenzie. Journal for the Study of the Old Testament Supplement Series 268. Sheffield: Sheffield Academic, 1999.

Winston, David. *Logos and Mystical Theology in Philo of Alexandria.* Cincinnati: Hebrew Union College Press, 1985.

———. "Philo's Ethical Theory." *ANRW* 21.1:381–88. Part 2, *Principat,* 21.1. Edited by H. Temporini and W. Haase. Berlin: de Gruyter, 1984.

———. "Response to Runia and Sterling." *Studia Philonica Annual* 5 (1993): 141–46.

————. "Two Types of Mosaic Prophecy According to Philo." Pages 442–55 in *SBL Seminar Papers, 1988.* Society of Biblical Literature Seminar Papers 27. Atlanta: Scholars Press, 1988.

Wise, Michael O. "The Covenant of Temple Scroll XXIX, 3–10." *Revue de Qumran* 14 (1989): 49–60.

————. *A Critical Study of the Temple Scroll from Qumran Cave 11.* Studies in Ancient Oriental Civilization 49. Chicago: The Oriental Institute of the University of Chicago, 1990.

————. "The Eschatological Vision of the Temple Scroll." *Journal of Near Eastern Studies* 40 (1990): 155–73.

Wolff, Hans W. "Das kerygma des deuteronomistichen Geschichteswerkes." *Zeitschrift für die alttestamentliche Wissenschaft* 73 (1961): 171–86.

Wolfson, Elliot R. *Through a Speculum that Shines: Vision and Imagination in Medieval Jewish Mysticism.* Princeton: Princeton University Press, 1994.

Wolfson, Harry Austryn. *Philo.* 2 vols. Cambridge, Mass.: Harvard University Press 1947.

Woodmansee, Martha, and Peter Jaszi, eds., *The Construction of Authorship: Textual Appropriation in Law and Literature.* Durham, N.C.: Duke University Press, 1994.

Würthwein, Ernst. "Die josianische Reform und das Deuteronomium." *Zeitschrift für Theologie und Kirche* 73 (1976): 395–423.

Yadin, Yigael. "Is the Temple Scroll a Sectarian Document?" Pages 153–69 in *Humanizing America's Iconic Book.* Edited by Gene M. Tucker and Douglas A. Knight. Chico, Calif.: Scholars Press, 1980.

————. *The Temple Scroll.* 3 vols. Jerusalem: Israel Exploration Society and the Shrine of the Book, 1983.

————. *The Temple Scroll: The Hidden Law of the Dead Sea Sect.* New York: Random House, 1985.

Zeitlin, Solomon. "The Beginning of the Day in the Calendar of Jubilees." *Journal of Biblical Literature* 78 (1959): 153–57.

————. "The Book of 'Jubilees' and the Pentateuch." *Jewish Quarterly Review* 48 (1957–58): 218–35.

INDEX OF AUTHORS

SUBJECT INDEX

INDEX OF PRIMARY TEXTS

OTHER SECOND TEMPLE LITERATURE

SUPPLEMENTS

TO THE

JOURNAL FOR THE STUDY OF JUDAISM

64. LIESEN, J.W.M. *Full of Praise.* An Exegetical Study of Sir 39,12-35. 1999. ISBN 90 04 11359 2

65. BEDFORD, P.R. *Temple Restoration in Early Achaemenid Judah.* 2000. ISBN 90 04 11509 9

66. RUITEN, J.T.A.G.M. van *Primaeval History Interpreted.* The Rewriting of Genesis 1-11 in the book of Jubilees. 2000. ISBN 90 04 11658 3

67. HOFMANN, N.J. *Die Assumptio Mosis.* Studien zur Rezeption massgültiger Überlieferung. 2000. ISBN 90 04 11938 8

68. HACHLILI, R. *The Menorah, the Ancient Seven-armed Candelabrum.* Origin, Form and Significance. 2001. ISBN 90 04 12017 3

69. VELTRI, G. *Gegenwart der Tradition.* Studien zur jüdischen Literatur und Kulturgeschichte. 2002. ISBN 90 04 11686 9

70. DAVILA, J.R. *Descenders to the Chariot.* The People behind the Hekhalot Literature. 2001. ISBN 90 04 11541 2

72. SCOTT, J.M. (ed.). *Restoration.* Old Testament, Jewish, and Christian Perspectives. 2001. ISBN 90 04 11580 3

73. TORIJANO, P.A. *Solomon the Esoteric King.* From King to Magus, Development of a Tradition. 2002. ISBN 90 04 11941 8

74. KUGEL, J.L. *Shem in the Tents of Japhet.* Essays on the Encounter of Judaism and Hellenism. 2002. ISBN 90 04 12514 0

75. COLAUTTI, F.M. *Passover in the Works of Josephus.* 2002. ISBN 90 04 12372 5

76. BERTHELOT, K. *Philanthrôpia judaica.* Le débat autour de la "misanthropie" des lois juives dans l'Antiquité. 2003. ISBN 90 04 12886 7

77. NAJMAN, H. *Seconding Sinai.* The Development of Mosaic Discourse in Second Temple Judaism. 2003. ISBN 90 04 11542 0

78. MULDER, O. *Simon the High Priest in Sirach 50.* An Exegetical Study of the Significance of Simon the High Priest as Climax to the Praise of the Fathers in Ben Sira's Concept of the History of Israel. 2003. ISBN 90 04 12316 4 (*In preparation*)

79. BURKES, S.L. *God, Self, and Death.* The Shape of Religious Transformation in the Second Temple Period. 2003. ISBN 90 04 12954 5 (*In preparation*)

ISSN 1384-2161

Lightning Source UK Ltd.
Milton Keynes UK
UKOW01f1154240817

307886UK00001B/270/P